Multi-cloud FinOps Handbook

FinOps Frameworks, multi-cloud cost optimization, and cloud governance

Satyendra Pasalapudi

Venkat Reddy Chintalapudi

Anirudh Sharma Valiveti

bpb

www.bpbonline.com

First Edition 2025

Copyright © BPB Publications, India

ISBN: 978-93-65894-417

To View Complete
BPB Publications Catalogue
Scan the QR Code:

Dedicated to

Vanitha Devi Pasalapudi (Wife)
PVN Bharat and Chandra Varnika (Children)
Pasalapudi Chandrakala (Mother), and PVN Murthy (Late Father)
- Satyendra Pasalapudi

Srujana Chintalapudi (Wife)
Sai Lokesh Reddy Chintalapudi and Manish Reddy Chintalapudi (Sons)
Savithri Chintalapudi and Venkata Reddy Chintalapudi (Parents Late)
- Venkat Reddy Chintalapudi

Malathi (Mother), Bhanu Tejaswi (Wife), and
my mentors – Venkat Chitturi (CEO of Technoidentity) and
Brajesh KR (Founder of Reshape Nation)
- Anirudh Sharma

About the Authors

- **Satyendra Pasalapudi:** Is an Oracle ACE director alumni and MBA graduate with 26+ years of diversified international experience in the IT industry that spans across multiple continents. He is an accomplished cloud, database professional, author, and speaker with the right blend of business and technology skills. Pasalapudi has bootstrapped various strategic business units in cloud, big data, Oracle support services, real-time reporting, and monitoring products in his career and is currently working as a managing director at Inflolob Global to lead the cloud business. Recently, he has worked at Oracle Consulting Solution Centre as director-platform architecture services, responsible for Oracle Cloud Infrastructure solutions. Prior to Oracle, he had worked at Apps Associates Pvt Ltd as director cloud services, heading their infrastructure managed services and cloud services at GDC, and had also worked with APTS, Pointsoft, Kenexa, DELL, and Megasoft in his earlier assignments.

  He is a high-performing technology management executive with 25+ years of achievement, driving impactful business change by leveraging and creating technology and data assets. Superb leadership and communication skills to forge strong relationships that drive business-technology alignment and enable high-performing, motivated, innovative teams.

  Pasalapudi possesses immense business acumen, technology expertise, and a strong people connect. His ability to coach, guide, and provide direction to resources at all levels is commendable. He supported customers across INDIA, the US, the UK, and the Middle East. His areas of strength include cloud, big data, performance tuning, capacity planning, architecting enterprise systems, infrastructure design, solutioning and datacenter operations. He has strong domain skills in Telecom, finance, and banking. Pasalapudi is the co-founder and immediate past president of the **All India Oracle Users Group** (**AIOUG**) and is a frequent speaker at the Oracle Open World, AIOUG Sangam, IOUG Collaborate, and other conferences.

- **Venkat Reddy Chintalapudi:** With over 25+ years of experience in various leadership roles in the software industry, Venkat Chintalapudi is a seasoned and passionate product management specialist who thrives on bringing ideas to life, delivering awesome products, and building world-class engineering teams.

  His entrepreneurial mindset drives the enterprises to instill FinOps discipline and transform their financial structure to save huge on increasing cloud costs. As a certified product owner, scrum master, and project management professional, his experience in driving cross-functional global teams at scale creates value for customers and stakeholders with simple and elegant solutions. His insights in this book are the crucial components that help enterprises to go beyond their operational lifecycle and investigate synergies with FinOps revolution.

- **Anirudh Sharma Valiveti:** A passionate writer by choice, Anirudh Sharma comes with 8 years of experience, where his writings on philosophy, mentorship, and technology have sparked the interest of people. He drives the content roadmaps at scale as a strategist for enterprises with a vision to create an impact globally. With strong hands in research, his insights and creative writing style in this book serve the purpose of active engagement of readers in every way possible.

Anirudh Sharma's extensive research skills, along with industry-leading authors, are the value drivers that made us explore the best touchpoints around FinOps.

Acknowledgements

We would like to express our sincere gratitude to all those who contributed to the completion of this book.

First and foremost, we extend our heartfelt appreciation to our family and friends for their incredible support and encouragement throughout this journey. Their love and encouragement have been a constant source of motivation.

We would like to extend our special thanks to the Heeddata Team and FinOps organization for bringing great adoption practices and wealth of information.

We are thankful to BPB Publications for their guidance and support in bringing this book to fruition. Their assistance has driven through the review and publishing process, making it go live in most of the online and offline stores.

We would express our mighty gratitude to the readers who have shown interest in our work. Your support and continuous encouragement have been soulfully embraced and appreciated.

Thank you to everyone who has played a part in making this book a reality.

Preface

In a world where digital transformation and business enablement is the core motive for enterprises of all types and sizes, the cloud has emerged as the cornerstone of modern enterprise infrastructure. With great capabilities and power comes great complexity, especially when businesses go beyond single-vendor cloud adoption and choose multi-cloud ecosystems. As cloud footprints increase, so do the growing costs, scattered visibility, and operational inefficiencies. This is where FinOps – a cultural, strategic, and transformative framework evolves in cloud financial management.

This book has risen with an aim to truly optimize multi-cloud investments for enterprises while being agile, efficient, and financially accountable. Powered by real-world insights, proven practices, and frameworks, this book explores in-depth dynamics of technology, finance, and strategy in a multi-cloud world.

Serving as a compass, this book navigates cloud architects, CFOs, FinOps practitioners, CIOs, and business leaders through multi-cloud cost optimization. Starting from foundational concepts to cost governance strategies, we bring on the tools, models, and cultural shifts necessary to drive necessary, accelerated, and real impact.

As we go through the chapters, our goal is to inspire a new wave of financial accountability, operational excellence, and strategic foresight in cloud computing.

Chapter 1: Cloud Computing Fundamentals– This chapter is the foundation for cloud computing and the essence of multi-cloud environments that covers how innovation with cloud has begun, envisioning the cloud as a multiplied business value investment and a transformative engine for enterprises, cloud computing characteristics, how businesses can fetch maximum value through cloud adoption, various cloud deployment models and their key characteristics, importance of IaaS, PaaS, and SaaS across enterprise IT architecture, core concepts of cloud computing, such as containerization, microservices architecture, shared responsibility model, cloud management and orchestration, APIs and automation, and the future of cloud computing.

Chapter 2: Introduction to Multi-cloud Environments– This chapter explores the transformative potential of FinOps within multi-cloud environments, offering strategies and tools to master cost management and resource optimization. By embracing these principles, organizations can achieve sustained growth, competitive advantage, and a future-proof cloud strategy.

Chapter 3: FinOps Foundations– This chapter delves into the core of FinOps, highlighting its role in maximizing the business value of cloud investments. By fostering financial accountability and data-driven decision-making, FinOps ensures that organizations align their cloud spending with business objectives. The approach emphasizes flexibility, transparency, and collaboration to optimize cloud usage effectively.

Chapter 4: FOCUS: Transforming FinOps for Business Success– This chapter introduces the concept of FOCUS, emphasizing its role in creating synergy between cloud providers, enterprises, and FinOps practitioners. The chapter explores how major cloud providers integrate FOCUS into their ecosystems. Google Cloud champions FOCUS by offering robust tools for real-time cost analysis, while Microsoft Azure builds its strategy around FOCUS to ensure financial discipline. AWS leverages FOCUS to redefine cost and usage transparency, enabling enterprises to maximize their ROI. **Oracle Cloud Infrastructure (OCI)** incorporates FOCUS to make multi-cloud FinOps seamless and efficient.

Chapter 5: Cloud Financial Management and Budgeting– The chapter explores the evaluation process for adopting FinOps tools, guiding enterprises to make informed decisions on whether to build custom solutions for complexity or buy off-the-shelf tools for efficiency. Revolutionary FinOps tools have evolved to address the challenges of multi-cloud environments, offering advanced features like cost allocation, reporting, and resource optimization. By leveraging the power of cloud cost management tools, organizations can foster multi-cloud FinOps practices, optimize resource utilization, and enhance financial transparency. These tools empower enterprises to accelerate their FinOps journey, gain better traction, and achieve sustainable cloud financial management outcomes.

Chapter 6: Cloud Cost Allocation– This chapter covers the three pillars of cost allocation – strategy, tagging, and shared costs that are emphasized as a robust cost allocation framework, the fundamentals of breaking down cloud costs to determine who pays for what, ensuring every stakeholder has a clear understanding of their financial responsibilities, actionable insights into developing cloud cost allocation strategies, including practical approaches to maximize financial efficiency and align with business objectives, and real-world use cases of FOCUS with cost allocation models illustrate how this approach empowers businesses to achieve financial success while maintaining cost visibility.

Chapter 7: Cloud Cost Optimization Strategies– This chapter begins by defining cost optimization and emphasizing its necessity in today's cloud-centric landscape. It highlights the importance of a well-defined cloud cost optimization strategy to control expenses while maintaining performance and operational excellence. The chapter explores key questions organizations must address for effective optimization, such as understanding consumption patterns, identifying cost drivers, and balancing performance with cost. It differentiates between a strategy (long-term planning) and techniques (specific actions) while presenting actionable strategies for reducing cloud costs. This chapter equips enterprises with the mindset, tools, and strategies needed to navigate cloud cost optimization effectively and achieve sustainable business growth.

Chapter 8: Building a Multi-cloud Cost Optimization Plan– This chapter provides an architectural overview of multi-cloud, delving into its dynamic ecosystem and the growing adoption of platform as a service and infrastructure as a service beyond traditional SaaS models. It emphasizes the transformative potential of multi-cloud strategies for businesses but also highlights the greatest challenges associated with adoption, such as cost management, interoperability, and governance complexities. The chapter also showcases the top five benefits of a multi-cloud cost optimization strategy powered by FinOps. These include enhanced cost visibility, improved performance, agility in vendor selection, risk mitigation, and seamless resource allocation.

Chapter 9: FinOps Processes in a Multi-cloud Environment– This chapter delves into the three core stages of FinOps: inform, optimize, and govern, providing a structured approach to mastering financial operations in multi-cloud environments. The inform stage emphasizes gaining visibility into cloud usage and costs, empowering teams with actionable insights. The optimize stage focuses on reducing costs and improving efficiency, ensuring that resources are used strategically. Finally, the govern stage enforces policies and controls to maintain alignment with organizational goals and compliance standards. The chapter also addresses the unique challenges of implementing FinOps in a multi-cloud environment, such as inconsistent cost metrics, data silos, and varying pricing models. It offers actionable insights into implementing FinOps processes, emphasizing collaboration across teams and leveraging the right tools to streamline operations.

Chapter 10: Monitoring, Measuring, and Reporting Cloud Costs and Savings– This chapter underscores the critical importance of monitoring, measuring, and reporting cloud costs in a multi-cloud environment. It begins by highlighting the challenges of neglecting these practices, such as overspending, inefficiencies, and missed opportunities for optimization. The chapter explores how enterprises can standardize monitoring practices, enabling consistent tracking across diverse cloud platforms. Granular visibility and unit economics are emphasized in the context of multi-cloud cost measuring, ensuring that organizations understand the true cost drivers and optimize accordingly. This chapter equips readers with best practices and methodologies for establishing an effective framework to monitor, measure, and report cloud costs. By adopting these strategies, organizations can make informed decisions, enhance cost efficiency, and maximize the value of their multi-cloud investments.

Chapter 11: Cloud Security, Governance, and Compliance– This chapter delves into cloud governance, its significance, and how to implement it effectively in a multi-cloud environment. It defines cloud governance as the framework of policies, processes, and controls designed to ensure responsible cloud usage, cost efficiency, and compliance with organizational goals. The chapter emphasizes why cloud governance is critical, especially in managing complex multi-cloud setups, where mismanagement can lead to inefficiencies and soaring costs. A cloud governance checklist is introduced, providing a structured approach to ensure accountability, compliance, and transparency. Key principles for cloud cost governance are explored, along with essential components like access controls, compliance policies, cost tracking, and reporting mechanisms. The chapter outlines a roadmap to implementing a cloud governance framework, emphasizing automation for efficiency and enterprise-wide scalability.

Chapter 12: Case Studies and Real-world Examples of Multi-cloud FinOps– This chapter explores the practical implementation of FinOps across small-scale, mid-scale, and large enterprises, showcasing how organizations of varying sizes can leverage FinOps to achieve cloud cost optimization and operational efficiency. It also introduces the FinOps Playbook in action, offering actionable strategies for integrating FinOps into business processes. It emphasizes the importance of aligning FinOps principles with organizational goals, fostering collaboration between finance, operations, and IT teams, and utilizing data-driven decision-making to enhance cloud cost management.

Chapter 13: Future Scopes and Trends in Multi-cloud FinOps– The final chapter envisions the transformative future of FinOps, where innovation merges with financial stewardship to address emerging challenges and opportunities in cloud cost management. With advancements like AI-powered cloud search engines and automation, FinOps is poised to deliver unparalleled efficiency and precision in resource optimization. The chapter explores the integration of FinOps with edge computing, superclouds, and industry-specific clouds, highlighting how these trends are reshaping the landscape of financial governance in cloud environments. It emphasizes the rise of GreenOps, focusing on sustainability, and the growing importance of multicurrency and globalized governance frameworks in a connected world.

Coloured Images

Please follow the link to download the
Coloured Images of the book:

https://rebrand.ly/t9q3wkg

We have code bundles from our rich catalogue of books and videos available at https://github.com/bpbpublications. Check them out!

Errata

We take immense pride in our work at BPB Publications and follow best practices to ensure the accuracy of our content to provide with an indulging reading experience to our subscribers. Our readers are our mirrors, and we use their inputs to reflect and improve upon human errors, if any, that may have occurred during the publishing processes involved. To let us maintain the quality and help us reach out to any readers who might be having difficulties due to any unforeseen errors, please write to us at :

errata@bpbonline.com

Your support, suggestions and feedbacks are highly appreciated by the BPB Publications' Family.

Did you know that BPB offers eBook versions of every book published, with PDF and ePub files available? You can upgrade to the eBook version at www.bpbonline.com and as a print book customer, you are entitled to a discount on the eBook copy. Get in touch with us at :

business@bpbonline.com for more details.

At www.bpbonline.com, you can also read a collection of free technical articles, sign up for a range of free newsletters, and receive exclusive discounts and offers on BPB books and eBooks.

Piracy

If you come across any illegal copies of our works in any form on the internet, we would be grateful if you would provide us with the location address or website name. Please contact us at business@bpbonline.com with a link to the material.

If you are interested in becoming an author

If there is a topic that you have expertise in, and you are interested in either writing or contributing to a book, please visit www.bpbonline.com. We have worked with thousands of developers and tech professionals, just like you, to help them share their insights with the global tech community. You can make a general application, apply for a specific hot topic that we are recruiting an author for, or submit your own idea.

Reviews

Please leave a review. Once you have read and used this book, why not leave a review on the site that you purchased it from? Potential readers can then see and use your unbiased opinion to make purchase decisions. We at BPB can understand what you think about our products, and our authors can see your feedback on their book. Thank you!

For more information about BPB, please visit www.bpbonline.com.

Join our Discord space

Join our Discord workspace for latest updates, offers, tech happenings around the world, new releases, and sessions with the authors:

https://discord.bpbonline.com

Table of Contents

CHAPTER 1
Cloud Computing Fundamentals

Introduction

For decades, the soundtrack of every enterprise was *running on the massive rhythms of the data center*. Rows upon rows of servers, blinking lights, the whir of cooling fans—a physical manifestation of the digital world. Owning and operating this infrastructure was the price of admission for doing business in the modern age. It was a capital-intensive game, a heavy lift that demanded significant upfront investment and ongoing maintenance. However, the landscape has shifted dramatically. The cloud has arrived, and it is not just a passing shower; it is a paradigm shift.

This chapter serves as the bedrock for our journey into the world of multi-cloud FinOps. Before we can effectively manage the financial intricacies of a multi-cloud environment, we must first understand the fundamental principles of cloud computing itself. Think of it as learning the alphabet before attempting to write a novel. We will explore the core concepts, dissect the various service models, and trace the evolutionary arc that has brought us to this pivotal moment.

The story of cloud computing is not one of overnight success. It is a tale of incremental progress, of visionaries pushing boundaries, and of necessity giving birth to invention. It began with the simple idea of sharing computing resources, which dates to the early days of mainframe computing. Time-sharing allowed multiple users to access the same machine, maximizing utilization and minimizing costs. This principle, though rudimentary in its initial form, planted the seed for what would eventually blossom into the cloud revolution.

As the internet gained traction, the stage was set for the next act. The rise of web services and the increasing demand for scalable infrastructure created a fertile ground for innovation. Companies like *Amazon,* with its massive e-commerce operations, faced the challenge of managing fluctuating workloads. They needed a solution that could scale up rapidly during peak seasons and scale back down when demand subsided. This need gave rise to the concept of utility computing, where computing resources are treated like a utility, much like electricity or water; that is, you pay for what you use.

The emergence of virtualization technology was another critical catalyst. Virtualization allowed multiple virtual machines to run on a single physical server, further optimizing resource utilization and reducing costs. This technology was a game-changer, enabling the creation of dynamic and flexible infrastructure.

These interwoven threads, time-sharing, utility computing, and virtualization, formed the tapestry of early cloud computing. What was once a niche concept, primarily used by tech-savvy companies, has now become mainstream. Today, organizations of all sizes, across all industries, are leveraging the cloud to drive innovation, improve agility, and reduce costs.

This has led to the nuke and big bang of cloud computing, where innovation has taken its birth, scalable platforms have emerged, agility has evolved, ease-of-access has magnetized to company's app development lifecycles, and the entire IT infrastructure has transformed with this seismic shift as it gave a full throttle to unparalleled business advantage and value.

Necessity of cloud computing

We envision the cloud as a place of holistic transformation with multiplied business value. That is when we build a better future where humanity thrives and industries celebrate success. The main reason why industries became heavily reliant on cloud is due to one critical aspect, that is, agility. In today's lightning-fast developments and dynamics of the economy, speed is prominent. The ability to rapidly develop and deploy applications and services shows a clear difference between leading the edge and remaining a failure. The cloud, with its self-service provisioning and automated infrastructure management, empowers organizations to move at the speed of business. It is like going from dial-up internet to broadband; that is, the increase in speed and responsiveness is transformative:

Figure 1.1: Introduction to cloud computing

The other two essential traits of cloud are unparalleled security and elasticity. Imagine a retailer experiencing a sudden surge in traffic during the holiday season. With on-premises infrastructure, they would need to over-provision to handle peak demand, leaving much of that capacity unused for the rest of the year. The cloud, however, allows them to scale up their resources seamlessly during peak periods and then scale back down when demand subsides. This elasticity ensures that they always have the right amount of capacity without wasting money on idle resources. It is like having a rubber band that can stretch to accommodate any load.

The cloud also simplifies IT management. Maintaining on-premises infrastructure requires a dedicated team of experts to handle everything from server maintenance to security patching. With cloud, much of this heavy lifting is offloaded to the cloud provider, freeing up IT teams to focus on more strategic initiatives. It is like outsourcing your plumbing; you do not need to worry about the intricacies of pipes and drains, and you can focus on running your business.

In essence, the cloud has emerged as the answer to many challenges facing modern businesses. It offers a more cost-effective, agile, scalable, and manageable approach to IT. Companies shift to the cloud due to its limitless functionality and capabilities, enabling organizations to undergo business transformation. It is about empowering organizations to innovate more quickly, respond to market changes more effectively, and ultimately achieve their business objectives.

Every now and then, challenges boom out of nowhere, business disruptions happen, and so do cyberattacks. With the evolution and adoption of the cloud, industry experts and researchers are handling all of these. However, industries are adopting the cloud to a greater extent, its capabilities still remain undermined by many. Though multiple cloud leaders, such as *Oracle, Google, Amazon, Microsoft, IBM,* and others, are set in action mode to address government and private industrial challenges, there are many industries restricting the change. According to our research, this is due to a lack of expertise and a fear of change. With the most highly skilled players operating at the industrial core, a disruptive transformation is underway for industries to thrive soon.

Characteristics of cloud computing

When cloud is creating a huge impact, knowing its self-governing characteristics helps us understand the overall FinOps practice as well. These key characteristics lay the strong foundation for financial management strategies, which we will explore in later chapters of the book.

The cloud is a distinct computing paradigm with its own set of defining characteristics. Understanding these fundamental traits is crucial for anyone venturing into the world of Multi-cloud FinOps. Just as a doctor needs to understand the intricacies of human anatomy, a FinOps practitioner must grasp the core principles that underpin cloud computing. This chapter explores the key characteristics that distinguish the cloud from traditional IT, laying a solid foundation for the financial management strategies examined later in this book. These characterstics, displayed in the following figure, are not merely technical details; they are the DNA of the cloud, shaping its capabilities and influencing its economics:

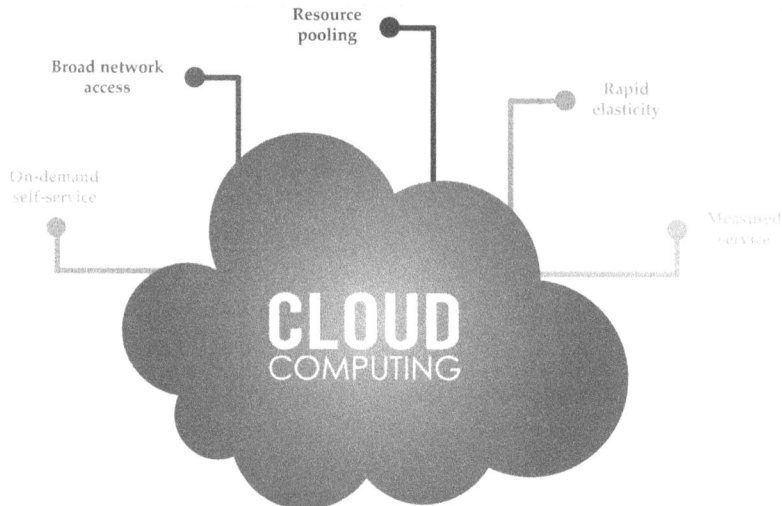

Figure 1.2: Characteristics of cloud computing

Let us go over the characteristics:

- **On-demand self-service**: Imagine ordering a pizza. You do not call the restaurant and ask them to build a pizza oven in your backyard. You simply place your order, and the pizza arrives at your doorstep. Cloud computing operates on a similar principle. Users can provision resources such as compute power, storage, and network capacity, as needed, without requiring human interaction with the service provider. It is all automated, like a vending machine for IT resources. This self-service model empowers users to quickly adapt to changing needs, avoiding the bottlenecks and delays associated with traditional IT procurement processes.

- **Broad network access**: The cloud is accessible from anywhere with an internet connection. Whether you are using a laptop, a smartphone, or a tablet, you can connect to cloud-based resources. This ubiquitous access is a game-changer, enabling remote work, collaboration, and global reach. It is like having a universal power outlet, that is, you can plug in your devices anywhere and access the cloud. This broad accessibility fuels innovation and breaks down geographical barriers.

- **Resource pooling**: Cloud providers maintain large pools of resources, such as servers, storage devices, and networking equipment, that are shared among multiple tenants. This multi-tenancy model allows providers to maximize utilization and achieve economies of scale. It is like living in an apartment building where you share common resources, such as the building structure and elevators, which reduces the cost for everyone. Resource pooling is a key driver of the cloud's cost-effectiveness.

- **Rapid elasticity**: The cloud is like a rubber band; it can stretch or shrink as needed. Resources can be scaled up or down quickly and automatically based on demand. This elasticity ensures that users always have the optimal amount of capacity, avoiding both over-provisioning and under-provisioning. It is like having a car that can transform into a truck when you need to haul cargo and then back into a compact car when you are navigating city streets. Rapid elasticity is crucial for handling fluctuating workloads and optimizing costs.

- **Measured service**: Cloud resources are measured and metered, just like utilities like electricity or water. Users pay only for the resources they consume. This pay-as-you-go model provides transparency and accountability, allowing users to track their spending and optimize their cloud usage. It is like paying for the electricity you use, rather than paying a flat fee regardless of consumption. Measured service is essential for effective cost management and FinOps.

These five characteristics are the cornerstones of cloud computing. They are what distinguish the cloud from traditional IT and enable its unique capabilities. These principles influence the financial aspects of multi-cloud environments and FinOps practice, which together help us to navigate the complexities of cloud economics.

Business benefits of cloud computing

More than a powerful engine, cloud is a technological marvel of industrial transformation. It unlocks new realms of possibilities, drives innovation, and offers unprecedented levels of agility and efficiency. Now, let us see how the cloud can impact businesses at scale by creating a smooth friction with the following advantages:

- **Enhanced agility and speed**: The cloud empowers organizations to respond quickly to changing market conditions and customer demands. With on-demand resource provisioning and automated infrastructure management, businesses can deploy new applications and services in a fraction of the time compared to traditional IT. This agility translates to faster time-to-market, improved competitiveness, and increased responsiveness to customer needs.

- **Improved scalability and elasticity**: The cloud's ability to seamlessly scale resources up or down based on demand, ensures that businesses always have the right amount of capacity. This elasticity eliminates the need for over-provisioning and reduces the risk of performance bottlenecks. It is like having a dial that you can turn to adjust your IT resources as needed, ensuring optimal performance and cost efficiency.

- **Reduced costs and increased efficiency**: By shifting from CapEx to OpEx, the cloud allows businesses to avoid large upfront investments in hardware and software. The pay-as-you-go model ensures that organizations only pay for the resources they consume, eliminating the waste associated with over-provisioning. Furthermore, cloud providers achieve economies of scale, which translate to lower costs for cloud users.

- **Enhanced collaboration and accessibility**: Cloud-based applications and data are accessible from anywhere with an internet connection, fostering collaboration among geographically dispersed teams. This accessibility empowers employees to work remotely, collaborate more effectively, and access critical information regardless of their location.

- **Increased focus on core business**: By offloading IT management to cloud providers, businesses can free up their IT teams to focus on more strategic initiatives. This allows organizations to concentrate on their core competencies and drive innovation, rather than getting bogged down in the complexities of managing IT infrastructure.

- **Improved disaster recovery and business continuity**: The cloud offers robust disaster recovery capabilities, ensuring that critical data and applications are protected from outages and disasters. Cloud-based backups and replication services enable businesses to quickly recover from disruptions and maintain business continuity.

- **Enhanced security**: Cloud providers invest heavily in security measures to protect their infrastructure and their customers' data. While security concerns are often a barrier to cloud adoption, the reality is that cloud providers typically have more sophisticated security capabilities than many organizations can afford to implement on their own.

- **Global reach and expansion**: The cloud enables businesses to easily expand their global footprint without having to invest in building new data centers in different regions. Cloud providers have data centers located worldwide, enabling businesses to access new markets and serve customers globally.

- **Fostering innovation**: By providing easy access to cutting-edge technologies and a scalable infrastructure, the cloud empowers businesses to experiment, innovate, and develop new products and services more quickly and efficiently. It removes the barriers to entry for innovation, allowing businesses to explore new ideas without significant upfront investment.

- **Accelerated cloud-native apps development and deployment**: The cloud provides a fertile ground for cultivating cloud-native applications. Microservices architectures, containerization, and serverless computing, all hallmarks of cloud-native development, thrive in the cloud environment. This accelerates the development lifecycle, enabling organizations to introduce new features and applications to market more quickly, thereby gaining a crucial competitive edge. Here, the organizations shift from monolithic legacy systems to agile, adaptable applications that can evolve at the speed of business.

- **Streamlined workflows**: Cloud computing facilitates the automation and integration of business processes, leading to streamlined workflows. By leveraging cloud-based platforms and services, organizations can connect disparate systems, eliminate manual tasks, and optimize the flow of information. This not only improves efficiency but also reduces the risk of errors and improves overall process visibility. Imagine a factory floor where every step, from raw materials to finished product, is seamlessly orchestrated through cloud-connected systems.

- **Automated processes**: Automation is a cornerstone of the cloud paradigm. From infrastructure provisioning to application deployment, cloud empowers organizations to automate repetitive tasks, freeing up valuable human resources for more strategic initiatives. This automation improves consistency and reliability, minimizing the risk of human error. Let the machines handle the mundane so that people can focus on the meaningful.

- **Increased efficiencies**: The cloud's inherent characteristics, that is, on-demand resources, scalability, and automation, contribute to significant gains in efficiency. Organizations can optimize resource utilization, reduce waste, and streamline operations, leading to lower costs and improved productivity. It is about doing more with less, maximizing resources, and minimizing overhead.

- **Overall operational excellence**: By streamlining workflows, automating processes, and enhancing efficiencies, the cloud enables operational excellence. Organizations can achieve higher levels of performance, improve customer satisfaction, and gain a competitive advantage. Optimize relentlessly and leverage the cloud to empower your operations to the next level.

- **Increased developer productivity**: The cloud provides developers with access to a wide range of tools and services that simplify the development process. From pre-built APIs to serverless computing platforms, the cloud removes many of the traditional barriers to development, allowing developers to focus on writing code and building innovative applications.

- **Optimal ROI**: By reducing costs, improving efficiency, and driving innovation, the cloud can deliver a significant return on investment. The shift from **capital expenditures** (**CapEx**) to **operational expenditures** (**OpEx**), coupled with optimized resource utilization, enables organizations to maximize the value of their IT investments. Moreover, cloud investments translate into tangible business benefits.

- **Centralized infrastructure across the enterprise**: The cloud enables organizations to consolidate their IT infrastructure into a centralized platform, simplifying management and improving visibility. This centralized approach allows for better control over resources, improved security, and streamlined operations.

- **Scalable storage**: Cloud storage is virtually limitless, allowing organizations to store vast amounts of data without worrying about capacity constraints. This scalability is crucial for businesses that are generating and storing increasing volumes of data. This is where you will have the space you need, depending on the requirements, without the limitations of physical storage.

- **On-demand computational power accessibility**: The cloud provides on-demand access to vast amounts of computational power, enabling organizations to run complex simulations, analyze large datasets, and perform other computationally intensive tasks. This access to scalable computing resources is crucial for businesses that need to handle fluctuating workloads or require high-performance computing capabilities.

- **Greater adaptability and resilience**: The cloud's inherent redundancy and distributed architecture make it highly resilient to outages and disruptions. Cloud-based applications and data are replicated across multiple data centers, ensuring that they remain available even in the event of failure. This resilience is crucial for maintaining business continuity and minimizing downtime. Being prepared for anything will enable your business to withstand any storm with minimal hassle.

- **Seamless integration capabilities**: Break down the silos of data and applications by leveraging the connected ecosystem of applications and data, as cloud facilitates seamless integration between different applications and systems, both in the cloud and on-premises. This integration enables organizations to connect disparate data sources, automate workflows, and improve the flow of information across the enterprise.

Cloud deployment models

Empower yourself to decide on a cloud strategy. Though cloud brings many advantages for enterprises, it is not a one-size-fits-all solution. Depending on the diverse needs, varying levels of administrative control, and different security and compliance requirements, cloud computing offers various deployment models, each with its characteristics and trade-offs. Choosing the right deployment model is a critical decision that directly impacts cost, security, control, and scalability.

Cloud deployment models are classified into three types: public, private, and hybrid. Let us explore each one in brief to know the difference and how this helps frame a multi-cloud strategy.

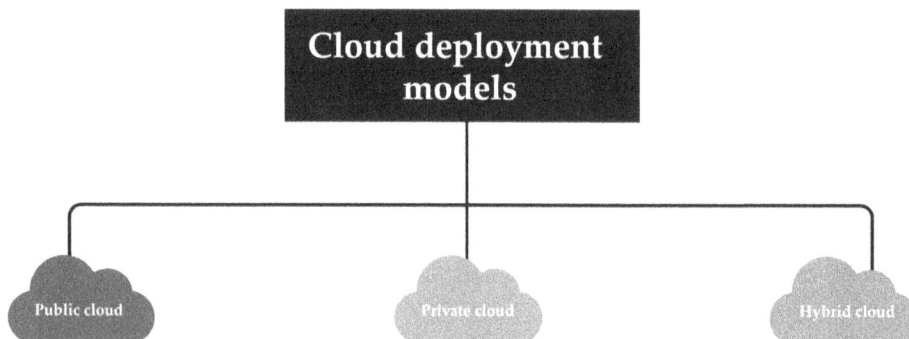

Figure 1.3: Cloud deployment models

Public cloud

The public cloud is the most common and widely recognized deployment model. In this model, a third-party provider owns and manages the infrastructure, including servers, storage, and networking. These resources are shared among multiple tenants, much like a large apartment building where residents share common facilities. Public cloud providers offer a wide range of services, from basic computing and storage to advanced analytics and machine learning.

Key characteristics

The key characteristics of the public cloud are as follows:

- **Shared infrastructure**: Resources are shared among multiple tenants, leading to economies of scale and lower costs.

- **Pay-as-you-go pricing**: Users pay only for the resources they consume, providing flexibility and cost efficiency.

- **Scalability and elasticity**: Resources can be scaled up or down quickly and easily to meet changing demands.

- **Limited control**: Users have limited control over the underlying infrastructure, as it is managed by the provider.

- **High availability**: Public cloud providers typically offer high levels of availability and redundancy.

Private cloud

A private cloud is a cloud infrastructure that is dedicated to a single organization. It can be located on-premises or hosted by a third-party provider. Unlike the public cloud, resources are not shared with other tenants, providing greater control and security. Think of it as a private mansion where you have complete control over the property.

Key characteristics

The key characteristics of a private cloud are as follows:

- **Dedicated infrastructure**: Resources are dedicated to a single organization, providing greater control and security.

- **Customization**: Organizations can customize the infrastructure to meet their specific needs.

- **Greater control**: Users have greater control over the infrastructure and its configuration.

- **Higher cost**: Building and maintaining a private cloud can be more expensive than using a public cloud.

- **Increased security**: Private clouds offer enhanced security due to dedicated resources and greater control.

Hybrid cloud

A hybrid cloud is a combination of public and private clouds. It enables organizations to leverage the benefits of both models, utilizing the public cloud for specific workloads and the private cloud for others. This approach offers flexibility, enabling organizations to tailor their cloud strategy to meet their specific needs. Imagine a house with a guest house. You use the main house for your primary needs and the guest house for specific purposes.

Key characteristics

The key characteristics of a hybrid cloud are as follows:

- **Combination of public and private clouds**: Combines the benefits of both public and private cloud models.

- **Workload portability**: Workloads can be moved between the public and private clouds as needed.

- **Flexibility**: Provides greater flexibility and allows organizations to optimize their cloud strategy.

- **Complexity**: Managing a hybrid cloud environment can be more complex than managing a single cloud.

The beauty of these cloud deployment models lies not only in their individual strengths but also in their ability to interoperate and form the foundation of a multi-cloud strategy. A multi-cloud approach involves leveraging services from multiple cloud providers, picking and choosing the best-of-breed solutions for specific needs. This might include using the robust computing capabilities of one provider, the advanced machine learning services of another, and the cost-effective storage solutions of a third.

Hybrid cloud models, in particular, act as a bridge between different cloud environments, enabling seamless data flow and application portability. This allows organizations to avoid vendor lock-in, maintain flexibility, and optimize their cloud investments by selecting the most suitable services from various providers.

Think of it like building a house. You would not necessarily buy all your materials from a single store. You might get the best lumber from one supplier, the most efficient windows from another, and the most stylish fixtures from a third. Similarly, a multi-cloud approach allows you to construct your ideal cloud environment by leveraging the strengths of different providers.

By understanding the nuances of each cloud deployment model, organizations can craft a tailored multi-cloud strategy that aligns with their specific business objectives, maximizes their return on investment, and unlocks the full potential of the cloud. This foundational knowledge is crucial for navigating the complexities of multi-cloud environments and harnessing the power of this transformative approach to IT.

Cloud service models

When organizations utilize the cloud effectively after conducting comprehensive research, they benefit from numerous advantages that we have discussed. However, the real challenge is in understanding the service models: **infrastructure as a service (IaaS)**, **platform as a service (PaaS)**, and **software as a service (SaaS)**, shown in the following figure. This will make the strategic wing more profound and optimize the cloud investments for enterprises.

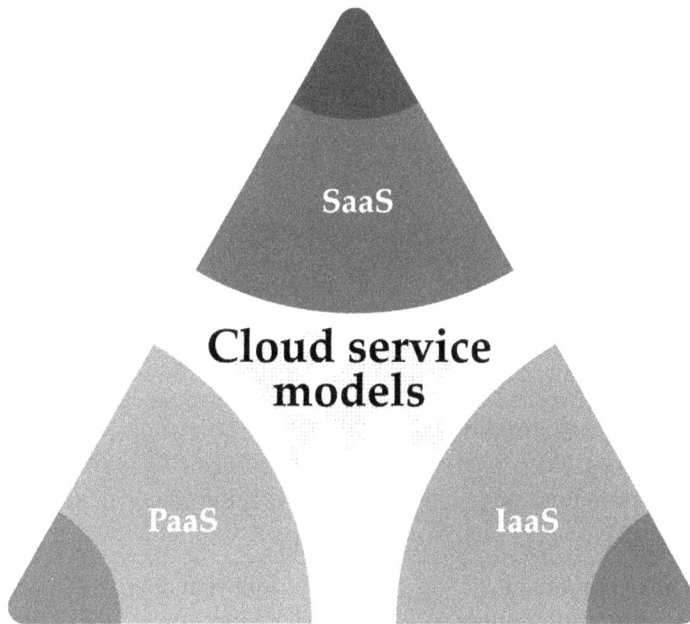

Figure 1.4: Cloud service models

Now, let us understand these models:

- **IaaS**: At the foundation lies IaaS, the raw building blocks of the cloud. IaaS provides on-demand access to fundamental computing resources such as servers, storage, and networking. It offers maximum flexibility and control, making it ideal for organizations with specific infrastructure requirements or those seeking to lift and shift existing applications to the cloud. However, it also demands a higher level of technical expertise and management overhead.

- **PaaS**: Building upon IaaS is PaaS, that provides a complete platform for developing, deploying, and managing applications. PaaS offers a pre-configured environment that includes the operating system, middleware, and runtime environment, allowing developers to focus on building and deploying applications without the complexities of managing the underlying infrastructure. PaaS accelerates the development lifecycle, reduces time-to-market, and simplifies application management, making it a popular choice for organizations seeking to build and deploy cloud-native applications.

- **SaaS**: At the top of the stack sits SaaS, the most user-friendly and accessible of the cloud service models. SaaS delivers software applications over the internet, eliminating the need for users to install or manage any software on their own devices. It is like using a streaming service; you can access a vast library of content without worrying about downloading or storing it locally. SaaS applications are typically subscription-based and centrally managed by the provider, offering ease of use, accessibility, and automatic updates. This makes SaaS ideal for organizations seeking to streamline operations, reduce IT overhead, and provide users with access to essential business applications.

The following *Table 1.1* provides the various features of the service models that we just discussed:

Feature	IaaS	PaaS	SaaS
Definition	Provides access to raw computing resources.	Offers a platform for developing and deploying applications.	Delivers software applications over the internet.
Examples	AWS EC2, Azure Virtual Machines, Google Compute Engine.	AWS Elastic Beanstalk, Azure App Service, Google App Engine.	Salesforce, Google Workspace, Microsoft 365.
Control	Highest.	Moderate.	Lowest.
Management	The user manages the operating system, applications, and data.	The provider manages the underlying infrastructure.	The provider manages the application and infrastructure.
Cost	Pay-as-you-go for resources consumed.	Pay for the platform and resources used.	Subscription-based or pay-per-use.
Scalability	Highly scalable.	Scalable.	Scalable.
Use cases	Hosting web applications, running enterprise applications, data storage.	Developing and deploying web and mobile applications, data analytics.	Email, collaboration, CRM, ERP.

Table 1.1: Features of the service models

Choosing the right cloud service model depends on a variety of factors, including an organization's specific needs, technical expertise, and budget. IaaS offers maximum flexibility and control, PaaS accelerates development and simplifies application management, and SaaS provides ease of use and accessibility. Understanding the nuances of each model is crucial for making informed decisions about your cloud strategy and optimizing your cloud investments.

Core concepts of cloud computing

From making informed decisions about your cloud strategy to harnessing the full potential of transformative technology, these core concepts drive the capabilities and shape your experience towards cloud. These five key pillars, containers, microservices, cloud security, cloud management and orchestration, and APIs and automation, set you on the path of adopting cloud or multi-cloud to capture maximum business value.

Containerization for packaging applications for portability and efficiency

Imagine shipping goods overseas. You would not send each item individually; you would pack them into containers for efficient transport. Containers in the cloud serve a similar purpose. They package applications and their dependencies into isolated units, ensuring portability and consistency across different environments. This eliminates the *it works on my machine* problem, allowing developers to seamlessly move applications from development to testing to production, regardless of the underlying infrastructure. Containers also optimize resource utilization, as multiple containers can share the same operating system kernel, reducing overhead and improving efficiency.

Breaking down monoliths for agility and scalability

Traditional applications were often built as monolithic structures, where all components were tightly coupled. This made them difficult to scale, update, and maintain. Microservices offer a different approach, breaking down applications into small, independent services that communicate with each other through APIs. This modular architecture allows for greater agility, as individual services can be updated and scaled independently without affecting the entire application. It is like building with Lego blocks; you can easily add, remove, or modify individual components without disrupting the overall structure. Microservices are a key enabler of cloud-native applications, providing the flexibility and scalability needed to thrive in the dynamic cloud environment.

Shared responsibility model in cloud security

Security is paramount in the cloud. However, the responsibility for security is shared between the cloud provider and the cloud user. Cloud providers are responsible for securing the underlying infrastructure, while users are responsible for ensuring their own applications and data. This shared responsibility model requires a clear understanding of security best practices, including access control, data encryption, and vulnerability management. Cloud security is an ongoing process that requires vigilance, adaptation, and a collaborative approach between providers and users.

Taming cloud complexity with automation using cloud management and orchestration

Cloud environments can be complex, with numerous resources, services, and configurations to manage. Cloud management and orchestration tools enable the automation and streamlining of these tasks, thereby reducing manual effort and enhancing efficiency. These tools would allow organizations to provision resources, deploy applications, monitor performance, and enforce security policies, all from a centralized platform. Cloud management and orchestration tools bring order to cloud chaos, allowing organizations to manage their cloud resources and optimize their cloud investments effectively.

APIs and automation

Application programming interfaces (**API**) are the connective tissue of the cloud. They allow different applications and services to communicate with each other, enabling automation and integration. Cloud providers offer a vast array of APIs that expose their services and data, allowing users to build custom applications, automate workflows, and integrate with other systems. APIs and automation are crucial for unlocking the full potential of the cloud, enabling organizations to create dynamic, interconnected systems that drive innovation and efficiency.

Future of cloud computing

The future of cloud computing is being shaped by a confluence of emerging trends that are pushing the boundaries of innovation and transforming how organizations leverage the cloud. Serverless computing, edge computing, and the rise of **artificial intelligence** (**AI**) and **machine learning** (**ML**) are just a few of the trends that are redefining the cloud landscape. Serverless computing abstracts away the underlying infrastructure, allowing developers to focus solely on writing code.

Edge computing brings computation closer to the data source, reducing latency and enabling real-time applications. AI and ML are being infused into various cloud services, empowering organizations to extract insights from data, automate processes, and personalize experiences. These trends are not merely technological curiosities; they are powerful forces that will shape the future of cloud computing and influence how organizations adopt and utilize cloud services.

Conclusion

The impact of cloud computing extends far beyond the realm of technology. It is reshaping industries, transforming business models, and redefining how we work and interact. Cloud computing is democratizing access to technology, empowering startups and small businesses with capabilities that were once reserved for large enterprises. It fosters innovation, enabling organizations to experiment with new ideas and bring products and services to market faster. It is also driving social change, connecting people and communities in unprecedented ways.

Moreover, the cloud landscape is in a constant state of flux, with new technologies, services, and providers emerging at a rapid pace. This dynamic environment requires organizations to be agile and adaptable, constantly evaluating their cloud strategies and adjusting their approaches to stay ahead of the curve. The rise of multi-cloud and hybrid cloud deployments, the increasing importance of data security and privacy, and the growing demand for sustainable cloud solutions are just a few of the factors that are shaping the evolving cloud landscape. Organizations that can navigate this evolving landscape, embrace change, and adapt to new realities will be best positioned to harness the full potential of the cloud and achieve their business objectives.

Understanding the future of cloud computing is not about predicting the future with certainty; it is about recognizing the forces that are shaping the cloud landscape and preparing for the challenges and opportunities that lie ahead. This forward-looking perspective is essential for establishing a FinOps culture that is aligned with business goals, adaptable to change, and capable of optimizing cloud investments in a dynamic environment.

Join our Discord space

Join our Discord workspace for latest updates, offers, tech happenings around the world, new releases, and sessions with the authors:

https://discord.bpbonline.com

CHAPTER 2
Introduction to Multi-cloud Environments

Introduction

Innovation appears to be increasing globally as the cloud unveils greater possibilities and enhancements for organizations, driving significant business value. By accelerating the transformative journey and becoming a rapid digital transformation force, every industry is leveraging the cloud's potential, making it a necessity for enterprises to drive their strategic initiatives. Additionally, investments in the cloud environment have increased ROI exponentially, driving overall efficiency and enabling companies to remain competitive in a landscape of infinite possibilities.

Moving beyond the cloud, multi-cloud and hybrid cloud have evolved to enhance computational power and meet ever-growing business needs. Keeping aside the hybrid cloud environment, multi-cloud usage was up by 74% in 2021, as per *Gartner*, as it enabled organizations to avoid vendor lock-ins and take advantage of the unique benefits and potential of various cloud providers.

A multi-cloud environment offers unparalleled flexibility to utilize any cloud based on the needed speed and computational power. Multi-cloud environments can also boost up the development and delivery of enterprise applications by leveraging cloud as IaaS and SaaS models.

We have seen that multi-cloud environments offer greater flexibility, they can handle a more significant number of workloads that a business requires, and they migrate, manage, and secure applications as soon as they are deployed. When the right implementation strategy is in place, multi-cloud architecture triggers enterprises to enhance speed, save costs, and reduce risks associated with the IT landscape.

In a multi-cloud environment, an organization can choose to utilize one provider's cloud services for specific workloads and another provider's cloud services for other workloads. This enables organizations to optimize their cloud usage and reduce their reliance on a single provider for all their computing needs. However, managing a multi-cloud environment can be complex, especially when it comes to cost management. Each cloud provider has its own pricing model, making it challenging to track usage and costs across multiple providers.

Origin and significance of FinOps

Since the implementation of multi-cloud environments within many enterprises, there has also come a necessity to trace cloud costs and governance. Tracking the resources that are being used, and the respective cost structure, became a crucial OpEx model for enterprises as it was observed that their budgets have been exceeding. Hence, to align the entire cloud cost structure, governance, and compliance, FinOps has taken its stand in the era of digital transformation, helping hundreds of organizations define frameworks and a set of principles to manage their entire cloud portfolio.

Financial operations (**FinOps**) is an operational framework and cultural practice that maximizes the business value of the cloud, enables timely data-driven decision-making, and creates financial accountability through collaboration between engineering, financial, and business teams as per *The FinOps Foundation*. In other words, it is a management practice that embraces shared responsibility for an enterprise's cloud infrastructure and associated costs.

To address cloud costs across the organization, the three departments, engineering, operations, and finance teams, collaborate using the FinOps framework as a go-to model. According to our forecast, the story of cloud started with AWS. If we consider the numbers, global cloud spending touched $1 billion in 2009, and it has only increased since then. By 2019, the global cloud spend has crossed $100 billion, which means a 100X increase from the former. Then, all the big cloud players entered the race. As far as we have observed, the current global spend on cloud services is estimated at $600 billion, projected to reach $2.5 trillion by 2030. Another curious aspect is that most enterprises have their workloads on on-premises. This shows that year-on-year cloud adoption is at 50%-52%. Hence, there is less dependency on on-premises, as cloud is being revolutionized by the industry of any type and scale, because cloud adoption is at 1%-2% growth every year. As this continues, it presents challenges to enterprises due to the widespread adoption of cloud. The predominant aspect is enterprises are expected to lose $1/3^{rd}$ of their cloud spends, though the spend stands at $180 billion. This is where accountability, visibility, and automation come into play, and they make enterprises save huge on their cloud spend.

As cloud expenses seem to be the top OpEx within organizations, they tend to expand their portfolios. Hence, FinOps culture becomes a disciplined practice that enables organizations to maximize value from their cloud spend, achieve increased ROI, and gain a competitive edge during high-stakes scenarios.

Dealing with these challenges requires considerable effort and time. However, thanks to a FinOps culture that aligns the organization's cloud spend with its business objectives and cross-functional teams working in collaboration to gain better control over cloud financials, products can be delivered faster. In short, the main objectives of FinOps are:

- 3x value gain for the investment made on cloud resources, that is, gaining maximum efficiency possible.

- Optimize cloud infrastructure to the best possible extent, particularly in terms of financials, which involves doing more with less, that is, achieving cost optimization.

- Continuous improvement opportunities in financial processes and achieve greater business outcomes.

Establishing a FinOps culture

The cloud is known for the **torrent of innovation**, offering organizations unprecedented agility and scalability, but this freedom comes with unrestrained cloud spending. Hence, FinOps fosters disciplined accountability into the very DNA of cloud operations. It encourages everyone to remain accountable for all that we do and respond to whatever is scattered around the cloud spending. It is more of creating a powerful movement to raise the pillars for cultures of accountability, so that FinOps taps the maximum business value for your enterprise.

Establishing FinOps steers the enterprise towards embracing a long-term roadmap of transformation and continuous improvement across all FinOps domains at each stage of FinOps maturity. All this is possible when you, as a FinOps enthusiast, find allies who oppose, win over detractors during times of change, and build communication programs to inspire the FinOps personas in your organization.

At its core, FinOps represents a cultural shift, as it embodies a dynamic approach to driving effective cloud financial management. This is made possible through the collaboration of finance, engineering, and executive leadership, facilitated by the FinOps framework:

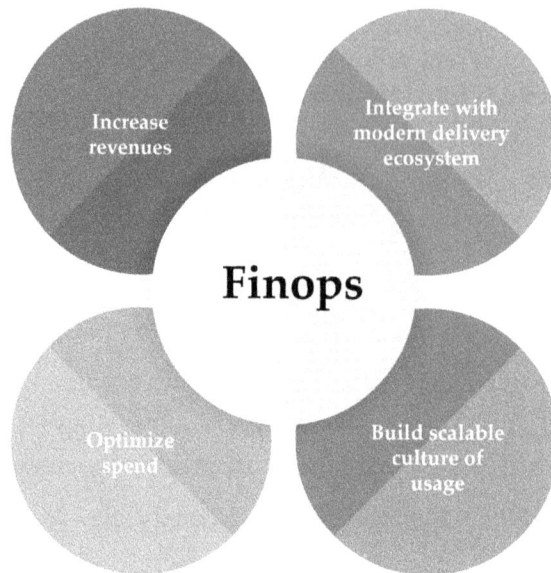

Figure 2.1: *FinOps culture*

Implementing FinOps culture

Aimed at saving infrastructure and operational costs for enterprises, establishing a FinOps culture is a strategic move that adds significant exponential value. Though the implementation of FinOps culture is associated with its own consequences, the potential benefits outweigh the rest. We recommend that enterprises enable the following blueprint, which helps them run FinOps smoothly and derive the best benefits for their businesses to thrive.

A strategic blueprint for FinOps culture

Embarking on the FinOps journey requires a well-defined strategy. This carefully crafted roadmap guides the organization toward a future where cloud financial management is deeply ingrained in its operational fabric. This initial phase, akin to laying the foundation for a skyscraper, is crucial for ensuring the long-term success and sustainability of your FinOps initiative. Let us understand the steps now:

1. **Deep dive discovery**: Before any transformative change can take root, a thorough understanding of the current landscape is essential. This involves delving deep into the organization's cloud cost dynamics, identifying key stakeholders, pinpointing pain points, and recognizing the individuals and teams most impacted by cloud expenditures. Begin by identifying the key players in this transformation, that is, the potential champions, advocates, and executive sponsors who will be instrumental in driving FinOps adoption. Engage them in insightful conversations to uncover

the challenges they face with cloud costs. Are cloud costs hindering business cases? Is there a pervasive perception of cost overruns? Do cloud consumers lack visibility into their spending? These pain points are the driving force for change, the fuel that will ignite the FinOps initiative.

2. **Crafting a bespoke roadmap**: With a deep understanding of the current state, it is time to paint a compelling vision of the future, a future where FinOps is not just a function, but a way of life. This vision should align with the organization's strategic goals, highlighting the tangible benefits of FinOps, including improved cost efficiency, increased agility, and enhanced innovation. This vision takes shape in a customized FinOps roadmap, a detailed plan that outlines the steps, milestones, and resources required to achieve the desired future state. This roadmap should be tailored to the organization's unique needs, considering its pain points, organizational structure, and corporate culture. It should identify the necessary tools, establish an organizational home for the FinOps function, and pinpoint suitable early adopter teams who will pave the way for wider adoption.

3. **Engaging the stakeholders**: A successful FinOps transformation requires buy-in and support from across the organization. This involves actively engaging key stakeholders, sharing a tailored roadmap, and highlighting the value proposition of FinOps. Present the roadmap to executive sponsors, champions, and potential early adopter teams, highlighting the current state, pain points, and potential opportunities. Illustrate the *Crawl, Walk, Run*, progression, demonstrating how the organization will gradually adopt and mature its FinOps practices. Solicit feedback, refine the roadmap, and ensure that stakeholders understand the tangible benefits of FinOps, such as the return on investment achieved by implementing a FinOps function compared to the ongoing costs of cloud overspend.

4. **Securing the resources**: FinOps requires resources, that is, budget, headcount, and tools. Executive sponsorship is crucial for securing these resources, enlisting the support of other leaders, and building a coalition for change. This coalition should comprise genuine organizational influencers and stakeholders who can champion the FinOps cause and drive adoption across the organization. Obtain budget approval for FinOps initiatives, allocate headcount for dedicated FinOps roles, and acquire new tools as needed to support cloud financial management. These resources are the fuel that will power the FinOps engine, enabling the organization to effectively implement and sustain its FinOps practices.

Socializing financial accountability

Building a FinOps culture is a collaborative movement that requires buy-in and support from across the organization. This stage, akin to igniting a spark that will eventually grow into a wildfire, involves effectively communicating the value of FinOps, sharing a compelling vision for the future, and establishing a meaningful dialogue with impacted teams. By fostering a shared understanding and enthusiasm for FinOps, organizations can lay the groundwork for successful adoption and cultivate a culture of collaboration, accountability, and cost-consciousness. Let us go over the following steps now:

1. **Communicate core values**: The first step in socializing FinOps is to communicate its core values and benefits effectively. This is about inspiring and motivating individuals to adopt FinOps as a means of achieving both personal and organizational objectives. Craft a compelling narrative that highlights the transformative potential of FinOps, emphasizing how it can empower teams to optimize cloud spending, drive innovation, and contribute to the organization's overall success. Present a high-level roadmap that outlines the vision for the future and illustrates how FinOps will play a pivotal role in achieving that vision. This roadmap should serve as a living testament to the evolving FinOps journey, continually adapting to new challenges and opportunities as they emerge.

2. **Engage impacted teams**: FinOps is a cross-functional endeavor that requires collaboration and alignment between finance, product, and engineering teams. Engage these teams in meaningful conversations, providing a clear understanding of FinOps principles, addressing their concerns, and demonstrating how FinOps can help them overcome their challenges. These conversations should be a two-way street, a dialogue that fosters mutual understanding and trust. Actively listen to feedback, adjust proposed KPIs based on insights gathered from these interactions, and establish a clear interaction model between the FinOps team and key partners. This collaborative approach ensures that FinOps is not perceived as an external mandate but as a shared responsibility that benefits everyone.

3. **Build the teams**: The success of FinOps hinges on the dedication and expertise of individuals who are passionate about cloud financial management. During the socialization process, identify potential members for the **cloud center of excellence** (**CCoE**) and the Executive Steering Committee. These individuals will be the driving force behind the FinOps initiative, providing guidance, support, and leadership. Look for individuals who possess a combination of technical expertise, financial acumen, and leadership qualities. They should be passionate about FinOps, committed to driving change, and capable of influencing others. Building a strong FinOps team is an investment in the future, ensuring that the organization has the talent and expertise needed to navigate the complexities of cloud financial management.

4. **FinOps model framework for success**: The FinOps framework, with its three phases of inform, optimize, and operate, provides a solid foundation for cloud financial management. However, it is not a one-size-fits-all solution. Customize the FinOps model to suit your organization's specific needs, taking into account its size, structure, and cloud maturity level. Identify the core FinOps team, leveraging internal transfers where roles or individuals overlap, and fill any remaining gaps through recruitment or contracting. Map the change network for FinOps across the organization, ensuring that sponsors, influencers, and adopters are all engaged

and aligned with the FinOps vision. This tailored approach ensures that the FinOps framework is a practical tool that drives tangible results.

5. **Training and communications strategy**: Applied knowledge is power, and empowering individuals with the knowledge and skills they need to embrace FinOps is crucial for successful adoption. Develop a comprehensive training and communications strategy that has the backing of the Steering Committee. This strategy should ensure that all impacted resources receive the necessary information and support to participate in the FinOps journey effectively. For large organizations, consider implementing a hub-and-spoke change management model to reduce dependency on the central team and empower local champions to drive FinOps adoption within their respective teams. This decentralized approach fosters ownership and accountability, ensuring that FinOps becomes deeply ingrained in the organization's culture.

Aligning the organization for FinOps success

Embarking on the FinOps journey is akin to preparing for a rocket launch. It requires meticulous planning, careful coordination, and a deep understanding of the complexities involved. Before igniting the engines of FinOps adoption, it is crucial to assess the organization's readiness, engage stakeholders, establish regular communication channels, and create a change management plan that navigates the complexities of cultural transformation. These preparatory steps are the bedrock upon which a successful and sustainable FinOps practice is built:

1. **Assess readiness**: Just as a pilot conducts pre-flight checks before takeoff, organizations must assess their FinOps readiness before embarking on the transformation journey. This involves evaluating the current state of cloud financial management, identifying areas for improvement, and ensuring that the necessary tools and processes are in place. Begin by establishing a clear taxonomy for tagging, metadata, and organizational structure. This will streamline cost allocation and reporting, providing a clear picture of cloud spending patterns. This data-driven approach ensures that everyone has access to the information they need to make informed decisions about cloud spending.

2. **Building alliances**: FinOps requires collaboration and buy-in from across the organization. Collaborate with early adopter teams to achieve quick wins, such as shutting down unused test environments or optimizing instance sizes. These early successes serve as powerful testimonials, demonstrating the tangible benefits of FinOps and encouraging wider adoption. Implement early governance wins, such as enforcing tagging policies or automating lease-to-live processes, to further showcase the value of FinOps and build momentum for the transformation.

3. **Regular meetings**: Effective communication is the lifeblood of any successful transformation. Establish a consistent cadence of meetings between the FinOps

team, business units, app teams, practitioners, and stakeholders. These regular touchpoints provide a forum for sharing updates, discussing challenges, and aligning best practices. Use these meetings to track KPIs, celebrate successes, and identify areas for improvement. Foster a culture of open communication and collaboration, ensuring that everyone feels heard, valued, and respected. These ongoing discussions are crucial for maintaining momentum, ensuring continuous improvement, and reinforcing the organization's commitment to FinOps principles.

4. **Change management plan**: A successful FinOps transformation requires a change management plan that acknowledges these differences and provides a roadmap for navigating the complexities of change. Adopt a phased approach, allowing teams to embrace FinOps at a pace that suits their needs and capabilities. Provide ongoing support, training, and resources to empower teams throughout the journey. Celebrate milestones, recognize achievements, and address challenges proactively. By incorporating a flexible and supportive change management plan, organizations can foster a smoother transition to a FinOps culture.

Cultivating a culture of continuous FinOps

Reaching the summit of FinOps maturity is not the end of the journey; it is merely the beginning of a new phase, one marked by continuous improvement, adaptation, and a relentless pursuit of cloud financial excellence. This ongoing process requires constant nurturing, careful monitoring, and a willingness to adapt to the ever-changing cloud landscape. By embracing a culture of continuous learning and refinement, organizations can ensure that their FinOps practices remain vibrant, effective, and aligned with their evolving business objectives. Let us understand the steps now:

1. **Tracking and measuring progress**: Just as a ship captain relies on navigational instruments to stay on course, organizations must track and measure their FinOps progress to ensure they are moving in the right direction. This involves regularly evaluating the effectiveness of FinOps initiatives, comparing **key performance indicators** (**KPI**) against initial goals and industry benchmarks, and identifying areas that require further attention.

2. **Identifying areas for improvement**: The pursuit of FinOps maturity is an ongoing quest for optimization, a continuous search for ways to improve cloud financial management practices. This involves analyzing data gathered through KPI tracking and other metrics, identifying inefficiencies, addressing knowledge gaps, and refining processes to leverage cloud financial management tools better. Here, we challenge assumptions, question existing practices, and seek innovative solutions that drive greater efficiency and value.

3. **Implementing improvements**: Identifying areas for improvement is only the first step; the real value lies in implementing the necessary changes to enhance FinOps maturity. This may involve refining the FinOps framework, adopting new tools or

technologies, or providing additional training and support to team members, thus transforming knowledge into tangible improvements.

4. **Encouraging continuous learning**: Foster a culture of continuous learning by providing opportunities for team members to expand their knowledge and skills in FinOps. This may include attending industry conferences, participating in workshops, or enrolling in online courses. Investing in the professional development of your team is an investment in the future of your FinOps practice. It ensures that your team remains up to date on the latest FinOps best practices and technologies, enabling them to adapt to new challenges and seize new opportunities.

5. **Adapting to change**: As your organization's FinOps maturity grows, your objectives and challenges will evolve. Adjust your KPIs and goals to reflect these changes, ensuring that your team remains focused on driving continuous improvement and that your FinOps initiatives continue to deliver maximum value. This dynamic approach ensures that your FinOps practice remains aligned with your business goals and adapts to the changing cloud landscape, staying ahead of the curve, anticipating future needs, and proactively adjusting your FinOps strategy to maintain a competitive edge.

6. **Maintaining vigilance**: The journey towards FinOps maturity is an iterative process that requires constant vigilance and periodic reassessment. Regularly review your organization's FinOps maturity to ensure that you are maintaining best practices and adapting to any changes in the cloud cost landscape. This ongoing review process helps identify areas where your FinOps practice may be drifting off course, allowing you to make timely adjustments and ensure that your organization remains agile and efficient in managing cloud costs.

This approach to driving FinOps capitalizes significantly on cloud investments, enabling enterprises to make a smart difference by saving substantially and leveraging the cloud to accelerate business value. Establishing a FinOps culture is a strategic imperative for any organization that wants to thrive in the cloud era. It is about embedding financial accountability into the very fabric of cloud operations, empowering teams to make informed decisions about cloud spending, and maximizing the business value of cloud investments. By embracing FinOps, organizations can transform their relationship with the cloud, turning it from a potential cost center into a strategic asset that drives innovation and growth.

Redefining cloud cost optimization

Many enterprises fall into the misconception that cloud investment is a one-time expense. However, as they realize over time, it increases costs if it is unplanned or not included as one of the strategic imperatives. This is why FinOps redefines this approach by treating cloud cost optimization as a continuous and proactive process that aligns with the organization's broader business objectives and financial goals.

Let us now explore the factors that influence cloud costs and key aspects that are integral part of FinOps model.

Factors influencing cloud costs

The factors influencing cloud costs are as follows:

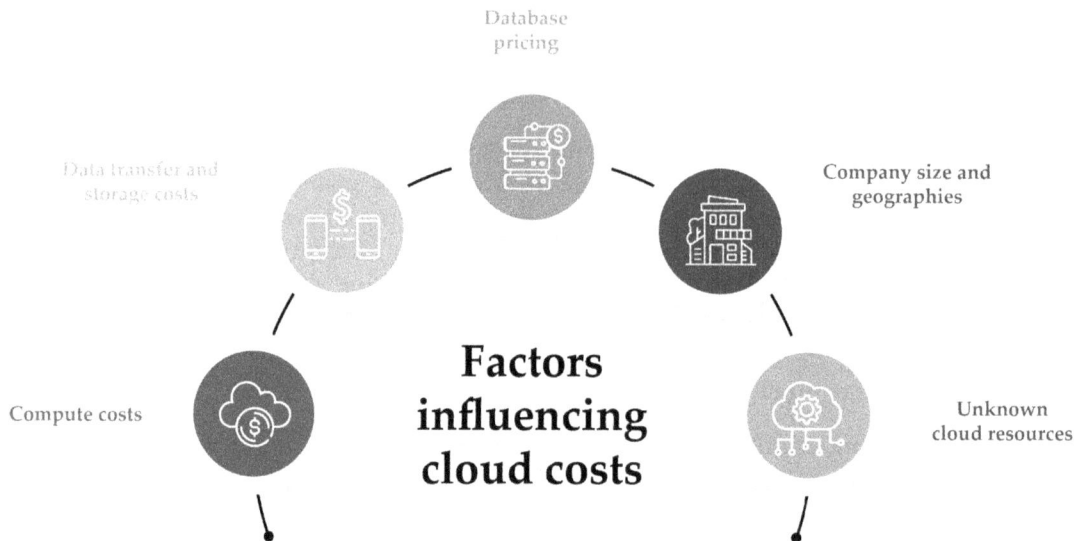

Figure 2.2: Factors influencing cloud costs

Let us look at the details:

- **Compute costs**: The costs associated with the processing power required to deploy or run applications in the cloud are known as compute costs. However, the price of computing costs relies on the type of **virtual machine** (**VM**) chosen, the geography where the application runs, and the operating system used. Enterprises have the flexibility to choose instances to be operated by deciding on their specifications and price, meeting their business needs.

  o   The instance type signifies the hardware of the hosting environment, that is, processor speed, networking capacity, storage type, and memory. As memory-intensive applications occupy a high capacity of networking and memory, various applications demand different types of instances.

  o   The geography also directly impacts compute costs. As cloud providers have datacenters across the globe (a few may have location constraints such as sticking only offshore), the price of instances varies based on region-specific operational costs.

- **Data transfer and storage costs**: Any enterprise needs storage that keeps expanding day after day. The storage costs of cloud services are primarily driven by enterprises' increasing reliance on and demand for data bandwidth in the cloud. Again, the region-specific and type of storage used come into play in this scenario. Although the cloud offers various storage options and corresponding pricing, their performance and characteristics differ. For example, if you have chosen block storage, it handles low latency and high **input/output operations per second** (**IOPs**) workloads. On the other hand, object storage is well-suited for storing unstructured data, such as images, videos, and various document formats.

- **Database pricing**: Every cloud-centralized enterprise needs to take advantage of managed database services and plan the associated costs as well. The database pricing includes the type of database service used, its capacity, performance, and the region where the database is hosted from.

- **Company size and geographies**: The best thing about cloud resources is that they can be scaled up or down depending on their usage. As the people within an organization scale up, cloud resources can be increased by scaling them up and the same goes for less in number. Whatever the instance, depending on the company's size and locations that it has been operating from, cloud costs have a significant impact on OpEx.

- **Unknown cloud resources**: A company conducts hundreds of thousands of operations in a single day or month. For every department, there can be multiple instances that need to be carried out, which depend on the cloud. As department operations continue to increase, so do the cloud resources. In a list of hundreds of cloud resources, it is a challenging and confusing task for enterprises to track how each of them is used and the associated costs. This is where the enterprises lack focus and run out of budgets, losing huge on their cloud costs.

The solution

As discussed, FinOps brings cloud cost discipline for enterprises, and a multi-cloud FinOps solution is a great option. From navigating through the cloud costs seamlessly with continuous optimization of cloud resources to tracking your expenses to a more granular level is how a multi-cloud FinOps solution contributes to these scenarios.

In an observation, a mid-sized IT company has faced similar challenges in terms of handling cloud costs and their integration of *Heeddata* and other tools, of course, have gained the traction. They have implemented it across the enterprise and observed the consistent reduction in their cloud costs. We will talk about this in upcoming chapters. When the market is equipped with such a potential solution that fosters a FinOps culture to a greater extent, that is where enterprises can rely, reducing their entire cloud spend by almost 30%.

Conclusion

The purpose of this book is to guide organizations in fulfilling FinOp's purpose, ensuring their cloud environment is safe and secure with the right optimization tools and standards. It also helps enterprises to focus more on their business operations than the cloud, as it can be handled by streamlining the FinOps culture.

Now, as part of establishing a greater purpose for organizations with a vision to enhance their cloud environment, this book delves into the best practices and tools for managing costs and optimizing resources in a multi-cloud environment using FinOps principles. We will cover cloud governance, cloud cost management, cloud cost allocation, optimization strategies, and more. By the end of this book, you should have a strong strategic approach to capitalize on multi-cloud environments, enabling you to sustain growth through ever-expanding cloud costs and overcome the challenges associated with FinOps and multi-cloud adoption.

Join our Discord space

Join our Discord workspace for latest updates, offers, tech happenings around the world, new releases, and sessions with the authors:

https://discord.bpbonline.com

CHAPTER 3

FinOps Foundations

Introduction

The exponential reliance to migrate, modernize, and innovate using cloud platforms for data storage, scalable infrastructure, intelligent application interfaces, and accessibility leaves organizations with significant challenges to strike the equilibrium between cost and performance. Maintaining this right balance is crucial for enhancing efficiency, resource utilization, and overall cloud value. To streamline everything together, FinOps is chosen as a compelling strategy.

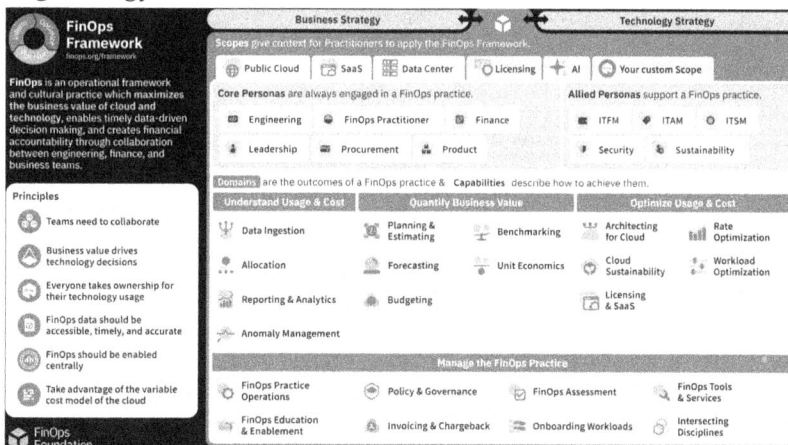

Figure 3.1: Complete FinOps framework

Managing and enhancing cloud spending, meeting the financial objectives along with operational goals, and streamlining cloud operations are three key areas where FinOps framework fosters. More than just understanding, delving into what FinOps holds in its core to unravel synergies for, as given in the following list, gives a visualization of how best FinOps fits into your enterprise's strategic imperatives and becomes a core operational value:

- Cost efficiency

- Optimal performance

- Unlocking full potential of cloud

- Accuracy about cloud usage

- Deriving maximum value through cloud

Slice and dice of FinOps framework

FinOps is a comprehensive discipline where strategies and principles imbibe to bring a balance for cloud operational and financial management. This culture is known for its efficiency and promotes greater collaboration between finance, operations, and technical teams to streamline cloud costs for substantial business outcomes.

Moreover, FinOps framework has its own significance: maintaining the right balance between innovation, speed, and adaptablity in cloud along with financial responsibility, promoting effective cross-collaboration across teams, breaking down the silos and establishing a unified approach to manage cloud costs, and aligning financial goals with enterprise global objectives, thus multiplying the value of the cloud.

In the essence of cultivating FinOps framework, our research into making it as an effective practice within enterprises has led to exploring the invaluable tools that balance FinOps culture and cloud resource utilization. In our innovation wing, we discovered that a multi-cloud FinOps platform, specifically Heeddata, brings greater balance and advantages to enterprises operating in the cloud.

Let us understand how FinOps optimizes cloud resource management while instilling financial discipline.

FinOps framework significance in cloud resource management

Owning the in-built capabilities to drive and streamline cloud resources in a way that enterprises can save huge on mounting cloud costs while dealing with underlying challenges and complexities is the paramount significance of FinOps framework.

Owing to these standards, the following essential facets have helped us unveil the FinOps significance for managing the cloud ecosystem of our clients:

- **Enhance the structure of cost visibility and transparency**: The cloud is not a cakewalk for many, especially when it has multiple architectures and pricing structures that challenge the monitoring of existing resources and expenses. This is where embracing FinOps lets you see your cloud spending which is cost visibility, allowing you to discover transparency across services and resources at the most granular level. What we have seen is that such transparency has become a power drive for small, medium, and large enterprises to be highly decisive, based on actionable insights, ultimately meeting the purpose of cloud spend optimization.

- **Foster ownership and accountability across enterprise**: Making teams accountable for uprising spend on the cloud involves a lot of challenges. However, fostering accountability shows the dynamics of internal leadership and management. Distributing cloud expenses across various functional units in your business, at least to the respective heads, drives them to take ownership of their responsibilities, and they will demonstrate a higher level of proactiveness in holding teams accountable for the cloud resources they use. This happens by making FinOps a bloodline for your teams where everyone is clear on financial objectives, aligns towards operational goals, and finds ways to optimize cloud computing and storage resources to the best possible scenario.

- **Strategize to optimize, not to disrupt cloud usage**: In our experience with implementing FinOps for enterprises, we have observed that these enterprises were attempting to break free from the constraints within the cloud, which has often led them into difficult scenarios. For instance, one of our healthcare technology pioneers approached us, quoting the problem of cloud usage disruption. When we deconstructed what happened, we noticed that with an aim to cut overhead cloud costs, this healthcare leader had disabled a few core operational resources that halted business continuity.

  o This case illustrates the importance of strategizing to optimize cloud resources, rather than simply reversing course because budgets are exceeding. Tapping into the right expertise to enable FinOps and prioritize constant optimization by examining every minute detail serves as a multiplier for your business, leading to the efficient use of cloud resources that align with your business objectives.

- **Collaborate seamlessly with cross-functional teams**: Communication is not only a skill; indeed, it is a way to take every aspect of business to the next level. Captivating cross-collaboration across the enterprise among teams is a type of synergy that bolsters business operations, engagement, and rapport. If cross-collaboration is not well established, operations become fragmented into individual functional units, and teams are hindered. No more exponential growth can be seen across your enterprise. To streamline FinOps and reduce business risks through cloud cost management, cross-collaboration must be a core operational practice for enterprises.

- **Adapt and evolve as dynamics of environment change**: The endless configurations and creation of resources as business evolves, along with the rapid scalability of the cloud environment, pose substantial challenges such as time consumption, involved costs, and complex scenarios. However, FinOps has its potential to recognize and embrace the ever-changing dynamics of cloud environment at ease, leaving you at peace. Adopting or embracing these changes, along with a FinOps discipline, complement organizations in scaling resources efficiently while handling cost-control mechanisms.

- **Compliance and risk mitigation**: We observed that overspending or inability to restrict cloud resources subjects enterprises to various risks, including compliance risks. Having FinOps in your business strategy plays a magnificent part in mitigating financial risks with cloud management, establishing governance policies, and implementing great control to keep your budgets under the threshold while meeting the regulatory requirements.

FinOps is an imperative strategy that must be fostered across the enterprise. Without FinOps, your cloud costs will always overrun, landing you in unexpected disruptive scenarios.

Though the significance of FinOps serves as the most potential framework for enterprises, all the following domains, capabilities, maturity model, phases, personas, best practices, and principles to fully complement your enterprise, leverage greater financial discipline for the cloud cost management and effectively utilize cloud resource management.

Best practices

In the cloud-powered world where enterprises relentlessly invest huge amounts in cloud operations, it is also essential to reduce cloud wastage and manage end-to-end commitments, sticking with the budgets and organizational objectives. As per the FinOps foundation report, almost 65% of enterprises are at *Crawl* phase in the maturity model. To toast the FinOps framework to the maximum, either elite expertise or an unmatchable platform that accelerates everything about FinOps serves the purpose. The goal of FinOps is to promote effective collaboration between engineering and finance teams to optimize cloud costs commendably.

Considering the importance of cloud cost management, industry-led best practices must be implemented across the enterprise to mitigate the surge in cloud costs and utilize resources effectively.

Let us now go over the seven proven and the unrivaled FinOps practices that serve organizations to save huge and scale high.

Cloud cost visibility

Visibility into cloud costs becomes a key challenge that beats hard for enterprises, leaving them clueless about what to do next.

The multi-cloud usage in most organizations makes it challenging to gain a clear understanding of their cloud costs, as visibility is limited. This challenge presents a challenge in identifying how resources are being used and where to scale down costs.

The rebelling aspects include:

- Resources used for the current product/service/application and respective costs.

- Personas responsible for activating so many resources and cloud costs and ways to allocate shared costs.

- Overrunning of costs in multi-cloud environments and how it serves in the coming months.

- Reasons for unexpected costs.

As we identified the root causes, the grounding solution is to gain consistent visibility into the cloud environment. How can this happen? What are the possibilities? Well, consistent visibility can totally allocate, monitor, analyze, and derive reports at the most granular level. *Unbeatable business decisions are taken when one completely understands cloud resources and personas responsible for utilizing them.* Let us now go over the various solutions:

- **Track hour by hour**: Track hour by hour of every resource that is being used, which is the right and best way to see patterns and high tides in usage. The cause behind unexpected costs and cloud spending by service, resource, or any other means, remain transparent when hourly tracking of the cloud environment is enabled.

- **Tagging is paramount to visibility**: The dimensions of cloud services, resources, type of operation, or usage cannot be seen or acted against. A tagging strategy magnifies meaningful information to organize cloud costs for diverse sets of stacks, customers, cloud environments, projects, departments, and teams.

- **Alerts and notifications**: What if the data transfer costs rise and turn the monthly budget of cloud upside down? The safest approach is to set thresholds for cloud spending and establish alerts and notifications within the environment, so that whenever there are cost overruns or unusual spending patterns, you receive an alert. This helps save even before billing surprises you.

Understanding multi-cloud pricing

In the dynamic world of multi-cloud environments, understanding pricing structures across multiple cloud providers is crucial to optimizing costs and maximizing value. Each cloud provider offers a plethora of services, each with its own pricing intricacies. To navigate this complex landscape, one must first grasp the foundational pricing models that most cloud providers utilize. Here is a breakdown of the major pricing types you will encounter in a multi-cloud environment:

- **On-demand**: The on-demand model epitomizes flexibility, enabling you to request cloud resources as needed without any long-term commitment. This model is ideal for unpredictable workloads where demand fluctuates, but it comes with a catch, that is, the cost. On-demand pricing is the most expensive option, as it charges a premium for the convenience of instant access to cloud resources. In a multi-cloud strategy, the goal should be to minimize reliance on on-demand instances, aiming for as close to 0% usage as possible to avoid unnecessary costs.

- **Reserved Instances**: **Reserved Instances** (**RI**) offer significant savings, sometimes up to 75% compared to on-demand pricing, in exchange for committing to a specific set of resources over a fixed term, typically one or three years. However, this model comes with limited flexibility, as the commitment is tied to specific parameters such as instance type, region, and operating system. In a multi-cloud environment, leveraging Reserved Instances across different providers can yield substantial cost benefits, but it requires careful planning and forecasting to avoid overcommitting resources that may not be fully utilized.

- **Savings Plans**: **Savings Plans** (**SP**) offer a middle ground between the flexibility of on-demand and the cost savings of Reserved Instances. By committing to a certain level of cloud usage over a one or three-year period, you can achieve discounts of up to 72% off on-demand rates. Unlike RI, SP are more adaptable, automatically applying discounts to the usage that provides the most significant financial benefit. In a multi-cloud environment, this flexibility is particularly valuable, as it enables more agile resource management across different cloud providers.

- **Spot Instances**: Spot Instances represent an opportunity to access cloud resources at a fraction of the cost. These are unused resources that cloud providers offer at a discount, with the caveat that they may reclaim the capacity at any time, potentially disrupting workloads. Spot Instances are an excellent choice for non-critical or fault-tolerant applications that can tolerate interruptions. In a multi-cloud setup, strategically deploying Spot Instances can further reduce costs, but it requires robust management practices to handle the inherent unpredictability.

- **Strategic commitment management**: The art of managing cloud costs lies in making informed commitments. In a constantly evolving cloud landscape, where systems are regularly modernized and resized, it is vital to strike a balance between overcommitting and under-committing. Overcommitting leads to wasted resources and unnecessary costs, while under-committing forces you to rely on expensive on-demand pricing for additional capacity.

  o To optimize your multi-cloud expenditure, start by moving stable workloads to RI or SP. This approach provides a predictable cost base, allowing you to take advantage of the lower pricing. For added flexibility and savings, consider using commitment management solutions that automatically optimize your purchases, sometimes offering buyback guarantees to further mitigate risk.

Mastering the art of cloud cost resource optimization through rightsizing EC2 instances

Have you ever heard of *Trimming the fat without cutting the muscle?* The core aspect of cloud cost optimization revolves around this single formula. However, the performance and workload requirements always grow at scale, leading to overprovisioning, although rightsizing is a viable option. This dynamic nature demands a vigilant, iterative approach to rightsizing.

So, how do we unlock the secrets of EC2 rightsizing in this new era of cloud computing? It all starts with getting up close and personal with your usage metrics. Monitoring tools are your best friends here: they are the unsung heroes that collect those crucial resource-level metrics. Compare your current usage with two yardsticks: your current instance type and the next size down. Here is where it gets interesting: if your max usage is sitting pretty at less than 40% of your current type, or you are only tapping into 80% of what the smaller instance offers, it is time to consider downsizing. Understand the nuances of your workload, the peaks and valleys of demand, and have the courage to make data-driven decisions.

Here are some advanced plays for the true cloud cost optimization maestro:

- **Embrace AI-driven rightsizing**: Embed AI/ML algorithms that automatically run instances to predict your resource needs before you even realize you have them.

- **Implement real-time rightsizing**: Never wait for monthly reviews through traditional ways, wondering at the last moment! Adjust the usage patterns and set your cloud portfolio in real time for accurate rightsizing.

- **Instance family selection**: Do not just focus on size: the right instance family can be a game-changer for performance and cost.

- **Leverage Spot Instances strategically**: For non-critical, interruptible workloads, Spot Instances can be your secret weapon for monitoring cloud costs.

- **Cultivate a FinOps culture**: Rightsizing is not an IT challenge anymore. It is a company-wide mindset where the culture brings accountability in a steward of cloud resources.

Scheduling resources for QA and dev environments

Scheduling the QA and dev environments is the goldmine of cost optimization, and most enterprises often neglect this aspect of cloud resource management. Unless your dev team is burning the midnight oil round the clock, your QA and dev environments are likely sitting idle for a significant chunk of the day. It is the equivalent of leaving all the lights on in your office building 24/7, a surefire way to inflate your utility bill unnecessarily.

Here is where the magic happens. By implementing a smart scheduling strategy, you are not just trimming the fat; you are potentially carving out a whopping 60-66% reduction in cloud costs for these environments. It is like finding money in the couch cushions of your cloud infrastructure.

Think about it: if your team typically puts in a solid 8-10 hour day, that leaves 14-16 hours where those environments are twiddling their virtual thumbs. Weekends are another 48 hours of potential savings just waiting to be tapped.

Now, you might think that you can manage this through the Cloud Console or CLI. Sure, you could. You could also choose to do your taxes with an abacus. However, why would you when there are better tools at your disposal?

This is where automation tools come into play, and they are not just a luxury. They are a necessity for any serious FinOps practitioner. Platforms like Heeddata are changing the game, making resource scheduling as easy as ordering your morning coffee.

Heeddata advantage

Let us talk about Heeddata for a moment. This is not just another tool in your FinOps toolkit; it is the Swiss Army knife you did not know you needed. With Heeddata, scheduling your resources is not a chore; it is a few clicks away from significant savings.

However, here is the kicker: it is not just about ease of use. Heeddata and similar platforms bring a level of precision and flexibility to your scheduling that manual methods simply cannot match. Want to automatically spin up your Dev environment at 8 AM sharp every weekday? Done. Need to keep certain critical systems running over the weekend for that big Monday release? No problem.

For the true FinOps virtuosos out there, basic scheduling is just the beginning. Here are some advanced plays to consider:

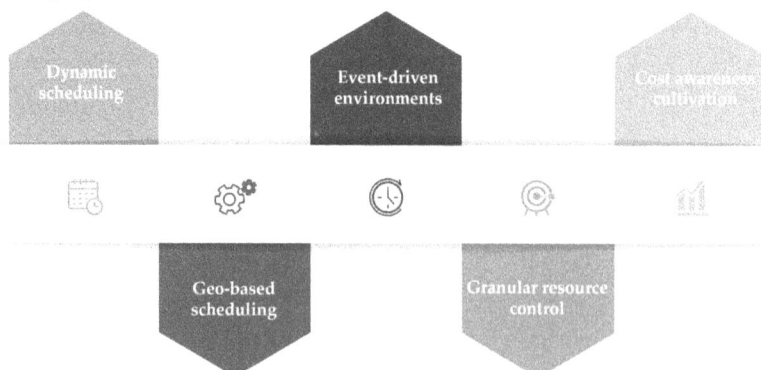

Figure 3.2: Heeddata's role in establishing FinOps

Let us look at the details:

- **Dynamic scheduling**: Use AI and machine learning to predict usage patterns and adjust schedules automatically.

- **Geo-based scheduling**: For global teams, implement schedules that follow the sun, maximizing resource utilization across time zones.

- **Event-driven environments**: Set up systems that spin up environments based on specific triggers, like code commits or pull requests.

- **Granular resource control**: Do not just schedule entire environments, get granular. Maybe your database needs to run 24/7, but your app servers can take a breather overnight.

- **Cost awareness cultivation**: Use scheduling as a tool to build cost awareness within your development teams. When they see the direct impact of resource usage on costs, you are fostering a culture of FinOps from the ground up.

Here is the thing about implementing smart scheduling for your QA and dev environments. It is not just about the immediate cost savings. You are setting in motion a domino effect of efficiency across your entire cloud strategy.

By optimizing these environments, you are freeing up resources and budget that can be reallocated to innovation, performance improvements, or even that machine learning project your team has been itching to start.

Moreover, you are sending a clear message throughout your organization: in the cloud, every resource counts, every dollar matters, and efficiency is not just encouraged—it is expected.

In the grand symphony of multi-cloud FinOps, scheduling your QA and dev environments may seem like a minor detail. However, as any maestro will tell you, it is often these small notes that elevate a performance from good to extraordinary. You might just find yourself leading the charge in the next revolution of cloud cost optimization.

Delete unused or underutilized resources

Every enterprise falls into this trap: cloud account as a sprawling digital city, with EC2 instances as buildings. Now, imagine half of those buildings sitting empty, lights on, AC running, but no one home. That is the reality for many organizations, and it is a FinOps nightmare.

These idle instances are the ghosts of projects past: remnants of overzealous auto-scaling, abandoned dev experiments, or the digital leftovers of completed migrations. They are not just costly; they are a monument to inefficiency.

Here is a mind-bender for you: for every dollar you save by stopping an idle instance, you are actually saving two. How? It is not just about the instance cost. You are also cutting out the associated storage, network, and database charges. It is like getting a two-for-one deal at the cloud savings buffet.

Now, let us talk about EBS volumes, the unsung heroes of cloud storage that often become the unintended villains of your cloud bill. These persistent block-level storage devices are like the hard drives of the cloud world. However, they outlive their usefulness.

In the fast-paced world of cloud computing, where EC2 instances come and go like tourists in *Times Square*, **Elastic Block Store** (**EBS**) volumes often get left behind. It is like leaving the meter running on a taxi long after you have reached your destination.

The culprit? That innocuous little checkbox labeled **Delete on Termination**. Unless you tick that box when launching your instance, terminating an EC2 does not delete its associated EBS volume; it just detaches it. The result is a digital wasteland of idle volumes, silently siphoning your budget month after month.

So, how do we turn this ship around? It is time for a FinOps revolution, and it starts with these game-changing strategies:

- **Implement a use it or lose it policy**: Set strict guidelines for resource provisioning and usage. If it is not actively used within a set timeframe, it gets the axe.

- **Automate the cleanup**: Leverage tools and scripts to automatically identify and flag (or even delete) unused resources.

- **Regular cloud audits**: Schedule monthly or quarterly spring cleanings of your cloud environment. It is not glamorous, but neither is a bloated cloud bill.

- **Educate your team**: Foster a culture of cloud cost awareness. Every developer should understand the impact of leaving resources running. Bring the fiscal responsibility into the core.

- **Tagging for accountability**: Implement a robust tagging strategy. Every resource should have an owner, a purpose, and an expiration date. It is like putting a best by date on your cloud resources.

- **Leverage Reserved Instances wisely**: For those long-running workloads, RIs can be a godsend. However, use them judiciously. An unused RI is just as wasteful as an idle on-demand instance.

- **Implement auto-scaling**: Do not just set it and forget it. Regularly review and refine your auto-scaling policies to ensure they are aligned with actual usage patterns.

When enterprises delete their unused resources, more than immediate cost savings, it is all about enhancing efficiency that permeates every aspect of your cloud strategy. Keep your applications lean, deploy more thoughtfully, and then your team will take care of the real costs associated with their work.

Through deletion of unused resources, your FinOps is embraced where financial accountability meets cloud operations.

Architected review of cloud usage

The cloud well-architected framework is revolutionizing how we build and run applications in the cloud. Think of it as our North Star, guiding us toward creating secure, high-performing, reliable, scalable, and cost-efficient workloads. However, here is the unsolved puzzle: how does it fit into your FinOps strategy?

The well-architected review serves as your trusted compass, guiding you through the complex terrain of your cloud environment. You will gain clear and deep insights into how your cloud usage is measured against industry standards.

The cloud usage review should provide a comprehensive overview of your entire cloud ecosystem. Through the series of targeted questions, you will have an overview of optimization potential of the cloud ecosystem.

Now, let us talk about the two crucial factors: the optimization of performance and cost. It is the holy grail of cloud architecture, and the well-architected review is your map to find it. This is not about penny-pinching or cutting corners. It is about striking that perfect balance where your applications perform great, and your CFO objectives meet.

At the heart of the well-architected framework lie its pillars. Think of them as the load-bearing columns of your cloud strategy. Each cloud provider may have its own interpretation of these pillars, but they all share a common goal: to elevate your cloud capabilities to new heights.

As you work through the review, each question is a steppingstone, leading you to a deeper understanding of how well your architecture aligns with these pillars. It is like holding up a mirror to your cloud strategy, reflecting both its strengths and areas for improvement.

Maximize cloud ROI by converting insights into actions

Selecting the launchpad for action is what a well-architected review is all about. To make transformation happen, it will lead you to focus on deriving greater value from every cloud penny spent. Make it as a roadmap to cloud nirvana, be it rightsizing your instances, optimizing your storage strategy, or fine-tuning your network configuration, every action on the cloud that is taken, is a step towards a more efficient, cost-effective cloud presence.

Armed with the insights from the well-architected review, you become the translator, the mediator between IT and finance. You are not just speaking the language of cloud; you are articulating its value in terms that resonate across the entire organization.

As you embed this practice into your FinOps strategy, you are not just keeping pace with the cloud; you are setting the pace. You are creating a culture where efficiency is not just a goal; it is a way of life. And in doing so, you are not just optimizing your cloud spend: you are positioning your organization at the forefront of the digital revolution.

Understand how optimized your cloud costs are

We are creating a culture where financial efficiency is baked into every decision, where every dollar spent in the cloud is a dollar invested in the company's future.

In the high-stakes game of cloud computing, understanding your cost optimization efforts is like trying to read the wind in a sailing race. It is subtle, crucial, and can make or break your performance. However, here is a little secret that might just give you the edge you have been looking for.

Take a good, hard look at your discount utilization. It is like a financial health check-up for your cloud strategy, providing a snapshot of how savvy your spending really is and here is the kicker: your goal should be to whittle down that full-price, on-demand spend until it is as close to zilch as humanly possible.

Why, you ask? Well, every dollar spent on full-price, on-demand resources is like leaving money on the table. In the cloud game, discounts are not just nice-to-haves; they are the secret sauce of cost-effective operations.

Some of you might think it is easier said than done and you are right. Navigating the labyrinth of cloud pricing models and discount options can feel like trying to solve a Rubik's cube blindfolded. However, here is where the rubber meets the road: mastering this art can be the difference between a cloud strategy that is merely functional and one that is a true competitive advantage.

Your cloud infrastructure must deliver the highest performance possible by leveraging discounted resources, while also outpacing the competition without breaking a sweat. Though this action is great, at the end, what matters is what you want to accomplish with it: either contributes to effective FinOps practice, with knowledge in action or leads your engineering team into nightmares.

This is where we enter the realm of automated cloud cost optimization platforms. These not only provide a comprehensive view of your garden-variety cost calculators, but they are also powerhouses equipped with sophisticated, AI-driven algorithms that can transform your cost optimization efforts from a manual slog into a well-oiled machine.

Imagine a world where optimizing cloud costs is as integral to the engineering process as writing clean code or running tests. Where every deployment comes with an automatic assessment of its financial impact and where finding a more cost-effective solution is celebrated as much as solving a tricky technical challenge.

This shift is not just about saving a few bucks here and there. It is about fundamentally changing how organizations view and interact with their cloud resources. It is about transforming the cloud from a cost center into a value creator, a platform for innovation and growth that pays for itself through intelligent, optimized usage.

By embracing these principles and leveraging cutting-edge tools, you are revolutionizing your entire approach to cloud computing.

FinOps capabilities

In a multi-cloud environment, where organizations leverage services from multiple providers, such as AWS, Azure, Google Cloud, and others, FinOps serves as a strategic framework for managing cloud costs, optimizing resource use, and aligning spending with business value. The FinOps Foundation defines key areas of focus, called domains, each supported by specific capabilities, which are actionable practices or skills. We will now outline the primary FinOps domains and highlight the capabilities within each, emphasizing their relevance to multi-cloud operations.

Understand cloud usage and cost

This domain focuses on gaining visibility into how cloud resources are consumed and what they cost across multiple providers. In a multi-cloud setup, this means untangling complex billing data, tracking usage patterns, and ensuring transparency for stakeholders.

Capabilities covered include:

- **Data ingestion**: Collecting and processing usage and cost data from various cloud providers into a unified system, handling differences in formats and granularity.

- **Allocation**: Assigning costs to specific teams, projects, or departments using tags, labels, or account structures, despite varying provider conventions.

- **Reporting and analytics**: Creating clear, actionable reports that consolidate multi-cloud spending and usage for decision-makers.

- **Anomaly management**: Detecting unexpected cost spikes or usage irregularities across providers and addressing them promptly.

Optimize cloud usage and cost

This domain is about taking action to reduce waste and improve efficiency while maintaining performance. In multi-cloud scenarios, optimization requires balancing provider-specific tools and pricing models to achieve cost savings.

Capabilities covered include:

- **Resource optimization**: Rightsizing instances, shutting down unused resources, or selecting cost-effective services across clouds.

- **Rate optimization**: Leveraging discounts (for example, Reserved Instances, Savings Plans) and negotiating rates where possible, tailored to each provider.

- **Cloud sustainability**: Minimizing environmental impact by optimizing workloads, a growing concern across multi-cloud deployments.

- **License and SaaS management**: Optimizing software licenses and third-party SaaS costs integrated with multi-cloud environments.

These capabilities ensure organizations extract maximum value from their multi cloud investments without compromising operational needs.

Quantify business value

This domain ties cloud spending to measurable business outcomes, ensuring that multi cloud investments align with organizational goals. It shifts the focus from pure cost-cutting to value creation.

Capabilities covered include:

- **Planning and estimating**: Developing cost projections and resource plans for multi-cloud environments by analyzing historical usage trends and anticipating future workload demands. This capability leverages provider-specific pricing models to estimate expenses accurately and guide optimization efforts.

- **Budgeting**: Setting and tracking budgets that reflect business priorities across multiple clouds.

- **Forecasting**: Predicting future costs and resource needs based on historical multi-cloud data and growth plans.

- **Unit economics**: Calculating the cost per business unit (for example, cost per customer, transaction, or product) by correlating multi-cloud spending with operational metrics. In a multi-cloud setup, this involves normalizing data across providers to measure how resource usage drives value at a granular level.

- **Benchmarking**: Comparing cost and performance metrics internally across teams or externally with industry peers using similar multi-cloud setups.

Manage the FinOps practice

This domain centers on building and sustaining a FinOps culture within the organization. In a multi-cloud world, it ensures consistency, collaboration, and governance across diverse platforms.

Capabilities covered include:

- **FinOps practice operations**: Establishing processes, tools, and teams to oversee multi-cloud FinOps activities.

- **FinOps education and enablement**: Training staff on multi-cloud cost management principles and provider-specific nuances.

- **Assessment of FinOps practice**: Evaluating the maturity of FinOps efforts and identifying gaps in multi-cloud execution.

- **Cloud policy and governance**: Defining rules for resource usage, cost accountability, and compliance across providers.

- **Intersecting disciplines**: Coordinating with IT, finance, and procurement to align multi-cloud efforts with broader goals.

- **FinOps tools and services**: Selecting and integrating tools that support multi-cloud cost visibility and optimization.

- **Invoicing and chargeback**: Managing the process of generating internal invoices or chargebacks based on multi-cloud usage, ensuring accurate cost distribution to teams or business units. This involves reconciling provider bills, applying allocation rules, and integrating with financial systems for seamless accountability.

- **Onboarding workloads**: Guiding the process of deploying new workloads into the multi-cloud environment with cost management in mind. This includes setting up tagging strategies, selecting cost-efficient services from available providers, and establishing governance to prevent cost overruns from the start.

FinOps domains form a comprehensive framework for mastering financial operations in a multi-cloud environment. Leveraged by capabilities, these domains enable organizations to achieve visibility, efficiency, strategic alignment, and operational excellence. Together, they transform multi-cloud complexity into a structured advantage, ensuring cost accountability, resource optimization, and business value realization.

FinOps principles

Let us now go over the various FinOps principles.

Collaborate

The cloud never operates for the purpose of quarterly reports or annual budgets; it is a living and breathing entity that evolves and revolutionizes as you play with it. At every instance or, say, every minute, enterprises live with it and spend dollars to launch innovations and develop the remarkable. In this landscape, collaboration is the livelihood of successful cloud operations.

As your finance team has their hands on the pulse of cloud spend versus focusing on monthly bill rolls in, and as your tech team lands on crucial decisions with a clear-cut understanding of financial implications, this is where the teams interact to reinvent the features with a keen awareness bringing best of both worlds, that is, technical feasibility and cost efficiency, a reality of FinOps collaboration.

Then, how do we foster such collaboration that drives towards a culture of continuous communication and shared responsibility? Here are the breakdowns for FinOps leaders like you to make it happen:

- **Shared dashboards**: Implement real-time cost and usage dashboards accessible to all teams. When everyone can see the impact of their decisions, things turn beneficial.

- **Cross-functional FinOps teams**: Form dedicated FinOps squads with representatives from each department, that is, action-oriented task forces.

- **Continuous education**: Make cloud cost optimization part of everyone's job description. From developers to product managers, everyone should speak the language of FinOps.

- **Incentivize collaboration**: Align team KPIs across departments. When cost efficiency becomes everyone's goal, silos naturally crumble.

- **Automate communication**: Use chatbots and automated alerts to keep all teams informed of significant cloud events or spending anomalies.

When teams collaborate in this way, you create a flywheel effect of efficiency and innovation. It is not a zero-sum game of cost-cutting versus feature development. Instead, it is a virtuous cycle where efficiency fuels innovation, and innovation drives further efficiency. Here is the cycle explained:

- When developers understand cost implications, they architect more efficient solutions from the get-go.

- When finance teams understand technical constraints, they can suggest more nuanced cost optimization strategies.

- When product teams are in the loop on both technical and financial aspects, they can prioritize features that deliver the most bang for the buck.

Accelerate your business, optimize your company's ability to innovate and compete by fostering the first principle of FinOps, that is, collaboration

By tearing down those silos and embracing the collaborative future of FinOps, your cloud—and your bottom line—will thank you.

Decisions are driven by business value of cloud

Where every cloud decision becomes a business imperative, and where ROI creates value, are the two big tasks for CFOs and CTOs to break the ice. Next is value-based metrics, where questions like the following are addressed:

- What is the cost per transaction?

- How much revenue does each dollar of cloud spend generate?

- What is the customer acquisition cost in relation to our cloud infrastructure?

These metrics reflect the business impact as the cloud spend directly influences the business outcomes, driving massive growth. In the cloud, every decision is a balancing act between cost, quality, and speed. Many times, this becomes exciting, challenging, and potentially disastrous if you cannot understand what you are into. However, FinOps principles, when come into action, they drive the most value for your business at any given moment.

When your enterprise needs a new feature to market rapidly, the prioritization is speed over cost optimization; when they deal with a sensitive workload, quality must take the precedence; and to scale a product, keep your focus on cost efficiency. The conscious trade-off with a clear understanding of business implications strikes the right balance within your cloud environment.

As we have seen and experimented so far, the visionary FinOps teams see cloud as an innovation engine where they:

- Experiment with new ideas at a fraction of the cost of traditional infrastructure.

- Scale from concept to global deployment in record time.

- Access cutting-edge technologies without massive upfront investments.

When you view the cloud through this lens, every dollar spent is not just a cost, it is an investment in your company's future. The question shifts from *How can we spend less?* to *How can we leverage the cloud to drive more value?*

Cloud Unit Economics

> *Remember, in the world of FinOps, the true north is not the lowest possible cloud bill—it is the highest possible business value. Keep your eyes on that prize, and you will navigate the complexities of cloud economics with the finesse of a true FinOps maestro.*

To truly embrace this approach, we need a fundamental shift in how we think about FinOps, and the first rule that comes into play is unit economics.

Cloud Unit Economics is a system that maximizes profitability based on objective measurements of how your enterprise performs best against market needs and FinOps goals. Achieving these goals through Cloud Unit Economics is possible by sweeping through the marginal cost calculation and marginal revenue that is specific to cloud-based software development and delivery. By calculating the difference between marginal cost and revenue, you can easily determine the point at which cloud operations either disrupt or generate profit, which is a crucial aspect in economics and one of the effective ways to drive data-based business decisions as your business capitalizes on cloud investments.

In simple terms, the Cloud Unit Economics helps the enterprises know the reason behind their increased cloud costs for the same set of resources being used from that of the previous month. With FinOps, now it is simple to know the reality of cloud spend. Moreover, Cloud Unit Economics delivers the following sentinels:

- **Quantification of cloud in your financial performance**: Let your company's management, investors, and employees take the great advantage of Cloud Unit Economics to understand your financial performance.

- **Forecast profitability**: The unit cost analysis embedded in unit economics reveals the profitability and the timeline to achieve it, along with factors that impact its desired goals.

- **Plan for cloud cost optimization**: It helps the enterprises to understand the scope of their product, that is, whether it is undervalued, overpriced, or balancing in the marketplace.

- **Evaluation of a product's future potential**: Enterprises that rely on Cloud Unit Economics can clearly understand the products and features that their customers are using, driving the changes in the product roadmap and engineering mechanisms without much effort.

- **Induce responsibility among cloud users**: Measuring the end-user behavior on cloud costs is one of the primary reasons why Unit Economics has evolved. Hence, this drives cost-conscious behavior across the enterprise, spotlighting the opportunities for efficient usage and the areas where governance is needed through throttling or incentivizing changes in behavior.

The capabilities of Unit Economics are needed because:

- To map current business demand and cloud costs at all levels, that is, per customer, per feature, per product, and so on.

- To know the impact on future cloud costs caused by the predicted changes in business. This is derived from status quo composition, architecture, provisioning patterns, and more.

- To understand future cloud costs, where undefined spend can be minimized by optimization, wise consumption from the end-user, and using efficient architectural patterns.

The value-based decisions within cloud can benefit enterprises when they make the following shifts in strategic ways possible:

- **From cost control to value creation**: Instead of asking *How much are we spending?*, ask *What value are we getting?*

- **From reactive to proactive**: Do not wait for the bill to make decisions. Use predictive analytics to anticipate needs and optimize proactively.

- **From IT metric to business metric**: Cloud efficiency should be a KPI not just for the tech team, but for every department that leverages cloud resources.

- **From restriction to enablement**: FinOps should not be about saying *no* to cloud usage; it should be about saying *yes, and here is how we can do it efficiently*.

- **From static to dynamic**: In the cloud, change is the only constant. Your FinOps strategies should be as dynamic and flexible as the cloud itself.

So, the next time you are poring over cloud metrics, take a step back and ask yourself: Are we just counting dollars, or are we measuring value? Are we making decisions based on sticker shock, or on strategic impact?

Everyone takes ownership for their cloud usage

Take complete ownership of your outcomes by holding no one but yourself responsible.

– Gary W. Keller.

This is where cloud economics turn in favor for you. Decentralization of accountability, rather than delegation, is the core aspect of this FinOps principle. It has been pushed to the very edge of the organization, so that code development meets the ever-expanding cloud. Here, the role of allied and core personas is vital as they not only spin up the instances but they do so with the precision of a Swiss Watchmaker and are mindful of the cost implications.

From the moment architecture is designed or planned to the execution of operations, cost is involved in every decision, every line of code, and every deployment. The core aspect of ownership is about empowering engineering teams with the knowledge and tools to make cost-effective decisions in real-time.

In the FinOps utopia, feature and product teams must masterfully manage cloud usage against predefined budgets. Some might believe that this is restricting innovation, but it is a culture of responsible innovation. When teams get involved in their own cloud budgets, your enterprise will be in line with the FinOps vision. Here, the teams bring their creative spark, finding ingenious ways to deliver out-of-the-box features while keeping costs in check. Hence, this entire empowerment is an immune booster of accountability.

However, the seismic shift in decision-making occurs when there are no bottlenecks related to cloud costs, where engineers, product managers, and DevOps wizards make informed decisions about cost-effective architecture. When the core and allied personas consider resource usage and optimization, it becomes the centralized idea of driving ownership. When this is decentralized across the enterprise, that is where controlled empowerment happens.

Though performance and scalability are the top-rating enterprise-wide goals to be achieved via cloud-native developments, cost is also a dominant factor. Throughout the software development lifecycle, the cost must be tracked to ensure that resources are utilized effectively and that responsibilities are clearly defined. This is where rethinking into software development whirls in:

- Architecture reviews now include cost projections.

- Sprint planning takes into account the cost implications of new features.

- Code reviews look at resource efficiency alongside functionality.

- Performance testing includes cost metrics alongside response times.

- We are not just building software anymore; we are crafting cost-effective, cloud-native solutions that deliver maximum value for every dollar spent. Every decision to use cloud resources becomes an investment decision. Teams now start asking themselves:

- o What is the ROI on this extra instance?
- o How can we optimize this database to deliver more value per dollar?
- o Is this serverless function really the most cost-effective way to achieve our goal?

This shift does not happen overnight. It requires education, reinforcement, and yes, sometimes a bit of tough love. However, when it clicks, when everyone from the CEO to the newest intern starts thinking about cloud usage in terms of value generation rather than cost center, that is when the real impact happens.

As we stand on the brink of this FinOps revolution, one thing is clear: the future of cloud cost management is not about tighter controls or more stringent policies. It is about unleashing the collective power of your entire organization to drive value from your cloud investment.

In the future, cloud cost optimization is not a chore; it is a competitive advantage. It is not a monthly review meeting; it is a daily practice that every member of your team embraces. It is not about restriction; it is about amplification, using cost-awareness as a catalyst for innovation and efficiency.

So, are you ready to take the plunge? Are you prepared to transform your organization into a lean, mean, cloud-optimizing machine where everyone, yes, everyone, takes ownership of their cloud usage?

The cloud is no longer just IT's playground. It is a shared resource, a shared responsibility, and ultimately, a shared success story.

FinOps data should be accessible and timely

Cloud spending is a fiscal responsibility of an enterprise, and to course FinOps into the veins of your organization, one must understand the pulsing heart of it, which is data. Without the data, there is nothing. So, to understand the cloud costs of real-time data processing and sharing, an ecosystem is needed that disciplines financial intelligence and autonomously drives better cloud utilization. Indeed, when data is given importance, the entire FinOps keeps your enterprise on edge.

Now, let us talk about feedback loops. In the old world, feedback on cloud spending was like sending a message in a bottle: you would toss it out and hope someone finds it eventually. In our brave new world of FinOps, we are talking about feedback loops tighter than a Formula 1 pit crew.

When engineers can see the cost impact of their decisions in real-time, they can analyze their resources more effectively. The unnecessary prod environment spinning up on non-business hours and overprovisioned databases that consume your budgets can be eliminated and minimized through rightsizing.

These rapid feedback loops do not just change behavior; they revolutionize it. They turn every member of your team into a cost-conscious cloud expert, making micro-optimizations that add up to macro savings.

Here is the radical question: what if everyone in your organization, from the newest intern to the CEO, had visibility into cloud spend? We are not talking about dumping raw cloud environment bills on everyone's desk. We are focusing on the intelligent, contextualized, role-appropriate visibility that turns cloud costs from an IT problem into an organizational opportunity.

When the marketing teams can see how their latest campaign impacts cloud costs, when the product team understands the infrastructure implications of their roadmap, and when the C-suite can correlate cloud spend with business outcomes, that is when your FinOps implementation has served the purpose.

This level of visibility empowers individuals and fosters a culture where everyone feels ownership over cloud costs, as they can see their direct impact.

If your cloud cost forecasting still involves Excel and a lot of squinting at trend lines, you are doing it wrong. In the world of modern FinOps, forecasting is a real-time, AI-driven art form.

Here, the systems predict based on historical data by factoring in everything from product roadmaps to market trends. Systems will tell you what your bill might be next month and help you understand why and, more importantly, what you can do about it.

Creating, monitoring, and continuously improving these forecasting models is a competitive necessity because in the cloud, those who can see the future are the ones who can shape it.

Trending and variance analysis is the unsung hero of FinOps, where it helps you understand why your costs shot up; the right reason why costs have been exceeded.

By correlating cost data with application metrics, deployment logs, and business events, you turn variance analysis from a headache into a goldmine of insights. Each spike or dip becomes a learning opportunity, a chance to fine-tune your cloud strategy.

This is where we recommend following internal benchmarking. This enables us to identify the best practices, celebrate wins, and create a culture of healthy competition, which will maximize cloud cost savings.

With industry benchmarking, you have a chance to see if you are a cloud cost champion or if you have got some catching up to do. It is not just about bragging rights (though those are nice); it is about understanding where you stand in the broader ecosystem and identifying opportunities for improvement.

As we stand on the brink of this data revolution in FinOps, one thing is clear: the organizations that will thrive in the cloud era are not those with the most significant budgets, but those with the best data practices.

In this future, FinOps data is not just a tool for cost control; it is the foundation of business intelligence where we drive innovation, inform strategy, and create competitive advantage.

The cloud has turned traditional IT economics on its head. It is time our approach to financial management followed suit. Welcome to the age of data-driven FinOps. The data is out there.

Remember, in the world of FinOps, data is not just the king; it is the kingdom, the army, and the crown jewels all rolled into one. So let it flow, let it shine, and watch as it transforms your organization from a cloud cost center into a lean, mean, value-generating machine.

Driving FinOps with a centralized team

Strategize to make your FinOps team centralized to achieve cloud financial excellence across your entire organization. Here, we highlight why this team can be the cloud cost champions for streamlining your FinOps. Be it SMBs or large enterprises, embedding the best practices, data insights, and a passion for cloud cost optimization will be taken care of by these dedicated teams. These teams are the evangelists of efficient cloud usage, the harbingers of a new era of shared accountability.

Like a championship sports coach, this central team does not play the game for you; they give you the playbook, train you in the fundamentals, and cheer you on from the sidelines. They are creating a culture where everyone, from the greenest junior developer to the most seasoned architect, feels not just responsible but empowered to optimize their cloud usage.

Think of them as the FinOps version of your security team. Just as everyone knows not to use *password123*, soon everyone will instinctively know not to leave that development environment running over the weekend. It is about creating a shared consciousness, a collective responsibility for cloud costs that permeates every corner of your organization.

Now, let us talk about the elephant in the room: executive buy-in. You can have the most brilliant FinOps team on the planet, but without the backing of the C-suite, they are just tilting at windmills. *The fundamental shift in how your organization views cloud costs and transforms cloud spend into a strategic lever for business success lies in securing executive buy-in.* It is as crucial as your CEO believing in your product or your CTO believing in your tech stack. When your executives are all-in on FinOps, magic happens. Suddenly, cloud cost optimization is not just an IT initiative; it is a business imperative, discussed in board rooms with the same gravity as revenue growth and market expansion. While we advocate for decentralized responsibility in cloud usage, when it comes to rate negotiations, commitment planning, and discount strategies, centralization is essential.

This is because there is power in numbers. When you consolidate your cloud purchasing power, you are not just a customer; you are a force to be reckoned with. Your centralized FinOps team becomes the master negotiator, leveraging your entire organization's cloud usage to secure rates that would make even the toughest cloud providers weak at the knees.

However, it is not just about flexing muscles in negotiations. A centralized approach to commitments and discounts allows for a holistic, strategic view of your cloud usage. It is the difference between each department buying its own office supplies and having a central procurement team that can buy in bulk, standardize equipment, and leverage company-wide deals.

This centralized team can play three-dimensional chess with your cloud commitments, balancing the needs of different departments, projects, and workloads to maximize savings across the board.

Now, here is a radical thought: what if we told your engineers and ops teams that they never had to think about rate negotiations or commitment planning again?

By centralizing these complex, organization-wide optimizations, along with leveraging economies of scale, we are liberating our technical teams to focus on what they do best: building awesome products and optimizing their own environments. It is a win-win scenario. Engineers get to focus on technical excellence and usage-based optimization, while the FinOps team handles the organizational-level financial strategies. The result is a harmonious blend of bottom-up optimization and top-down strategic financial management.

As we peer into the crystal ball of FinOps future, one thing is clear: the organizations that will thrive are those that master the art of being centrally decentralized. A strong, empowered central FinOps team that drives best practices handles organization-wide optimizations and fosters a culture of shared responsibility, combined with decentralized execution where every team and individual is empowered to optimize their own cloud usage.

So, as you embark on your FinOps journey, remember: a strong centralized team empowers, enables, and excels in your enterprise cloud financial goals. A FinOps culture that permeates every level of your organization drives true business value.

The future of cloud financial management is here, and it is being driven by these unsung heroes: your centralized FinOps team. Be ready to unleash their potential and transform your organization's approach to cloud costs? The cloud awaits, and with the right central FinOps team, you are poised to conquer it.

Take advantage of the variable cost model of the cloud

The key is to shift from the fear of unpredictability to capitalizing on flexibility, making every dollar work harder as you scale. By maximizing resource efficiency, you enhance your ability to innovate, experiment, and deliver faster. The freedom to scale up when demand spikes and scale down when it's quieter lets you ride the waves of demand with confidence.

Let us now understand this final principle:

- **The variable cost model of the cloud should be viewed as an opportunity to deliver more value, not as a risk**: Too often, businesses perceive the variable cost model of the cloud as a potential risk, one that might spiral out of control if left unchecked. However, that mindset holds you back from unleashing the full potential of cloud economics. In reality, this model is a golden opportunity to deliver greater value by aligning spending directly with business outcomes. It is about transforming cloud costs into a strategic lever for growth, not a liability to be managed.

- **Embrace just-in-time prediction, planning, and purchasing of capacity**: The traditional approach to infrastructure planning, where organizations buy far more than they need *just in case*, belongs to a bygone era. In the cloud, you no longer must make those costly, upfront investments in fixed capacity. Instead, you can adopt a just-in-time approach to prediction, planning, and capacity purchasing. This means forecasting demand with greater precision, acquiring resources only when they are needed, and dialing back when they are not. It is a model that puts you in the driver's seat, enabling you to fine-tune consumption and costs on the fly. By leveraging real-time data and advanced analytics, organizations can make smarter, faster decisions that deliver optimal value with minimal waste.

- **Agile iterative planning is preferred over static long-term plans**: Long gone are the days of rigid, long-term IT plans that try to predict the future of technology and business demands years in advance. With the cloud's variable cost model, agility is the key to success. Static, long-term plans often fall short, leaving organizations scrambling to adjust as circumstances change. Instead, embrace agile, iterative planning, that is, a model where you constantly evaluate, adapt, and optimize based on real-time insights. This enables your organization to pivot quickly and allocate resources where they are needed most. It is about staying nimble and keeping costs aligned with immediate needs, all while fostering a culture of continuous improvement.

- **Embrace proactive system design with continuous adjustments in cloud optimization over infrequent reactive cleanups**: A proactive approach to cloud system design means you are ahead of the curve, not playing catch-up. Instead of relying on reactive, infrequent cleanups, where you only optimize when costs have already ballooned, FinOps best practices call for continuous optimization. This involves designing systems that are *built to be adaptable* from day one, with an eye on efficiency. Regular fine-tuning and adjustment ensure that your cloud environment stays lean, cost-effective, and performance optimized. It is far more efficient to trim the fat before it accumulates, making small, strategic adjustments over time rather than dealing with a bloated system later. Proactive is your best defense against waste, and when done right, it can keep your costs in check while delivering top-notch performance.

    o   This principle enables you to fully leverage the cloud's variable cost model, transforming potential pitfalls into opportunities for innovation, agility, and value creation. When embraced thoughtfully, the variable cost model empowers you to do more with less, ensuring your organization remains competitive in an increasingly dynamic digital world.

Conclusion

The FinOps principles and best practices bring disciplinary FinOps transformation, may not be overnight but at a gradual pace. To make the cloud environment dynamic and ensure your core operations remain tracked with complete resource utilization, FinOps Principles and involved best practices are your shifters. A single action either costs you double or more or saves you from infinite casualties.

With a focus to enhance and deliver 3X business value for cloud-centralized organizations, we are here with simple aspects that streamline your cloud operations scenario.

Join our Discord space

Join our Discord workspace for latest updates, offers, tech happenings around the world, new releases, and sessions with the authors:

https://discord.bpbonline.com

CHAPTER 4

FOCUS: Transforming FinOps for Business Success

Introduction

The **FinOps Cost and Usage Specification** (**FOCUS™**) is a game-changer for FinOps practitioners worldwide. Designed with simplicity in mind, this open-source specification tackles one of the most time-consuming tasks in cloud cost management: normalizing and analyzing disparate billing data from various vendors. By setting a universal standard, FOCUS enables practitioners to spend less time resolving data inconsistencies and more time making strategic, data-driven decisions.

At its core, FOCUS addresses a problem that has plagued the FinOps community for years: getting different clouds and vendors to speak the same language. The four largest cloud platforms, that is, AWS, Microsoft Azure, Oracle Cloud Infrastructure, and Google Cloud, each service provider has its own way of reporting costs and usage, complete with unique terminology and metrics. However, FinOps practitioners must spend hours just gathering the data into actionable formats even before analysis begins. It is like trying to decode different dialects to extract meaningful insights.

FOCUS simplifies this by providing a standardized set of 43 columns, each with a distinct name, ID, and purpose. It is the difference between swimming against the tide and catching the current, allowing practitioners to immediately dive into the valuable work of improving FinOps capabilities and optimizing cloud spend.

FOCUS is not just a tool; it is a lifeline for FinOps professionals and the broader cloud community. The idea behind it is simple: unified billing data leads to unified insights. FinOps practitioners can now operate with data that speaks the same language, no matter the vendor. They can stop reinventing the wheel every time a new cloud service provider enters the picture. Instead, they can roll out consistent processes that deliver actionable insights faster. This means less time on the grind of normalization and more time on activities that move the needle, such as improving cloud governance and cost efficiency.

Cloud service providers (**CSP**), SaaS vendors, and **independent software vendors** (**ISV**) benefit from FOCUS by reducing the friction involved in onboarding new clients. The adoption of FOCUS ensures that vendors' billing data can be quickly understood and leveraged by any organization, driving up usage of their cloud infrastructure and software solutions. As the old saying goes, *a rising tide lifts all boats*. When the process of consuming cloud data becomes frictionless, everyone benefits, from the vendors to the end-users.

Empowering FinOps tool providers

For FinOps tooling vendors, FOCUS relieves the burden of building data normalization capabilities from scratch. Instead of burning development cycles on data parsing, they can focus on adding higher-value features to their platforms. In other words, FOCUS lets them *stick to their knitting*, building best-in-class tools that help organizations maximize their cloud investments, as shown in the following figure:

Figure 4.1: FinOps focus

The great thing about FOCUS is that it is already supported by the largest cloud providers, that is, AWS, Google Cloud, Microsoft Azure, and Oracle Cloud Infrastructure. These CSPs offer FOCUS-formatted billing data exports directly from their consoles, making it easier than ever to get started. The FinOps Foundation and we are also tracking the growing number of tools and vendors adopting FOCUS, with plans to offer an official certification to signify platform conformance. It is the dawn of a new era in FinOps, where consistency and transparency are finally within reach.

Portable skills and increased innovation

FOCUS offers FinOps practitioners something invaluable: the ability to transfer their skills across clouds, tools, and organizations. Learning to query billing data becomes a one-size-fits-all process, eliminating the steep learning curves that once came with switching vendors or platforms. Like seasoned travelers who know the lay of the land, practitioners can hit the ground running, no matter where they go. This portability of skills not only opens career mobility but also drives business continuity, as organizations no longer must spend time and resources retraining new hires on cloud billing schemas.

The benefits do not stop there. With consistent and reliable data, organizations can make smarter decisions more quickly. By enabling leadership to look at the big picture rather than isolated cloud environments, FOCUS empowers better data-driven decision-making, paving the way for increased innovation. Cloud offerings, once viewed merely as a utility, have become strategic assets for driving business growth.

FOCUS is not just a solution for today's challenges. It is built to evolve, with new columns and use cases on the horizon. As the ecosystem expands to include SaaS, PaaS, licensing, and even sustainability metrics, FOCUS will remain the foundation upon which future cloud cost management innovations are built. By adopting it today, organizations are investing in a future where cloud spend is not just managed, but optimized, streamlined, and primed for growth.

In short, FOCUS simplifies the complex, turning cloud cost management from a daunting task into a strategic advantage. It is the key to unlocking the full potential of the cloud, and it is here to stay.

Transforming FinOps centralized enterprises with FOCUS

FinOps adopting enterprises have already ingested the FOCUS into their core, and the widespread adoption can be seen as a paradigm shift for cloud-centralized industries. It is a one-time adoption, however, eliminating the need for normalization within cloud-powered enterprises. This change of removing time-intensive and complex processes from the FinOps practice enables the wheels of adoption to move faster and value realization of cloud resources, services, and tools quicker.

Focus on what truly matters, discipline what exactly brings value, and streamline to maximize FinOps capabilities.

More gain for FinOps practitioners

For FinOps practitioners, FOCUS is a game-changer. It turns what used to be a highly fragmented and complex process into a unified, streamlined experience. Now, practitioners can leverage a single approach to querying cloud billing data, irrespective of the cloud platform or vendor. This not only simplifies their work but also makes their skill set far more portable across industries, clouds, and tools. In essence, they can hit the ground running no matter where they go.

The beauty of FOCUS lies in the way it allows practitioners to shift their attention from mundane tasks like data normalization to more strategic activities. Instead of getting bogged down in aligning disparate data sets, they can channel their energy into fine-tuning FinOps capabilities that deliver real value to the business. It is akin to spending less time tuning the engine and more time accelerating the vehicle. Let us now go over some benefits:

Benefit	Description
Data-driven decision-making in a multi-cloud environment	A consistent reporting that FOCUS drives across cloud vendors with the help of data normalization enables the leadership to analyze the complete environment, thus breaking the silos of looking into each vendor or cloud. The better the data is, the better and smarter the decisions are, meeting the goals faster.
Scaling down the complexity of billing files	A unified columnar set applies across enterprise-wide cloud billing data, even for a multi-cloud/multi-vendor environment. Hence, FinOps practitioners have minimum terminology to learn, driving the most effectiveness.
Consistency and accuracy in reporting	Consistency format in billing files standardization minimizes inconsistencies in reporting that cause discrepancies in terminology and definitions of columns across external vendors or internal teams.
Seamless integrations with fresh vendors	Future-proofing your enterprise highly relies on the changes vendors make. As a new vendor gets added to the ecosystem, the organization will already have a defined format to convert the data into actionable insights. Time spent on figuring out how the data can be transformed to make seamless integration with other data sources is eliminated.
Innovation multiplied	The understanding of cloud value paves the way for using cloud offerings to make innovations and drive business growth. FOCUS plays a role in accessing normalized data in a timely state, unleashing an opportunity to leverage the cloud as a strategic ecosystem for innovation.
Price-for-data processing	FOCUS adjoins actual billed costs and amortized costs into a single dataset, drastically minimizing the computing and storage costs needed for this data to be processed.

Benefit	Description
Transferable knowledge and skills	FOCUS leads practitioners to perform a FinOps activity through learning a single process, leading to faster time to value and pays off for both the practitioner and their organization: • **Job mobility**: Easy for practitioners to change between companies without learning a new normalization scheme. • **Business continuity**: New FinOps practitioners familiar with FOCUS save time and efforts for enterprises as they need not invest on training these people on normalizing billing data. • **Tool flexibility**: The single set of columns can be transferred across cloud and third-party tool providers, making it easy for individuals to change providers as organizations remain flexible to adjust their toolkits as time evolves.
Beyond the cloud	As years pass by, we expect FOCUS to include SaaS, PaaS, licensing and software, and on-premises costs in addition to public cloud spending. This boosts the power of having a normalized, single accurate data set from which the value-based decisions can be taken.
Ground language with external people	Open discussions with other enterprises as well, when FOCUS is adopted, using common terms with a base understanding across various cloud and tooling vendors that every enterprise may be using.

Table 4.1: Benefits and their descriptions

FOCUS also democratizes reporting within the organization. Practitioners can easily train stakeholders across different levels to run FinOps queries using a standard process. This self-service model becomes crucial as companies scale, allowing more people to access the data they need without placing additional burdens on the FinOps team.

Benefits for cloud vendors

From the vendor's perspective, adopting the FOCUS format offers a strategic advantage. By delivering billing data that conforms to FOCUS, cloud service providers make it easier for customers to integrate that data into their broader ecosystems. It is like speaking the same language, enabling faster and more seamless integration.

With FOCUS, businesses gain a clear understanding of the costs and returns associated with each cloud vendor. This increased clarity not only boosts confidence but also drives higher adoption rates and accelerates account growth. Vendors that offer FOCUS billing data make it easier for their customers to gauge ROI, which leads to greater satisfaction and, ultimately, reduced churn. It is a win-win scenario: vendors get more stickiness with their customers, while customers experience smoother cloud adoption and management. The benefits are further described in the following table:

Benefit	Description
Increased adoption	We recommend your billing file in the FOCUS format so that your customers can integrate this billing data into their tools as they already understand terminology and definitions used in your billing file. Meeting your customers makes it simpler for them to quickly adopt your offering.
Accelerated usage	Billing data is a predominant accelerator for adoption and usage, and to establish this trust, understanding is needed. Embrace FOCUS as it simplifies FinOps for practitioners to navigate the ROI of investments in cloud infrastructure and software, helping businesses understand and trust cloud vendors. When a customer's leadership is trustworthy and delivers a positive ROI, they tend to use your offering more frequently. Hence, the usage of cloud infrastructure and software makes it easier for businesses to understand the value of cloud usage.
Reduced account churn	Comparing cost and usage data across different vendors is no longer a hustle with the consistency in vendor billing files. One can easily find the vendor that best meet their needs, reducing the account churn within the industry.

Table 4.2: Benefits and their descriptions

Turning it as a cakewalk for FinOps tool vendors

FinOps tool vendors also stand to gain from FOCUS. Tools that adopt FOCUS are inherently easier to use because they align with the standardized terminology and structure that customers already know. This familiarity reduces the friction of adoption and encourages customers to bring more data into the tool, that is, fueling more usage and making the tool more sticky. Let us understand the benefits in this scenario as well:

Benefit	Description
Adoption and consumption	FinOps tools and FOCUS together make the customers adoption easy as the terminology used in reports of the tools can be understood without much effort. On the other hand, they add more data into the tool, increasing usage and stickiness.

Benefit	Description
Simple to add integrations	FOCUS brings various formats for billing data together, removing the need for normalization and enables FinOps vendors to integrate with more vendors.
Shift development resources to valuable features	With FOCUS, FinOps vendors need not spend on developing resources to build data normalization functionality. Instead, these resources can support other FinOps capabilities that customers need.

Table 4.3: Benefits and their descriptions

Moreover, by reducing the time and effort needed for data normalization, FinOps vendors can allocate more resources to building out high-impact features. Instead of reinventing the wheel, they can focus on improving their core offering, expanding support for additional vendors, or developing new FinOps capabilities. This, in turn, allows vendors to stay ahead of the competition by continually enhancing their tools' value proposition.

Multi-cloud vision must be fulfilled, and as enterprises increase their resourcefulness and expand their operations into other cloud environments, FOCUS must become multi-cloud. In this regard, the vision is almost fulfilled as FOCUS is supported and its features are embraced across all four clouds, that is, **Amazon Web Services** (**AWS**), Microsoft Azure, Oracle Cloud, and Google Cloud. Earlier this year, all four cloud platforms went big about extending their massive support for the activities that FOCUS takes forward. It is a multi-cloud vision; it is the momentum that industry needs, and it is the core business value where financial discipline fosters and operational excellence mounts. This multi-cloud feasibility accelerates FinOps adoption as well.

Google Cloud support towards FOCUS

Google Cloud has aligned with the FOCUS based on an updated BigQuery view, and a new Looker template generates a table to have a consolidated view of FOCUS data in Looker.

Google's new Looker template helps in visualizing the open billing data and producing a table by deriving insights from a FOCUS query. This is achieved through the LookML code where the creation and management of table is automated, eliminating the manual efforts. This template gives a glimpse of the possible scenarios to visualize cost trends across services, SKUS, zones, regions, and resource types, offering:

- **Multi-featured template**: The templates give you an immediate access to pre-built visualizations that show you cost trends, breakdowns by charges, regions, and services. The need to wait for custom dashboards can be eliminated.

- **Easy to filter**: This template never demands you to be a data analyst. Looker interface is intuitive and lessens the learning curve. It will filter the specific time periods or services and gives the granular details in just a few clicks.

- **Customizability**: The template is a wonderful beginning as its flexibility allows to specifically tailors the views to your needs. Be it adding custom metrics, change the visualizations, or integrate the dashboards into your existing workflows, it is easy to do.

Moreover, Google offers three ways to export cost and cloud billing data to BigQuery: Standard Billing Export, Detailed Billing Export, and Price Export. The new BigQuery view reflects the results of a SQL query, transforming data towards FOCUS Preview format.

Coming to BigQuery, the views are stunning because the virtual table where queries are executed contains only the data obtained from the tables and fields specified in the base query that defines the view. As BigQuery views are virtually represented tables, they come with no additional costs for data storage if you are using Billing Export to BigQuery. The BigQuery assists you with:

- Viewing and querying Google Cloud Billing data that is aligned towards FOCUS specification.

- Using it as a data source to visualize using tools such as Looker Studio.

- Analyzing Google cloud costs atop data from multiple providers with the help of common FOCUS format.

Working principle of FOCUS BigQuery on Google Cloud

The FOCUS BigQuery view functions as a virtual layer over your existing Cloud Billing data, creating a streamlined way to interact with your financial data. Think of it as a bridge between complex billing exports and the actionable insights you need to manage your multi-cloud environments efficiently. To make the most of this, you will need both Detailed Billing Export and Price Exports enabled. By using a base SQL query, FOCUS maps your raw billing data into a unified schema, transforming disparate datasets into a format that speaks the same language, regardless of the cloud provider.

What this does is eliminate the need for constant data wrangling. You can query and analyze costs from different cloud providers as if the data were native to FOCUS. In other words, it takes the heavy lifting out of cloud cost analysis, letting you focus on higher-value activities rather than piecing together disjointed billing information.

When it comes to the Looker template, there are some key distinctions to note. First, it is important to recognize that the Looker template is compatible with Looker and Looker Core, but not Looker Studio. If you want to hit the ground running with this template, you will need to have Detailed Billing Export and Pricing Export enabled, just like with BigQuery. Additionally, the right permissions are crucial; you will need access to create a new Looker Project and Connection to fully utilize the template.

The real advantage of this Looker template is its use of temporary tables. While BigQuery Views provide a persistent layer for data analysis, the Looker template further simplifies the process by automatically generating and managing temporary tables using the provided LookML code. This means you can skip the tedious manual setup and dive straight into analyzing your data.

In essence, we have pitched the perfect plan, with Google rolling out the red carpet, to help you harness the full potential of FOCUS, whether you are using BigQuery or Looker, through an easy, step-by-step guide that walks you through every stage. The combination of these tools and FOCUS offers a fast track to making data-driven decisions without the usual headaches.

With this, enterprises can reduce the latency in cloud billing data by 30%, embrace AI-powered anomaly detection, and gain granularity into metadata for CUD management.

Moreover, we envision to concretize the standards of open billing along with maintaining the standards of our customers, beloved partners, FinOps practitioners, expert heads in the industry, and more, to make your cloud costs unified today with this single, powerful innovation.

Microsoft hardwired its belief around FOCUS

By removing the complexity around cloud cost data normalization, FOCUS breaks down one of the biggest barriers to cloud adoption. Organizations can now focus on making better data-driven decisions, translating cloud usage into tangible business value, whether on the Microsoft Cloud or beyond.

Ever questioned why Microsoft would join the feat of adopting FOCUS and be in the same line as of the other cloud vendors?

It is because Microsoft believes *consistent cloud billing brings innovation and experimentation that Azure is architected to provide.* Developing and optimizing the applications in Azure, iteratively implementing the modern architectures, becomes more manageable when your enterprise understands how the billing cycle happens and balances costs equally among other business priorities in developing those systems. Therefore, a better collaboration between business, technical, and finance teams exponentially increases the overall productivity of the organization, which, in turn, maps to the core mission of Microsoft: *to empower every person and every organization on the planet to achieve more.*

The widespread adoption of FOCUS marks a turning point in how organizations handle cloud financial management. Imagine a world where allocating, analyzing, monitoring, and optimizing costs across multiple providers is as seamless as managing costs with just one provider. FOCUS makes that vision a reality, allowing organizations to do more with fewer resources. With this new standard, FinOps skills become highly portable, meaning practitioners, vendors, and consultants can easily transition between different organizations, regardless of the cloud or SaaS products being used. This eliminates the need for learning proprietary data formats, freeing up time for value-added activities that truly drive business outcomes.

Beginning phase with FOCUS

The FOCUS 0.5 release in June 2023 introduced a game-changing, standardized way to describe essential cloud cost concepts that apply universally across providers. At its core, FOCUS organizes resources by **ResourceId** and **ResourceName**, which are then sorted into their respective **ServiceName** and **ServiceCategory**. This hierarchy simplifies how organizations categorize costs, creating a top-level framework consistent across different cloud environments. For example, you can view key details like the region where a resource was deployed, the **PublisherName** of the service provider, and the **ProviderName** of the cloud used.

Additionally, every charge is associated with a **ChargeType**, defining whether it is based on usage or a purchase. Billing periods are clearly marked with **ChargePeriodStart** and **ChargePeriodEnd**, while costs are broken down into **BilledCost** and **AmortizedCost**. This is a major departure from current cloud cost management systems. Instead of pulling data from separate actual and amortized datasets, FOCUS allows you to query all your cost data in one go. This unified approach accelerates data processing and reduces storage requirements for organizations that previously had to manage multiple datasets.

Redefine the billing structure

FOCUS also simplifies the billing structure. It links charges to a specific **BillingAccountId** and **BillingAccountName**, reflecting the scope of your invoices. For more granular management, it introduces **SubAccountId** and **SubAccountName**, which drill down to the subscription accounts where individual resources are managed. This level of detail allows you to tie your charges directly to the right billing profile, which is particularly useful for customers using Microsoft Cloud.

For those using the **Microsoft Customer Agreement**, FOCUS makes a key distinction: your **BillingAccountId** is now tied to your billing profile, streamlining the connection between your cloud usage and invoices. The **SubAccountId** is similarly linked to your subscription, establishing a new cross-cloud term for easier cost allocation and chargeback tracking.

However, this is just the beginning. We are excited to be part of the FinOps community as FOCUS evolves toward its milestone. The upcoming specification is being shaped by squads of project members who are working from the perspective of FinOps practitioners' real-world use cases. Our practitioners are determining the specific columns and data points they need to perform consistent cost allocation, manage commitment-based discounts, and define uniform unit cost metrics and KPIs.

The FOCUS squads are building a specification that addresses real needs, ensuring consistent usage, pricing, and cost metrics across the board. They are also focused on the inclusion of credits, discounts, and prepaid cost elements, ensuring that every aspect of cloud costs is accounted for accurately and uniformly.

Setting the new standards for the industry

The FOCUS initiative represents an important step forward, not just for Microsoft but for the cloud industry. It lays the foundation for global FinOps adoption, creating a common language and structure that can be adopted by organizations worldwide. As a proud member of the FOCUS Steering Committee, the Governing Board, and the Technical Advisory Council of the FinOps Foundation, Microsoft is committed to shaping this future.

We invite you to join us in setting a new global standard for cloud financial management through FOCUS, helping organizations everywhere make better decisions, drive efficiency, and unlock the full potential of their cloud investments.

Redefine cost and usage transparency with FOCUS on AWS

The contribution towards the FOCUS initiative on AWS helps the customers to derive AWS cost and usage data with the FOCUS schema. However, the summed bill costs of FOCUS must align with the customers' invoiced costs. With the granularity on an hourly basis event at the resource-level, the data can be exported. As Data Exports for FOCUS, it offers the following advantages:

- **Standardized cost columns**: All the involved costs such as `ListCost`, `BilledCost`, `EffectiveCost`, and more are standardized within the columns and are referenced with reliability within or across the sources. All the discounts you have can be validated in one go.

- **Consistency in schema**: A standardized schema used by FOCUS makes each type of billing data appear in the same column, breaking the silos or inconsistencies.

- **Common set of values**: The fields, service category or usage quantity have this advantage so that mappings or conversions are eliminated for aggregations on specific columns.

FOCUS on AWS is more than just a technical solution; it is a game-changer for how businesses approach cloud cost management. By simplifying and standardizing data exports, it enables organizations to spend less time reconciling discrepancies and more time making strategic, value-driven decisions. As we move forward, the synergy between FOCUS and AWS will continue to evolve, setting the stage for more intelligent, agile financial operations that scale effortlessly across the cloud landscape.

Simplified multi-cloud FinOps support with FOCUS on OCI

Almost 98% of companies are willing to go multi-cloud, and multi-cloud strategies are hotcakes in the market right now. The need for business continuity and the opportunity to promote best-in-class services from various cloud vendors are driving enterprises. This seismic shift is recognized by *Oracle* in developing the on-the-hook solutions, empowering the businesses to thrive in the multi-cloud environment.

However, managing multiple cloud providers, SaaS services, and hybrid infrastructures brings a unique set of challenges. Each cloud provider has its own operational model, and services are billed differently, depending on a variety of factors. The complexity of monitoring, allocating, and optimizing costs across platforms can quickly become overwhelming. This is compounded by the fact that every cloud provider presents its billing and usage data in proprietary formats, making comparisons and reconciliations a daunting task.

FOCUS acts as a game-changer by addressing these pain points. It establishes a vendor-agnostic framework that simplifies how organizations handle cloud costs across multiple providers. Rather than getting bogged down in the minutiae of reconciling differences across proprietary datasets, enterprises can now focus on what truly matters: prioritizing investments that deliver business value.

In the case of **Oracle Cloud Infrastructure (OCI)**, users can access detailed cost breakdowns in a convenient, standardized format. OCI already generates CSV files multiple times per day, offering per-resource, per-hour usage details. These reports can be accessed via the Oracle Cloud Console, under Billing and Cost Management, and then Cost and Usage Reports. Additionally, these files are organized within a FOCUS-specific folder structure, making it easy to pinpoint cost reports for any given day.

Whether accessed programmatically or via Oracle's CLI, the FOCUS reports can be imported into any data warehouse solution, enabling businesses to integrate their cloud cost data seamlessly. By adopting the FOCUS format, companies can break free from the limitations of proprietary cost reports and move towards a more unified and actionable view of their cloud investments.

The beauty of FOCUS lies in its standardization. Oracle's proprietary cost report, with headers like **`ResourceName`**, **`ServiceCategory`**, and **`UsageQuantity`**, is mapped into the FOCUS schema, allowing for consistency across providers. This unified approach does not just make life easier for FinOps teams, it also accelerates decision-making, driving cost optimization and operational efficiency.

Here is a sample OCI column to FOCUS column mapping:

OCI column header	FOCUS column header
product/availabilityDomain	AvailabilityZone
cost/subscriptionId	BillingAccountId
lineItem/intervalUsageStart	ChargePeriodStart
lineItem/intervalUsageEnd	ChargePeriodEnd
usage/billedQuantity	PricingQuantity
product/resourceId	ResourceId
lineItem/tenantId	SubAccountId

Table 4.4: Sample OCI column to FOCUS column mapping

FOCUS is a milestone and crucial when it comes to standardizing cost reporting across diverse cloud environments, enabling FinOps practitioners to maximize business value and scale across all providers. Now, Oracle Cloud takes pride in its support for FinOps and FOCUS.

Now, let us see how FOCUS benefits FinOps practitioners in gaining promising cloud momentum.

Elegant aspects of FOCUS for FinOps practitioners

With FOCUS, FinOps practitioners unlock a new level of agility, allowing them to seamlessly transition their skills across different platforms and vendors. No longer bound by the intricacies of individual cloud billing formats, they can now rely on a single, streamlined process to query cloud billing data. This shift enhances the portability of their expertise across clouds, FinOps tools, and organizations, enabling them to contribute value wherever they go.

FOCUS is not just about simplifying data; it transforms how practitioners approach their work. By reducing the time spent on mundane data normalization tasks, practitioners can channel their energy into higher-value FinOps capabilities. In essence, they can shift their focus from troubleshooting billing discrepancies to driving meaningful insights and improvements in cloud spend efficiency.

Conclusion

A game-changer for self-service reporting, FOCUS empowers not just practitioners but entire organizations. The ability to teach stakeholders a single method for querying FinOps data means that, as companies scale, everyone, from leadership to individual teams, can generate insights independently. This decentralization of data analysis enables quicker decision-making while maintaining consistency in how data is interpreted.

Standardization, another hallmark of FOCUS, minimizes the risk of discrepancies that can arise from inconsistent terminologies or definitions across different vendors. Whether it is list cost, usage charges, or discounts, the standardized schema ensures everyone is working from the same playbook, enhancing both accuracy and confidence in reporting.

Moreover, FOCUS is an educational cornerstone, allowing practitioners to master a singular approach to cloud billing data management. This learning investment pays dividends, increasing job mobility for practitioners who can now transition effortlessly between companies without the steep learning curve associated with new data formats. For organizations, this continuity minimizes downtime and training costs, especially when onboarding new hires.

The self-service aspect extends even further, simplifying reporting for broader teams, allowing core and allied personas to create their own reports with minimal oversight. This ability to decentralize reporting empowers teams to answer their own FinOps questions, reducing bottlenecks and accelerating business decisions.

FOCUS also tackles the complexity of billing head-on, offering a unified set of columns across an organization's entire multi-cloud environment. Gone are the days of mastering cloud-specific terminologies and schemas. Instead, FinOps practitioners can operate with a concise, consistent dataset, drastically cutting the effort required to manage and analyze costs across multiple vendors.

From a cost perspective, FOCUS delivers tangible savings by combining billed and amortized costs into a single dataset. This consolidation reduces both the compute power and storage needed to process vast amounts of billing data, helping organizations keep costs in check while scaling their FinOps operations.

Most importantly, FOCUS enables better decision-making at the leadership level by providing a holistic view of multi-cloud environments. Instead of analyzing each cloud in isolation, executives can derive actionable insights from unified data, leading to more informed decisions and faster progress towards strategic objectives.

As the cloud becomes an engine for innovation, FOCUS paves the way for organizations to unlock its full potential. By demystifying the value of cloud services, FOCUS accelerates the journey to FinOps excellence, transforming the cloud from a cost center into a strategic enabler for growth and innovation.

Join our Discord space

Join our Discord workspace for latest updates, offers, tech happenings around the world, new releases, and sessions with the authors:

https://discord.bpbonline.com

CHAPTER 5
Cloud Financial Management and Budgeting

Beware of little expenses. A small leak will sink a great ship.

– Benjamin Franklin

Introduction

Here we are talking about finances. However, what kind of finances are these? We are talking about cloud financials. Is there a need to talk about these or tell you how to manage these? Well, when experts are involved, every word becomes a quote, and every strategy leads to greater wins. The cycle of cloud finance revolves around establishing and operating with control, cost transparency, planning, and optimization for your cloud environments.

However, **Cloud Financial Management** (**CFM**) spins in agility, innovation, and scale of cloud environments, maximizing the business value through cloud. More than just caring about cloud costs, drive it as a strategic asset to foster discipline across the enterprise.

In today's dynamic business environment, focusing on CFM is a strategic imperative, and not just a best practice. It allows enterprises to stay ahead of financial pitfalls, unlock the full potential of their cloud investments, and drive innovation with confidence.

The involved risk that spirals up here is sticking to traditional and static waterfall planning, IT budgeting, and cost assessment models. These will not cope with dynamic cloud usage, with you ending up with inaccurate planning and near-to-no visibility. The chaos of static models and dynamic cloud kicks out the opportunity, with ineffective optimization and control over costs and unrealized long-term business value. So, to break the barriers, one must be proactive to manage costs, as long as cloud is the centralized force that drives business operations.

From transforming enterprises through cost transparency, providing great control over resources, forecasting, and optimization, to establishing a cost-consciousness that fosters accountability across all teams and business functions, CFM solutions focus on identifying areas where costs spike. This enables operations to run smoothly with minimal unexpected expenses, be prepared for changing cloud dynamics, and save from overrunning expenses while teams are on their feet scaling cloud adoption. When all these aspects are shared with engineering teams, a financial context is necessary for resource selection, usage, and optimization.

Need for extreme CFM focus

As enterprises continue to scale and embrace the cloud, the complexity of managing cloud costs becomes increasingly apparent. CFM is no longer optional but a critical necessity for any organization aiming to maintain financial health and competitive advantage. Let us break down the reasons why enterprises need to focus on CFM to ensure both immediate savings and long-term strategic success:

- **Averting cloud cost chaos**: The on-demand nature of cloud services makes it all too easy to fall into the trap of overspending. Without effective CFM practices, organizations often end up with unused resources, escalating costs, and a lack of visibility into where their funds are being allocated. CFM acts as a safeguard, helping businesses avoid this cloud cost chaos by providing structured, actionable insights into cloud usage and spending patterns.

- **Maximizing the value of every dollar spent**: Cloud spending is only justified if it delivers value. CFM enables businesses to fine-tune their investments, ensuring that every dollar spent on cloud services generates maximum return. By aligning cloud spending with business objectives, enterprises can optimize their use of cloud resources while making sure they pay only for what they need and when they need it. In this way, CFM ensures that cloud resources are not just a cost center, but a driver of value.

- **Gaining full visibility into multi-cloud environments**: With the rise of multi-cloud strategies, it is no longer enough to manage a single cloud platform. Enterprises need visibility across all platforms to avoid blind spots and identify inefficiencies. CFM provides a single pane of glass, enabling teams to gain full visibility into multiple cloud environments. This visibility is crucial for decision-makers to identify trends, forecast future expenses, and allocate resources strategically.

  o Automation is to retrieve data from data lake to generate rapid and dynamic reports.

- **Empowering data-driven decision-making**: Good decisions require good data, and CFM provides just that. Through CFM, organizations gain access to a treasure trove of financial insights that allow leadership to make informed decisions about their cloud strategy. Whether it is scaling resources, renegotiating vendor contracts, or shifting workloads to optimize costs, having solid financial data at your fingertips ensures that these decisions are data-driven, not gut-driven.

- **Streamlining collaboration between finance and IT**: One of the most significant benefits of CFM is its ability to bridge the gap between finance and IT departments. Historically, these two functions have operated in silos, but cloud adoption demands greater collaboration. CFM fosters communication between these teams, ensuring that financial decisions are made with a clear understanding of technical requirements and that IT initiatives are aligned with budgetary constraints. This unity prevents costly misalignments and improves organizational agility.

- **Accelerating innovation with financial discipline**: Enterprises are increasingly leveraging cloud resources to fuel innovation. However, innovation without financial discipline can lead to runaway costs. CFM brings a layer of governance that enables businesses to innovate faster and more effectively without the fear of breaking the bank. By providing clear guidelines for spending and resource allocation, CFM allows companies to pursue bold new initiatives while maintaining financial control.

  o For example, developers use cloud resources for rapid deployment purposes. Cloud model is paper use. Maximum innovation happens in non-prod environments. In a week of 40 hours, most of the hours will be focused on developments and the rest of the hours must be focused on innovation. At a maximum, only 20 hours/week will be spent on the cloud innovation engine. Due to a lack of visibility and governance, 744 hours will be considered into billing, which is losing 80%-90% costs for enterprises.

- **Building a scalable foundation for growth**: As enterprises grow, their cloud usage will naturally expand. CFM helps businesses build a scalable foundation for this growth. Instead of grappling with ballooning cloud costs, organizations can leverage CFM to maintain cost efficiency even as they scale their operations. This ensures that as businesses grow, they can continue to innovate and expand without being hampered by financial inefficiencies.

- **Achieving sustainable cloud cost optimization**: Sustainable growth requires more than just one-off cost savings. CFM creates a framework for continuous optimization, ensuring that cloud costs remain manageable over time. Through regular monitoring and fine-tuning, enterprises can achieve ongoing savings that fuel long-term success. This commitment to sustainable optimization is what sets high-performing organizations apart from their competitors.

- **Gearing up for future-proof financial health**: The cloud landscape is constantly evolving, with new services, pricing models, and innovations emerging regularly.

CFM ensures that enterprises are not only prepared for these changes but can also take full advantage of them. By adopting robust CFM practices, organizations position themselves to adapt to future challenges and opportunities, ensuring their financial health remains secure in the face of rapid technological change.

CFM as a strategic imperative

Balance with cloud financials can be possible when it is directed as a strategic imperative and that is how FinOps culture is embraced and built on. To navigate this and induce into the nerves of your enterprise, a few aspects influence it. As this is a top-down approach, the involvement of stakeholders and how this strategic imperative supports your vision must be analyzed in a clear manner. After seeing and driving CFM in multiple enterprises, here are the five key strategies which when aligned, your cloud financial management remains stable, and this is the promising aspect we are hard striking on:

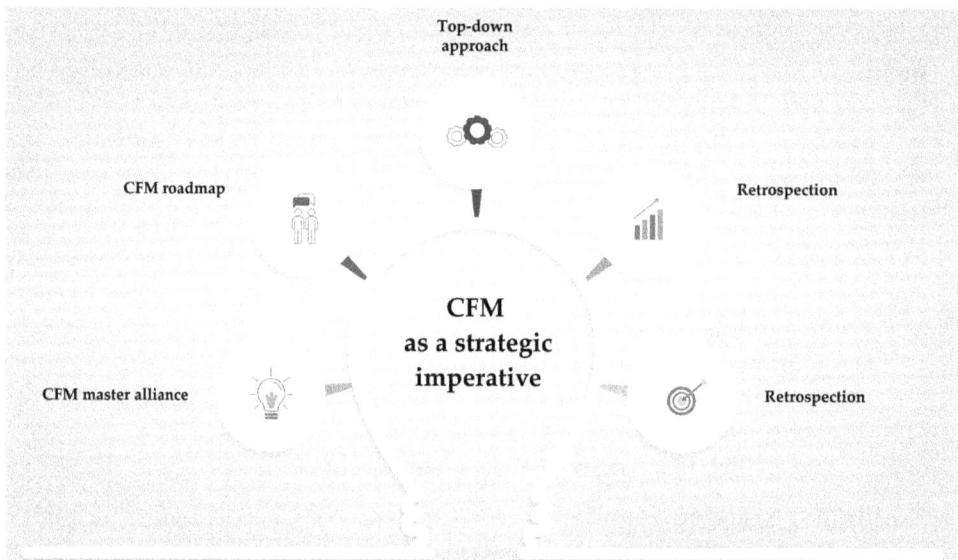

Figure 5.1: *Strategies to consider for cloud financial management*

Let us look at the strategies in detail:

- **CFM master alliance**: A group of experts, be it within the enterprise or external individuals, can imbibe the effective practices to understand and discipline cloud financials. It requires significant effort, as enterprise stakeholders must analyze the capabilities, track records, success rates, and impact that this group of individuals has created and can create through their working style, particularly as CFM experts. Taking help of tools is common, but more than that, driving efficiency with tools plays a major part. So, form an internal and external CFM master alliance where resources that increase cloud costs and quarterly cloud financials can be planned in control.

- **CFM roadmap**: Aligning to the business objectives, define CFM objectives or goals that align with yours as well. Now, define the ways you can manage and optimize cloud financials by engaging in insightful discussions with experts. Now, identify the opportunities where CFM is implemented effectively by involving the above group of leaders, accelerating the cloud resource dynamics. Once this is clear, a CFM roadmap is easy to frame that makes you achieve goals under it, including the following:

    o   Maximizing the current business value.

    o   Sustaining growth for years to come.

    o   Reducing the cloud costs.

    o   Establishing complete control over cloud costs.

    o   Planning to establish strategies that create a financial impact.

- **Top-down approach**: Every decision should flow from top to bottom and every strategy must be driven in the same way, as middle-level change is unacceptable. This is the nicest way to foster accountability and drive the change needed where cloud financial management touches the heights. Every CFM expert is responsible for the decision and strategy made and implemented enterprise wide. Here, there will be no excuses or escapes from the scenarios as everyone is held accountable for what they have been assigned to effectively manage cloud financials.

- **Retrospection**: We are following the roadmap, meeting our goals, and establishing a well-disciplined process for the effectiveness of CFM. However, there can be unexpected changes and challenges that your enterprise might face. In these cases, business objectives and the CFM roadmap will also be adjusted accordingly. This is where you must retrospect, that is, diagnose how things are moving around, analyze the responsibilities of the board, consider the business value, and most of all, how your CFM score is! This will keep you on track without any deviations. Review your CFM strategy every quarter and decide what is working, what could be done to make it better, how it could be done, and what the consequences are. When such retrospection is performed by involving top-level individuals, there is less worry and more impact.

- **Implementing the changes**: Whatever is done in retrospection, implement those changes. If the impact of CFM strategy seems promising and elevates the business to new heights, no second thought is needed! Jump into action. Define a map that measures business impact against CFM effectiveness. This map clearly shows you how the change in strategy will affect you. Bring in all the aspects, that is, market needs, customer requirements, internal changes, process improvements, accountability, and so on, so that implementation goes smoother while allowing you to strike the right balance between overrunning cloud costs and disrupting business scenarios.

By making CFM a cornerstone of your operations, businesses can navigate the complexities of the cloud with clarity, discipline, and agility. The road to cloud success is paved with smart financial management, and those who embrace it will reap the rewards for years to come.

Breaking the silos of cloud financials with FinOps tools

To maintain the balance of success while adopting FinOps and monitor and measure the ever-evolving organization needs, tools and services in FinOps become indispensable components. Acting as catalysts and piloting the FinOps discipline, these tools drive it so incredibly. However, organizations are blessed with multiple options to leverage cloud provider tooling, third-party tools, in-house tools, or customized integrations. The real challenge arises when people in the enterprise are unable to understand the purpose of the tool in the first place.

The extreme purpose of tool is to make collaborative decisions based on the value that the tool creates. Evaluation, clear understanding of cost and value they add to your organization, and the necessity to integrate as your environment undergoes significant changes are the right key aspects to think through as you evolve FinOps practice when adopting these tools and services.

To shine a light for enterprises to integrate these tools, we delve deeper into:

- Process for evaluating tools and selecting the right one you need for your environment (tool procurement process, tool integration, and deciding about tools, tool selection process).

- Exploring different types of tools that embrace your FinOps practice (tool candidates).

- Articulating on how these tools can bring the maximum value for the investments you have made.

- Effective cloud financial management with the help of these tools.

Evaluation process to accelerate FinOps adoption with pitch-perfect tools

The first phase of selecting the tool is to drive the clear process for your enterprise. However, enterprises that are in the starting phases of FinOps or long-established have existing processes to acquire software and tooling. FinOps tooling must be centered within such processes while involving decisions from the persons involved. If procurement is isolated in an organizational silo, the FinOps teams will gather relevant opinions from the relevant stakeholders as well as needs. Whether integrating or acquiring FinOps tools, it requires greater collaboration with procurement personnel and involves numerous other activities and factors to select the right one. These factors include:

- Identify all stakeholders and decision-makers who can be involved in the selection process and clearly define their roles through proper documentation.

- Evaluate current applied tools and platforms in various functions of the organization.

- Empathize with the motivations that are driving tool developments, core competencies, and their alignment to the organizational-specific needs.

- Clearly see the organization's experience and maturity of stakeholders as they must equip the proven expertise, invest their significant time, and have a value-driven business perspective to select the correct tooling.

- Derive data that the procurement team needs to negotiate in the right ways with the vendors, including forecasting.

- Define the cost structure of tools and see if your enterprise can invest in them along with supportive payment models.

- Work on competitive sourcing and procurement regulations to be followed and communicate the same to stakeholders and involved personas.

- Lock the timelines and create a process document to share with everyone, tracking the procurement process.

Despite gathering functional requirements through needs-based assessment, the FinOps roadmap will demand non-functional requirements as well before tooling can be integrated. The challenges that harden your enterprise here include compliance and regulations, tool security and configuration, integration, accessibility, and data protection. To create breakthroughs, a great collaboration with the IT personas and aligned requirements with any potential tool enables effective use of FinOps tools across your enterprise. Let us go over the various challenges now:

- **Compliance and regulations**: Ensure that the FinOps tool you intend to use within your multi-cloud environment meets the standards, such as SOC, GDPR, FedRAMP, or other industry-specific regulations (PCI-DSS or HIPAA) for which the organization must comply with. Some enterprises also establish data sovereignty requirements well. When you would like to purchase or develop a tool, establish greater controls and structure processes to meet most of the compliance requirements.

  o   However, this is not a scenario with a few organizations. The twist here is there can be complex compliance requirements that may require the implementation of robust logging and monitoring mechanisms, triggering effective auditing and incident investigation and continuous security assessments.

- **Tool security and configuration**: FinOps tools have the access to potential sensitive data, and they tend to act autonomously in your cloud environment. Clearly define where the tool features must run, when access to data is required, the permissions they may need, and the security capabilities. While defining permissions, ensure they are in alignment, bringing the best to both, that is, your environment and the IAM systems of cloud providers.

- **Application integration**: When FinOps tools are used there can be no opportunity for enterprises to operate in silos or have an independent working mechanism. They must be integrated with one another while continuously monitoring how existing tools support the new tools, and how the process changes will lead to unexpected conflicts. Recently in our tooling implementation with a manufacturing industry, it proved that the FinOps tools capabilities expand through APIs integration to internal systems or data repositories.

- **Accessibility**: In earlier chapters, the context is clear. FinOps practices and principles promote cross-functional collaboration where access to timely and consistent data is the pinnacle of it. The same accessibility is what FinOps tools need to embrace on. This touches the iconicity of organizational accessibility, addressing:

  o Authenticating new methods of logging.

  o Granting permissions internal to your environment and IAM permissions.

  o Tooling feasibility through internet access policies when operated remotely.

  o Meeting the expectations that organizations enhanced on the tooling.

  o Security standards for all these accessibility requirements.

  When it comes to CFM, security is not just an afterthought, but rather, a foundational pillar. Implementing the principle of least privilege for FinOps tools is a key step toward securing sensitive financial data. This approach ensures that FinOps tools are granted only the minimum permissions required for them to function effectively, reducing exposure to potential risks. Granular access controls, privilege management solutions, and regular audits help prevent unauthorized access and privilege escalation. The principle of *trust but verify* is vital here, continuous monitoring and fine-tuning of access rights is a must.

- **Collaboration with security teams**: Bringing the **Chief Information Security Officer** (**CISO**) and IT security teams into the fold from day one can save enterprises a world of trouble down the road. These teams can help establish secure authentication mechanisms such as **multi-factor authentication** (**MFA**) and encrypted communication protocols. Regular meetings, ideally on a quarterly basis, with security teams ensure that the FinOps tools align with organizational policies and remain up to date with the latest security standards.

- **Data protection**: When choosing or developing FinOps tools, the importance of data protection cannot be overstated. Clear processes must be established to control the access granted to data sources and ensure that only the right people and systems have access. Billing data may contain sensitive information, such as **personally identifiable information** (**PII**), internal project names, or business-critical details, that are embedded in tags or resource names. It is crucial for organizations to carefully govern this data, especially in highly regulated industries such as finance or healthcare.

- **Role-based access and encryption**: For larger or security-focused organizations, **role-based access controls** (**RBAC**) and data encryption, both in transit and at rest, are non-negotiable. These mechanisms ensure that sensitive data is only accessible by authorized individuals, reducing the risk of breaches. Moreover, for companies operating across multiple regions, adhering to data locality regulations through geo-fencing or data residency controls is essential. Complying with privacy regulations, mainly when handling PII, can be achieved through anonymization or pseudonymization techniques, protecting individual privacy while allowing the organization to leverage billing data effectively.

  o In short, the security and protection of cloud financial data are not merely technical concerns; they are essential to the integrity and success of an enterprise's cloud financial management strategy. Ignoring these facets could lead to unnecessary risks, regulatory penalties, and ultimately, loss of trust. Prioritizing security and data protection allows businesses to manage their cloud investments with confidence.

So, if you are willing to adopt a FinOps tools, consider following the most puzzle-solving aspects.

Weighing the build vs. buy decision for FinOps tools

When deciding between building a custom FinOps tool or buying an off-the-shelf solution, there are several critical questions that organizations must address to make an informed decision. Let us go over them now:

- **Full cost of building and maintaining**:
  o Building a custom FinOps tool involves significant upfront investment, not just financially, but also in terms of time and expertise. Beyond the cost of the developers and team needed to create the initial application, there is the ongoing expense of maintaining and supporting both the tool and its underlying infrastructure. Maintenance is not just about keeping the lights on; it involves adapting to ever-evolving cloud usage patterns, data ingestion challenges, and potential scaling issues. Therefore, it is important to assess the long-term financial and operational impact of this route.

- **Mitigating the key-person risk:**

    o One often overlooked aspect of custom tool development is the key-person problem. What happens if the person or team responsible for building the tool leaves the company? Having a long-term succession plan is crucial to avoid this bottleneck, ensuring continuity without over-reliance on any individual.

- **Understanding the complexity of cloud data:**

    o Building a custom FinOps tool requires a deep understanding of the complexities involved in cloud billing data. It is essential to recognize that managing and analyzing cloud cost data is not a trivial task; other companies have faced pitfalls along the way. Speaking with experienced peers can help avoid common mistakes. The more complex your FinOps practice becomes, the more functionality your tool will need, raising the question of whether your development team has the bandwidth and expertise to support those growing needs.

- **Focus on core competency:**

    o A fundamental question is whether building a FinOps tool aligns with your company's core competency. If your business is centered around FinOps infrastructure and data analysis, developing a custom solution might make sense. However, for most companies, cloud financial management is a function rather than a focus. In such cases, investing time and resources in a custom tool may not be the most effective use of resources.

- **Comparing build versus buy:**

    o Another critical consideration is the cost comparison. Does building a custom tool deliver significantly more value than an off-the-shelf product that covers 80-90% of your needs? Many third-party tools or native CSP consoles already offer robust FinOps functionalities. In many instances, it is more cost-effective to purchase a pre-built solution and customize it with additional layers, rather than starting from scratch.

- **Adaptability to standard models:**

    o Organizations must also evaluate whether they can adapt their processes to align with standard models of FinOps practice. Custom-built solutions may seem appealing for organizations with unique requirements, but if your business can modify its processes to fit within an existing model, a third-party tool can meet most of your needs with far less effort.

- **Timeline for deployment:**

    o Lastly, how quickly does your organization need a FinOps tool to meet its operational requirements? Building a custom tool can be a lengthy process, while off-the-shelf solutions are ready for immediate deployment. Time-to-market can be a significant factor in your decision, particularly for organizations needing rapid FinOps capabilities.

Build for complexity, buy for efficiency

For larger, tech-driven organizations with complex use cases, building a custom tool might be justified. However, for smaller companies or those without deep technical resources, the burden of maintaining a custom-built system could outweigh its benefits. If your needs are unique and no third-party tool can meet them, then a custom solution may be necessary, but it is essential to plan for ongoing updates and expansion. Otherwise, an off-the-shelf solution might offer the best balance of functionality, cost, and speed.

Evolving FinOps with revolutionary tools

When embarking on the journey of FinOps tool selection, enterprises need a systematic approach. It all begins with a well-considered list of candidates tailored to the organization's needs and scope. Whether building from scratch or integrating existing tools, here are some key strategies to get started.

Building your list

Let us go over the following:

- **FinOps landscape**: Leverage the FinOps landscape to identify tools by capability, CSP, compliance, or specific features.

- **Commercial tools**: Evaluate commercial solutions from our FinOps experts and connect with our product leaders for insights.

- **Try before you buy**: Utilize free trials to test the tool's functionality in real-world scenarios, giving you first-hand insights.

- **Expert opinions**: Meet product professionals to understand their approach to FinOps, filtering the list to a smaller, focused subset.

- **Analyst reports**: Tap into industry insights through reports from Gartner, Forrester, or IDC for recommendations.

- **Community engagement**: Gain valuable insights from FinOps community members via Slack, meetups, or conferences like FinOps X.

- **Consult expert vendors**: Seek advice from current vendors or cloud service providers for recommendations like us.

Tool selection phase

Once a list of potential candidates has been compiled, the real work begins. The selection process is about narrowing down options based on features, costs, compliance, and long-term sustainability. The steps are as follows:

1. **Refinement**: Compare the tool's capabilities to your documented needs, keeping in mind the total cost of ownership.

2. **Collaboration**: Involve procurement teams, technical experts, and internal stakeholders for comprehensive decision-making.

3. **Trials and demos**: Consider trailing multiple tools with actual data to test them in your environment before making the final decision.

Implementation phase

Selecting a tool is just the beginning. Successful implementation hinges on proper user adoption and ongoing support. Let us go over the phases now:

- **Customize before rollout**: Before deploying, ensure that tool permissions and access levels are configured for different user roles. Tailoring these permissions ensures that users only have access to the data relevant to their functions.

- **Enable and train users**: Training and support are crucial. While some users may learn independently, most will benefit from structured enablement. Leverage the vendor's resources and internal training for a smoother adoption curve.

- **Stay mindful of organizational change**: Rolling out new tools can be challenging, especially for large organizations. It is essential to communicate clearly about changes, expectations, and the benefits of the new system.

- **Continuous evaluation and tool optimization**: The journey does not end with deployment. Continuous evaluation is crucial for ensuring that tools evolve in tandem with your organization's changing needs.

- **Assess and adapt**: Monitor adoption KPIs and tool performance. If the tool is not delivering as expected, determine whether it is due to misconfiguration, lack of training, or the need for further customization.

- **Evolving ecosystem**: The FinOps ecosystem is dynamic. As your organization grows, so will your tool needs. Regular evaluation will ensure that your toolkit stays up-to-date and continues to provide value. With this strategy, enterprises can seamlessly integrate FinOps tools into their operations, ensuring continuous value generation while adapting to evolving financial and operational needs.

Now, you have decided the tools and how these can be implemented but the conclusion of tooling is not there yet! The FinOps tools serve the purpose in many areas and therefore, the tools are categorized into various types, such as:

- Cloud cost management tools.
- Cloud resource optimization tools.
- Cloud governance tools.
- Cloud financial management tools.
- Cost allocation and reporting tools.

The impact that each of these tools create can be huge. It varies depending on what your enterprise wants to achieve through FinOps culture. The mix and match of these tools obviously set the direction right, delivering the expected outcomes. However, before selecting the tool, one must understand the differences each type of tool has, so that you are well-versed with the tool that best aligns with your FinOps culture.

Though there are many numbers of tools among the specified categories, our focus is restricted to CFM tools. For your reference, here we come up how each one of them can serve the enterprise needs atop focusing extremely on CFM tools.

Helping enterprises with cloud cost management tools

Cloud cost-effectiveness is the art and science in a dynamic multi-cloud environment. As your enterprise leverages diverse cloud platforms, the need to analyze spending patterns to avoid hitting with runaway costs is always at its peak. This is where cloud cost management tools like Azure Cost Management, AWS Cost Explorer, and Google Cloud Cost Management come into play. These tools not only track cloud usage and spending but also serve as the unsung heroes that enable financial governance, cost optimization, and operational efficiency across multiple cloud providers. As cloud environments evolve, organizations that invest in robust cost management practices will not only reduce waste but also position themselves for long-term success. The future of cloud financial management lies in mastering these tools to drive efficiency, collaboration, and innovation at every turn.

Power of cloud resource optimization tools

The sheer volume of cloud resources and associated costs can quickly spiral out of control if left unchecked. Here, the cloud resource optimization tools, such as CloudHealth, CloudCheckr, and ParkMyCloud, play a vital role. These platforms not only help streamline operations but also serve as a financial compass for organizations looking to gain better control over their cloud spending.

Cloud resource optimization tools automate the process of identifying underutilized or oversized resources, which, in turn, helps businesses avoid unnecessary expenses. The age-old saying, *A penny saved is a penny earned*, holds more weight than ever in the cloud ecosystem. By using these tools, organizations can continuously optimize their resources without having to manually monitor and adjust each element.

Gain FinOps traction with CFM tools

As enterprises embrace the cloud at scale, managing cloud finances has become as complex as it is critical. This is where cloud financial management platforms step in, acting as the linchpin for effective financial governance, cost optimization, and resource allocation. These platforms offer an integrated suite of tools designed to provide real-time visibility and control over cloud expenses. However, their impact goes far beyond cost management. They shape the way organizations plan, allocate resources, and strategize for long-term financial success in the cloud.

As cloud architectures grow, more complex and multi-cloud becomes the norm, these platforms will play a pivotal role in shaping the future of cloud financial management.

In our research, we have witnessed the most significant wins that these tools have brought to enterprises. Spotlighting these tools has helped businesses remain agile, adaptive, and equipped with the financial insights they need to thrive in a competitive digital environment. Now, let us see the capabilities that each tool has encompassed, so that your search and head-banging on which tool to use ends here, irrespective of rankings or ratings!

IBM Cloudability

In today's multi-cloud era, IBM Cloudability stands at the forefront of cloud financial management, seamlessly aligning technology investments with business priorities. It is not just a tool; it is a catalyst for cross-functional accountability and financial efficiency in hybrid IT environments. By empowering organizations to maximize their cloud investments, Cloudability transforms the way businesses manage and optimize cloud spending.

IBM Cloudability offers a unified, single-pane-of-glass solution for FinOps practitioners across all major cloud service providers. It enables businesses to take full control of their variable, consumption-based cloud costs. Through its intuitive business mapping engine, Cloudability ensures that every dollar spent is properly allocated, automating chargebacks to the appropriate teams with precision. AI-backed anomaly detection, customizable dashboards, and comprehensive analytics tools further enhance visibility, enabling teams to pinpoint inefficiencies and act swiftly.

The platform fosters team ownership of cloud spending, allowing businesses to monitor, manage, and improve their cloud economics. Teams can reduce cloud unit costs by up to 30%, achieve 100% cost allocation, and boost commitment coverage to over 90%.

By offering detailed forecasting, budgets, and curated reports, Cloudability equips businesses with the tools to make informed financial decisions that drive growth. As a FinOps leader, delivers actionable insights that ensure cloud resources are used efficiently and strategically, resulting in maximum return on investment.

The key features of IBM Cloudability are:

- Understand cloud usage and cost.
- Quantify business value.

- Optimize cloud usage and cost.
- Robust integrations.
- Collaborative FinOps.
- Enhanced operational efficiency.
- Forecast cloud costs with greater accuracy.

CoreStack

CoreStack, an AI-driven multi-cloud governance platform, empowers enterprises to take full control of their cloud environments. By providing continuous, autonomous cloud governance at scale, CoreStack enables businesses to leverage the cloud on their own terms, driving transformational outcomes across FinOps, SecOps, and CloudOps. With impressive results, including a 40% reduction in cloud costs, 50% improvement in operational efficiency, and 100% assurance of security and compliance, CoreStack is reshaping how enterprises govern their multi-cloud environments.

At the heart of CoreStack's offering is its NextGen FinOps solution, which equips enterprises with the tools to optimize cloud costs and achieve financial accountability across multi-cloud platforms. CoreStack helps organizations assess their FinOps maturity, offering unparalleled visibility and insights that allow for effective cost planning, optimization, and long-term efficiency.

By providing an intuitive and seamless experience, CoreStack empowers teams to manage cloud costs with precision, maximizing their financial governance while continuing to innovate in the cloud.

The key features of Corestack are:

- Next-gen cloud governance.
- Leverage AI to cloud spending.
- Assess FinOps Maturity to foster financial accountability.
- Autonomously govern security operations.
- Achieve continuous cloud compliance.
- Run highly available and lean operations at scale.
- Build an efficient and profitable cloud MSP practice.

Flexera

Flexera helps enterprises maximize the return on their technology investments by offering SaaS-based IT management solutions that provide total visibility into complex hybrid ecosystems. This visibility enables organizations to right size across all platforms, reallocate spend, and mitigate risks, including audits and security breaches, while optimizing their path to the cloud.

To unlock true value from every IT dollar, **Technology Value Optimization** (**TVO**) is the key. Flexera empowers organizations with the insights needed to make better-informed IT decisions, ensuring efficient resource allocation, risk reduction, and smoother cloud transitions. With a focus on IT transformation, Flexera's solutions are designed to integrate seamlessly with ITSM and ITFM platforms, enhancing their effectiveness.

Flexera One, Flexera's flagship SaaS solution, provides a unified interface to visualize and manage an entire IT estate. Tailored for enterprises with highly complex hybrid environments, Flexera One empowers game-changing IT decisions, enabling organizations to efficiently and strategically illuminate and transform their IT landscapes.

Flexera addresses key pain points, including:

- Outdated systems that track technological spending, especially in hybrid cloud environments.

- Wasted spend across desktop, data center, SaaS and IaaS/PaaS.

- Identification of unknown, vulnerable, unused, or obsolete assets in the IT environment.

- Managing unreliable **configuration management database** (**CMBD**) data.

- Shadowed IT assets.

- Lacking in maintaining comprehensive cloud cost governance.

- Running with the risks of unbudgeted spending.

- Understanding the environmental impact of the IT footprint.

CloudFix

CloudFix is the automatic, always-running solution for optimizing AWS costs. Created by founder *Rahul Subramaniam* to manage his own company's massive AWS spend, CloudFix now empowers global enterprises to achieve up to 30% savings per AWS service by continuously identifying and implementing AWS-recommended cost-saving measures. Its features are as follows:

- **A nonstop savings engine**: Unlike other tools that offer one-time savings suggestions, CloudFix is a self-sustaining cost-saving engine. It runs around the clock, scanning your AWS environment and applying the most relevant savings opportunities, just like compounding interest. This means your savings grow as CloudFix continuously discovers and fixes new cost inefficiencies without manual intervention.

- **Beyond visualization with automated fixes, and not just insights**: Many tools merely identify cost-saving opportunities, leaving you to manage the rest. CloudFix takes it a step further by automatically applying AWS-approved fixes, making it a hassle-free solution for FinOps practitioners. With over 50 new AWS advisories weekly, CloudFix ensures you stay on top of savings, with the ability to approve and implement optimizations instantly.

- **AWS-approved, risk-free optimization**: All CloudFix actions are based on AWS's latest advisories, ensuring full compliance and zero risk to your cloud environment. It integrates seamlessly across multiple AWS services, beyond just storage and compute, so your entire AWS ecosystem benefits from continuous, compounding savings.

- **Savings that grow over time**: CloudFix's compounding savings model is what sets it apart from traditional consulting engagements or static visualizer tools. As AWS publishes new advisories, CloudFix automatically adjusts your environment, enabling ongoing cost reductions that accumulate over time and maximize your AWS investment without interruption.

CloudFix unleashes its greatest benefits to DevOps, FinOps, IT, and Cloud Architect teams in ways possible. Let us now go over the various types of teams and the CloudFix advantages associated with them:

Types of teams	CloudFix advantage
DevOps teams	• Zero risk and minimal downtime. • Easy fixes can be automated. • CloudFix scans automatically with quick deployment options. • Easily manage security and compliance. • Retain complete control using AWS tools.
FinOps teams	• Quick wins of cost savings, saving more money. • Act on optimizations by going beyond visualization solutions. • Achieve continuous, non-stop savings. • Easily communicate with DevOps teams on suggested changes. • AWS-recommended cost savings helps you realize powerful ROI.
IT executives	• Explore new ways to reduce AWS costs without adding more resources. • Fill in the gaps in your existing cost optimization strategy and toolset. • Uncover both immediate and long-term savings. • Optimize AWS costs rapidly, easily, and securely. • Automate AWS savings at scale.

Types of teams	CloudFix advantage
Cloud teams	• Find and fix AWS-recommended savings opportunities. • Introduce new ways to optimize your AWS spend. • Complement native AWS cost optimization tools with intelligent automation. • Stay on track with the latest AWS offerings. • Implement AWS best practices with a least privilege permission model.

Table 5.1: *Teams and advantages offered by CloudFix*

CloudZero

CloudZero empowers engineering teams to take charge of cloud costs by directly linking technical choices to business outcomes. For software-driven companies seeking to boost profit margins, CloudZero's key advantage lies in its ability to provide real-time, hourly insights into cloud spend across all major providers. This enables teams to innovate rapidly without compromising on cost efficiency.

CloudZero offers precise cloud cost visibility tailored to business goals without the usual complexities of cost management. The platform organizes costs into meaningful unit metrics like cost per customer or cost per feature, no tagging required. Even in cloud-native architectures, where shared resources such as Kubernetes and microservices often create blind spots, CloudZero provides seamless clarity.

Built with engineering in mind, the platform is intuitive and automated, decentralizing cost control to development teams. This fosters a culture where cost efficiency becomes a natural part of the innovation process. Automated AI-driven alerts, integrated with Slack, keep teams informed about cost anomalies in real time, while deep integrations with CI/CD tools streamline the debugging of cost issues.

The key features of CloudZero are:

- A single pane of glass for cloud spends.
- Perfect allocation without perfect tags.
- Automatic shared cost allocation.
- Benchmarks for cloud spend efficiency.
- Best-in-category Kubernetes visibility.
- AI and human-driven cloud savings.
- Precise cloud budgeting and forecasting.
- FinOps enablement through human and automated analysis.

Vantage

Vantage revolutionizes cloud cost management by putting actionable insights into the hands of every engineer, accelerating the maturity of FinOps practices. Unlike traditional tools, Vantage is ready to use within minutes and integrates seamlessly with a wide array of cloud platforms.

Built on deep, native integrations, Vantage consolidates cost data across your entire tech stack into a single platform, currently supporting over 15 major services like AWS, Azure, Google Cloud, Snowflake, Datadog, and MongoDB. With customizable reports and rule sets, users can slice and forecast cloud costs in virtually any way, including detailed insights into Kubernetes and network costs, broken down by resource, team, or application.

Vantage also enhances cost governance through virtual tags, ensuring consistency in cross-provider tagging, while its Segments feature enables precise cost attribution and hierarchical reporting. Beyond visibility, Vantage automates savings by identifying optimization opportunities across services, and its Autopilot feature for AWS Savings Plans fully automates cost-saving purchases, maximizing efficiency across the board.

The key highlights of the Vantage tool are:

- Easily build complex reports.
- Allocate and report on costs by cluster, namespace, and label on Kubernetes.
- Maintain cross-provider comprehensive tagging coverage.
- Increased networking visibility to attribute the main drivers of network costs.
- Cost governance through cost attribution and hierarchical reporting.
- Set budgets and stay on alert if costs are trending over budget.
- Save on AWS through automated buying of AWS Savings Plans.
- Understand your discounted coverage and effective savings rate.
- Savings planner for modeling and forecasting future savings.
- Team access and management.

Harness

Harness is making waves in the software delivery space with its intelligent platform that streamlines software deployment, combining speed, quality, and ease. Its software delivery platform integrates continuous integration, continuous delivery, cloud cost management, and feature flags, enabling companies to fast-track their cloud strategies, especially with containerization and orchestration tools like Kubernetes and Amazon ECS.

Harness cloud cost management stands out by offering visibility and cost optimization, particularly for Kubernetes, without the need for resource tagging. Supporting AWS, GCP, and Azure, it simplifies cost control for customers, enabling them to derive more value with less effort. For example, Harness cuts its cloud expenses by $8,000 a day, saving $3 million over five months.

Harness covers three main areas:

- **Cost visibility**: Granular insights into container costs on Kubernetes and ECS, no tagging required.

- **Cost savings**: Significantly reduce container costs and avoid surprise spikes.

- **Cost forecasting**: Confidently predict future cloud costs for better capacity planning and budget control.

ProsperOps

ProsperOps offers a fully autonomous AWS cost optimization service that delivers maximum savings with minimal risk, that is, completely hands-off. Companies using ProsperOps achieve savings rates exceeding 40%, ranking in the top 1% of AWS optimizers, with commitments that adjust in real-time to shifts in usage.

For many organizations, AWS is a major cost driver, with compute resources alone accounting for around 60% of their bill. AWS offers various tools to reduce costs, but these tools come with trade-offs. Companies often under save or overcommit, leading to unnecessary expenses.

ProsperOps eliminates the guesswork. Its algorithms autonomously manage an optimized commitment portfolio that evolves with your usage, ensuring you save consistently without lifting a finger. Trusted by top brands, ProsperOps manages cost optimization for over $500M in cloud spend.

The benefits of ProsperOps are:

- **Greater savings, less risk**: The built-in algorithms maximize AWS and GCP discounts 24/7, and minimizes long-term and inelastic commitment risk, without any manual efforts

- **Zero friction for engineering and finance**: Engineering teams prefer solutions that do not create overhead and tech debt. ProsperOps runs in the background to save money on the cloud, being uncompromised or undistracted.

- **Seamless integration with finance and accounting**: The intelligence allocation of resources within AWS environment based on your business operations enables your finance and accounting teams to integrate ProsperOps wherever needed.

Heeddata

Right now, the global market has endorsed with a lot of FinOps tools and services but there should be one unique platform where the platform covers most of the FinOps capabilities, accelerating FinOps discipline across the enterprise and delivering the key functionalities such as accurate forecasting and budgeting, anomaly detection, optimizing cloud financial management, and more on multi-cloud.

This exploration has led us to Heeddata, a leading and phenomenal multi cloud FinOps platform that enhances CFM within enterprises at scale. Though unlisted in FinOps landscape, the platform's capabilities remain unmatched as it touches most of the FinOps capabilities that the previous tools could not. Based on our data and wide research into all these tools, Heeddata seems to be a potent solution for enterprises that wish to foster FinOps.

In the present day, it has been listed in the global marketplaces of Azure and Oracle, delivering a seamless experience to enterprises in FinOps adoption. The next two cloud global marketplaces will be in place by the end of this year, according to the company's recent update.

The company's product head, *Venkat Reddy Chintalapudi* said, *Heeddata is going to revolutionize the FinOps adoption for SMBs as well as for large-scale enterprises, meeting their requirements at scale. Complementing most of the FinOps capabilities and establishing every aspect of FinOps – Phases, Principles, Personas, and Domains, the process establishment is going to bring greater ROI for all the enterprises. And FOCUS is another major advantage where together they bring the supreme value to the enterprises.*

The FinOps capabilities complemented by Heeddata are:

- Allocation of resources
- Anomaly management
- Benchmarking
- Budgeting
- Cloud policy and governance
- Cloud sustainability
- Forecasting
- Rate optimization
- Reporting and analytics
- Unit economics

To know more about each one of the capabilities, refer to *Appendix A*.

Moreover, Heeddata integrates into all four major cloud environments, that is, Oracle, AWS, Azure, and Google Cloud. Proving its flexibility in every cloud at every instance within your ecosystem, it redefines your FinOps processes and reinvents with its out-of-the-box features that include:

- Multi-cloud governance
- Cloud cost optimization

- AI-powered recommendations
- Continuous monitoring and observability
- Cost map
- Cost explorer
- Multi-cloud visibility

Another milestone that Heeddata has achieved is, as we have highlighted in the introduction, the cloud spend is going to touch $180 billion by 2025. Heeddata's promising features and integration with cloud environments slash this cloud spend as much as 40%-50%. It fosters accountability, enhances granular visibility, and drives automation effectively. As far as our research is concerned, Heeddata is one such potential and uprising leader in driving your FinOps in the most effective way possible!

Here, we conclude that CFM platforms offer end-to-end visibility, control, and optimization of cloud costs, driving smarter financial decisions and fostering a culture of continuous improvement. Whether it is through budgeting and forecasting, cost allocation, or ongoing optimization, these platforms provide the foundation for financial governance in the cloud era. It is not just about saving money; it is about maximizing the value of every cloud dollar spent.

Role of cost allocation and reporting tools

As cloud adoption becomes the backbone of modern enterprises, keeping a tight rein on cloud costs is no longer a luxury but a necessity. Managing those costs, especially in a multi-cloud environment, can quickly turn into a tangled web of confusion. However, cost allocation and reporting tools such as CloudCheckr and FinanceManager provide the clarity and precision businesses need to track and manage their cloud spending effectively. These tools are game changers, offering granular insights into where cloud dollars are being spent, by whom, and for what purposes. They go beyond simply tracking costs; they enable organizations to drive accountability, transparency, and optimization at every level.

Cost allocation and reporting tools like CloudCheckr and FinanceManager provide businesses with the visibility, precision, and insights needed to manage cloud costs effectively. By enabling accurate cost allocation, fostering accountability, and delivering detailed reports on cloud usage, these tools empower organizations to take full control of their cloud spending. They drive not only financial discipline but also smarter decision-making, ensuring that cloud investments are aligned with business goals and optimized for success.

Fostering multi-cloud FinOps with powerful tools

Touching and exploring the horizons of FinOps is an innovative aspect, and all these FinOps tools and platforms help enterprises achieve the best with their promising features and capabilities. Solving the Rubik Cube of complexities in the multi-cloud world, these tools and platforms enable businesses to scale across multi-cloud providers, massively overcoming the challenges associated with cloud cost management, resource optimization, and financial governance. Blending financial accountability with cloud operations and driving companies to harness the true potential of multi-cloud strategy, FinOps is the true top-angle value-multiplying culture.

To embrace this FinOps, the following are the aspects that help enterprises to make multicolored FinOps adoption faster, driving the most value out of the cloud:

- **Fostering cost efficiency and accountability**: FinOps platforms provide real-time visibility into cloud spend across multiple providers, helping businesses make informed decisions. For small businesses, this means keeping a tighter rein on their budgets and scaling effectively without overspending. Large enterprises, on the other hand, can break down cloud costs by department, service, or product, ensuring each team is accountable for their usage. This visibility fosters a culture of shared responsibility, where both engineering and finance work together to achieve optimal outcomes.

- **Optimizing resources across providers**: Multi-cloud strategies enable enterprises to avoid vendor lock-in, but they also increase complexity. FinOps tools simplify this by offering a unified view of cloud usage and costs, regardless of the provider. They enable businesses to identify underutilized resources, eliminate waste, and apply Reserved Instances or Savings Plans where they make the most impact. For any enterprise, this capability translates into significant cost savings and more efficient resource utilization.

- **Driving innovation without financial risk**: The flexibility of multi-cloud environments allows enterprises to experiment, innovate, and leverage the best services from each provider. However, this can often lead to unexpected costs. FinOps platforms mitigate these risks by offering predictive insights and cost forecasting. Enterprises can confidently pursue innovation, knowing that they are safeguarded against cost overruns and inefficiencies.

- **Scaling cloud governance**: As organizations grow, maintaining financial governance across multiple clouds becomes a challenge. FinOps platforms automate cost governance by implementing policies that ensure financial best practices are followed at every level. Whether it is enforcing tagging standards, setting budget alerts, or automating compliance checks, these tools enable enterprises to maintain control as they scale their cloud operations.

Conclusion

More than cost-saving mechanisms, FinOps tools and platforms are the enablers of deploying multi-cloud strategies, especially for cloud cost allocation. These empower enterprises to maximize the value of their cloud investments while driving innovation and growth. Most importantly, they address ever-increasing cloud cost concerns and financials in the rapidly expanding dynamic cloud environments.

Join our Discord space

Join our Discord workspace for latest updates, offers, tech happenings around the world, new releases, and sessions with the authors:

https://discord.bpbonline.com

CHAPTER 6
Cloud Cost Allocation

Introduction

Cloud resources grow huge and increase by hundreds to thousands as organizations expand, and costs also increase in one way or another. As cloud resources grow, so does the cost, and many teams or individuals remain unaware of their resource usage and corresponding cloud costs. This is where cloud cost allocation takes the credit. Cost allocation is a critical practice in which cloud resources are classified and distributed based on resource usage. It effectively tracks cloud resource consumption at scale across different entities within an organization, including business units, projects, or departments. As soon as the usage is tracked, the respective departments are assigned the costs, ensuring everyone is accountable for their own cloud usage.

Let us open the threads of cloud cost allocation that enable effective FinOps by adoring one of the principles: *Everyone takes ownership for their cloud usage*.

When managing cloud costs, allocation is a critical strategy that ensures costs are distributed across the organization based on usage, accountability, and value. Done right, it aligns cloud expenses with the teams and projects responsible for them, fostering transparency and financial ownership. In FinOps, allocation goes beyond simply dividing costs; it brings to light the true cost of cloud resources to product managers, engineers, and other stakeholders, enabling them to make informed decisions.

Breaking down cloud costs

At its core, cost allocation involves assigning cloud expenses to the right teams, products, or departments. Whether done directly or by sharing common costs, allocation helps build a clear financial picture for everyone involved. This is not just about spreading out costs arbitrarily but understanding how to distribute expenses accurately by using account structures, tags, and metadata that categorize cloud resources effectively.

The more granular the cost breakdown, the better. This often means tagging or naming resources in a way that clarifies their ownership and purpose. Some organizations go even further by pulling data from CMDB, observability platforms, or utilization data, ensuring even shared costs are split fairly. The level of sophistication in cost allocation grows as organizations require more detailed reporting and insights.

Pillars of effective cost allocation

To fully embrace the power of cost allocation, organizations must adopt three key strategies:

- Allocation strategy
- Tagging strategy
- Shared cost strategy

Crafting the allocation strategy

The allocation strategy is all about defining how cloud costs will be mapped within the organization. Different stakeholders require different levels of insight. Finance teams may want a high-level overview divided by Cost Center, while engineering might demand a granular breakdown by application or project. Meanwhile, operations teams need a holistic view of production environments across the board.

This means there are often multiple layers of allocation at play, from dividing costs by R&D, operations, and customer-facing services, to creating chargeback models that ensure teams are financially responsible for their cloud usage. Showback and chargeback models can be vital tools to enhance transparency and drive accountability across departments.

Tagging strategy

The tagging strategy is the foundation of cost visibility. By leveraging tags, labels, and metadata, organizations can effectively classify cloud resources and associate them with specific teams or projects. However, this process is not as simple as it sounds. There are challenges in tagging compliance, consistency, and the limitations of tagging certain resources across different cloud platforms. Without proper tagging automation, such as **infrastructure as code** (**IaC**) or tools that manage tags post-launch, chaos can ensue.

Furthermore, tagging strategies should align not only with financial goals but also with the broader needs of the organization, from security and operations to automation. Collaboration across departments, particularly involving the CCOE, CloudOps, or DevOps teams, ensures a cohesive tagging approach that meets both cost allocation and other organizational needs.

Shared cost strategy

In every organization, there are shared costs, that is, resources or services that benefit multiple teams or departments. This includes things like centralized networking services, platforms, or containers. Allocating these shared costs can be a balancing act. While the goal is often full allocation, many organizations opt for a more pragmatic approach by budgeting shared costs centrally, especially in the early stages of FinOps, to avoid unnecessarily burdening individual cost centers. This is known as the **informed ignore strategy**.

However, as FinOps practices mature, organizations often adopt more sophisticated methods to distribute shared costs, such as fixed allocations, proportional splits based on usage, or using proxy metrics to determine variable proportions. Over time, as cloud usage grows and automation increases, the complexity of shared cost allocation will evolve as well, requiring regular reassessment and adjustments.

Importance of flexibility in cost allocation strategies

Cost allocation in cloud environments is not a static process. As an organization matures in its FinOps practice, it may implement multiple versions of allocation strategies simultaneously. This evolving nature makes it nearly impossible to achieve 100% consistency in tagging, allocation, or shared cost management. However, the primary goal should be to develop a system that provides actionable insights, enabling more intelligent decision-making at every stage of the organization's cloud journey.

In the world of FinOps, cost allocation is power. By mastering the art of allocation, through intelligent strategies, efficient tagging, and mindful distribution of shared costs, organizations can gain not only financial transparency but also a deeper understanding of their cloud investments.

Maturity assessment for cost allocation

Cloud cost allocation evolves through three stages: Crawl, Walk, and Run. Each phase reflects an organization's maturity in managing, distributing, and optimizing cloud costs. Let us explore the strategies for each phase and how they impact cloud financial management.

Crawl: Setting the foundation for cost allocation

At the Crawl stage, organizations are just starting to establish their cloud cost allocation practices. This is a simple allocation strategy, with room for improvement in structure and consistency. Let us go over the following:

- **Basic allocation setup:**
  - o Costs are assigned to business units, portfolios, or cost centers using known accounts.
  - o 50% of cloud costs can be allocated without needing metadata adjustments.

- **Tagging strategy:**
  - o Exists but is not uniformly applied across the board.
  - o Naming standards for resources, accounts, and projects exist, but they are not consistently adhered to.
  - o Challenges include identifying owners of untagged or unidentified accounts monthly.

- **Shared costs management:**
  - o Shared costs, such as support and taxes, are identified but allocated directly to central budgets.
  - o Product owners and engineers manage only direct costs, leading to inaccurate forecasts and budgets.

- **Tooling and KPIs:**
  - o Allocation tasks are primarily managed using cloud provider tools.
  - o KPIs for cost allocation are defined but created manually on an inconsistent basis.

Walk: Structured and documented allocation

At the Walk stage, the allocation strategy becomes more structured, documented, and applied, though inconsistencies may still exist. Let us go over the following:

- **Allocation strategy:**
  - o Well-documented allocation strategies cover multiple mechanisms for allocating cloud costs.
  - o 75% of cloud costs are allocated without requiring adjustments or deep investigation.
  - o Application and service-level allocation is introduced, improving accuracy.

- **Tagging strategy:**
  - o The tagging strategy is well-documented, and compliance is consistent in key areas.
  - o Legacy infrastructure may still require manual allocation or estimates.
- **Shared costs strategy:**
  - o Shared cost allocation models (proportional, fixed, even-split) are defined and used across the organization.
  - o Shared costs are fairly distributed among cost centers using documented models.
- **Tooling and KPIs:**
  - o A mix of cloud service provider tools, third-party, and custom tools are used for cost allocation.
  - o KPIs are understood but not yet fully automated.
  - o Discounts are proportionally spread across teams, reflecting fair allocation.
- **Awareness and planning**
  - o Product owners and engineers are aware of their shared platform costs and incorporate them into forecasts and budgets.
  - o Shared cost onboarding is documented, making it easier to bring new cost centers or business units into the fold.

Run: Advanced and automated cost allocation

At the Run stage, organizations have fully matured their cost allocation processes, making them highly granular, automated, and precise. Let us go over the following:

- **Comprehensive allocation:**
  - o Costs are allocated at any level of granularity the organization requires.
  - o 80-100% of FinOps-managed costs are allocated without needing manual adjustments or investigations.
- **Automation and tagging:**
  - o Automation ensures consistency in resources and account tagging.
  - o Metering tools are used to capture and attribute shared costs with greater accuracy.
  - o Mechanisms are in place to automatically correct tagging or augment cloud provider capabilities post-billing.

- **Shared costs strategy:**

  o The shared cost recovery process is automated, ensuring a fair share of costs and onboarding new cost centers efficiently.

  o Shared costs are recovered accurately, reflecting commercial and commitment-based discounts.

- **Real-time KPIs:**

  o KPIs are fully automated and provide near real-time insights, enabling product owners to understand monthly costs.

  o Product owners and engineers consider all shared costs during forecasting and budgeting.

- **Optimized tooling:**

  o Consistent use of cloud service provider tools, third-party tools, and custom tools ensures all costs are allocated efficiently.

  o Few scenarios exist where costs are unidentified or unallocated, and reporting time is drastically reduced.

The journey from Crawl to Run reflects an organization's evolution in cloud cost allocation. From manual, inconsistent processes to fully automated, highly accurate systems, each stage lays the groundwork for more informed decision-making, better forecasting, and cost transparency. The end goal is a robust FinOps culture that empowers teams to take charge of their cloud spend and optimize every dollar spent.

Defining KPIs for effective cloud cost allocation

The big challenge here is selecting the right KPIs for your FinOps practice, and identifying data sources to achieve visibility into each of these KPIs brings more complexity. The bridge to navigate these complexities is a set of KPIs that are effective for all organizations, regardless of their cloud service provider, industry size, or FinOps maturity. Let us go over them now.

KPI 1: **Usage or spend apportionment validation**

Method of apportioning shared costs based on usage or spend proportional amount.

Formula:

Total apportionment of shared costs/Total shared costs

Example: ACME Global Limited Shared cost for the month of July was $200,000 on cloud monitoring tools, security tools, cloud costs management tools, CSP Premium Support Fees. ACME Global Cloud bill for July came to $1,200,000, broken down per cost center/product/department as:

- Finance = $225,000
- Logistics = $225,000
- Commercial = $300,000
- Marketing = $450,000

Method for apportionment shared cost is cloud spend:

- Finance = ($225,000 / $1,200,000) $200,000 = $37,500
- Logistics = ($225,000 / $1,200,000) $200,000 = $37,500
- Commercial = ($300,000 / $1,200,000) $200,000 = $50,000
- Marketing = ($450,000 / $1,200,000) $200,000 = $75,000

  ($37,500 +$37,500+$50,000 +$75,000) / $200,000 x 100 = 100%

Data sources:

- CSP billing data
- Internal finance metrics

KPI 2: Percentage of CSP cloud costs where policy compliant is tagged

This KPI calculates the amount of compliance for cloud cost tagging and demands well-versed organizational tagging policy. The sophistication of determining what acceptable tag criteria is and the stringency of the KPI should evolve with the organization's FinOps maturity.

Formula:

(Total costs associated with tagging policy compliant CSP cloud resources during a period of time / Total CSP cloud costs during a period of time) x 100

Data sources:

- CSP billing data

KPI 3: Percentage of cloud costs associated with unallocated CSP cloud resources

Unallocated costs are the expenses incurred for undefined resources or services within specific projects, departments, or applications. These costs occur due to too many shared resources, lack of proper cost allocation mechanisms, or inefficiencies in resource management. Unallocated resources lead to cloud wastage, bringing the challenge of tracking and managing expenses accurately. Improving the cost allocation can only happen when unallocated costs are identified and reduced.

Formula:

Total costs associated with unallocated CSP cloud resources during a period of time / Total CSP cloud costs during a period of time

Data sources:

- CSP billing data

KPI 4: Percentage of unallocated shared CSP cloud cost

Expenses are indirectly attributed to a specific project, team, or department within an organization. Distribution of shared costs can be done by choosing a cost model such as shared costs that are evenly charged back across all consumers, proportionally charged back based on cloud consumption, or charged back by relying on any other metrics to determine cost allocation. Here, the aim is to limit the percentage of shared costs not being charged back as time passes.

Formula:

Percentage of unallocated shared CSP cloud cost = (Unallocated shared CSP cloud cost/Total CSP cloud cost)

Measure of success

Decreasing % of unallocated shared CSP cloud cost over time.

Data sources

- CSP billing data

- Cloud console

KPI 5: Percentage of costs involved with untagged CSP cloud resources

Implement the established organizational tagging policy to calculate the percentage of untagged resources. Acceptable tag criteria and the stringent KPI must be evolved and sophisticated with the FinOps maturity.

Formula:

(Total costs associated with untagged CSP cloud resources during a period of time / Total CSP cloud costs during a period of time) x 100

Data sources

- CSP billing data

Note: **Not all CSP cloud resources can be tagged.**

KPI 6: Fixed percentage apportionment validation

Method of apportioning shared costs based on fixed percentage.

Formula:

Total apportionment of shared costs / Total shared costs

Example: ACME Global Limited Shared cost for the month of July was $200,000 on cloud monitoring tools, security tools, cloud costs management tools, CSP Premium Support Fees. ACME Global Limited has 4 cost center/product/department, so the fixed percentage is 25%.

- *Finance = 25% x $200,000 = $50,000*

- *Logistics = 25% x $200,000 = $50,000*

- *Commercial = 25% x $200,000 = $50,000*

- *Marketing = 25% x $200,000 = $50,000 =*

  ($50,000 +$50,000+$50,000 +$50,000) / $200,000 x 100 = 100%

Data sources

- CSP billing data

- Internal finance metrics

In the realm of multi-cloud FinOps, these KPIs are more than just metrics; they are the pulse of an organization's ability to harness the full potential of its cloud investments. By continuously validating spend apportionment, tagging compliance, and allocation precision, organizations can illuminate areas of inefficiency and optimize cloud spend at a granular level. The key is to embrace these KPIs not just as benchmarks but as dynamic levers that drive accountability, transparency, and financial stewardship across every layer of cloud operations. In a cloud-driven world, mastering these KPIs is the cornerstone of sustainable, long-term financial success in the cloud.

Developing a cloud cost allocation strategy

What is the primary goal for your enterprise that you want to achieve with the cloud cost allocation strategy? Is it cost transparency, understanding why your resources are running high, supporting chargeback or showback models, or simplifying shared cost allocation? The goals with cloud cost allocation vary based on the enterprise's needs and what to consider through the implementation strategy.

Defining a cost structure for the resources is paramount for deploying the resources in any cloud environment. Establish the relationship between costs from cloud environment spend, how these costs aroused, and who or what is responsible for these costs. However, cost structure mechanisms greatly friction based on cloud solutions offering enterprises, accounts, environments, and entities within an enterprise. Moreover, cost structures are based on multiple attributes, allowing for cost examination in various ways or at different levels of granularity.

The cost structure mechanism must align with the desired outcomes: evaluating the cost allocation mechanisms on the simplicity of implementation vs. aimed accuracy.

Key cloud cost allocation strategies for financial success

Effective cloud cost allocation is the bedrock of sound cloud financial management, enabling organizations to optimize resources and drive accountability. The following are some key strategies that every cloud-driven business should incorporate to keep costs in check and drive growth:

- **Resource tagging for precision**: Resource tagging is the cornerstone of cloud cost allocation. By tagging cloud resources with key attributes like department, project, or cost center, businesses can allocate expenses with surgical precision. These tags provide the necessary metadata to tie costs back to the appropriate teams or initiatives, helping product managers and engineers take ownership of their cloud expenditures. Consistency and automation in tagging make this strategy even more impactful by minimizing errors and increasing visibility.

  o Here is a sample tagging strategy table that shows how tags can be divided into various categories and example values the tags might carry:

Tag	Description	Example value
Business tags		
Name	Name of the cloud resource.	ABCresource
Project/Business unit	Name of the project/app name.	healthapp
Environment	Defines the environment.	Production
Resource owner	Identifies who is accountable for the resource.	**Businessowner@myorg.com**
Cost center	Identifies cost center associated with a resource.	CC12345
Security tags		
Compliance	Identifies the level of compliance requirements (HIPAA, PCI, GDPR, and so on).	HIPAA, PCI, GDPR
Encryption	Identifies if a resource is encrypted or not.	Yes/No
Automation tags		
Date/time	Identifies when a resource was started, stopped, rotated, terminated, and so on.	03/10/2004 03:15:20 PM
Opt in	Indicates whether a resource should be automatically included in an automated activity.	Yes/No

Table 6.1: *Tags and their descriptions*

- **Defining cost allocation policies for greater impact**: Cost allocation policies are vital for shaping how cloud expenses are distributed. Whether allocating costs based on actual usage or a predetermined model, these policies create a clear roadmap for financial governance. Usage-based allocation provides greater transparency and fairness, while predefined models enable predictability in budgeting. The key is to find a balance that aligns with organizational goals, while offering the flexibility to adjust as needs evolve.

- **Choosing the right accountability model**: Implementing chargeback or showback models adds an additional layer of accountability to cloud financial management. Chargeback models enforce financial responsibility by billing departments for their specific cloud usage, ensuring each team understands the cost of their cloud consumption. On the other hand, showback models increase transparency by revealing usage patterns and associated costs without directly billing departments, which can serve as a softer introduction to financial accountability while still fostering cost-awareness.

- **Automating with cloud financial management platforms**: Cloud financial management platforms, such as Cloudability or Heeddata, streamline the allocation process by automating data collection, cost reporting, and optimization. These platforms provide real-time insights, enabling teams to identify inefficiencies and take corrective actions promptly. Automation not only reduces the manual burden but also ensures higher accuracy and timeliness in financial reporting, driving smarter cloud usage decisions across the organization.

- **Importance of cross-functional collaboration**: Cloud cost allocation is not just an IT responsibility; it is a business-wide imperative. Collaboration with business stakeholders is crucial to ensure that cost allocation strategies align with organizational objectives. When finance, engineering, and operations teams collaborate, it fosters a holistic understanding of how cloud costs impact business outcomes, promoting strategies that drive innovation while maintaining cost efficiency.

- **Reporting**: When it comes to managing cloud costs efficiently, all the cloud environments provide a robust ecosystem of tools and solutions to facilitate showbacks and chargebacks. These tools help organizations apportion costs fairly, monitor tagged resources, and ensure the effectiveness of their tagging strategies. Whether your goal is cost transparency, optimization, or accountability, third-party solutions can meet a variety of needs. Organizations face a key decision when implementing cost allocation strategies: invest in custom-built solutions or leverage Cloud Management Tools Competency Partners. Both approaches come with unique advantages, and the right choice depends on the organization's specific needs and objectives.

  o **Custom solutions**: For businesses seeking full control over their cost allocation parameters, cloud environments offer tools like the **Cloud Cost and Usage**

Report (**CUR**). CUR provides the most detailed data, enabling enterprises to create highly customized optimization dashboards that reflect their specific requirements. With CUR, businesses can filter and group cost data by account, service, cost category, or allocation tag, ensuring a granular understanding of cloud expenditure.

o   **Third-party tools**: If building in-house solutions is not ideal, the ecosystem of Cloud Management Tools Competency Partners offers turnkey solutions. These third-party tools are pre-configured to handle complex cost monitoring, tagging, and allocation needs, reducing the burden of developing internal tools.

o   For organizations leveraging CUR-based solutions, cloud also offers **Cloud Intelligence Dashboards** available on the **Well-Architected Labs**. These dashboards provide real-time insights into cloud costs, allowing you to track and optimize spending across multiple dimensions with minimal setup. They act as an out-of-the-box solution for businesses looking to enhance their cost visibility and management capabilities without the overhead of custom development.

• **Compliance and enforcement**: Technology alone can only go so far in enforcing tagging policies. The cornerstone of success lies in cultivating a FinOps culture across your organization. From engineers to product owners, every stakeholder must understand the role that tagging plays in cloud cost optimization. This cultural shift ensures that the strategy transcends a mere technical task and becomes a shared responsibility that drives operational excellence. To make this happen, education is key:

o   Educate engineers on the criticality of tagging new and existing resources.

o   Collaborate with teams to retroactively apply tags, resolving any existing gaps.

o   Create visibility through dashboards and reports that showcase compliance, triggering accountability and continuous improvement.

Enforcing tagging compliance requires diving into the capabilities offered by CSPs. AWS, Azure, and Google Cloud provide various tools to help identify untagged or non-compliant resources. For example, AWS **Service Control Policies** (**SCP**) can enforce tagging standards automatically, ensuring resources without tags are not created. The key steps to ensure robust tagging compliance include:

1.   **Identify untagged resources**: Understand which resources generate costs but remain untagged and define the financial impact.

2.   Custom tags for FinOps platform and link them to resources for effective allocation.

3. **Assess non-compliant tags**: Pinpoint resources with tags that do not align with your predefined categories and evaluate the risk they pose.

4. **Use dashboards to manage compliant tags**: Display tagging compliance through dashboards to stimulate internal discussions and create momentum.

5. **Intelligence wing**: The responsibility is to define the rules about crucial tags so that the missed tags will be redirected to corresponding resources. This creates an automatic report that goes to resources, making them responsible for untagged resources.

By marrying technical enforcement with a strong FinOps culture, organizations can achieve seamless cost allocation. This balance ensures tagging compliance becomes second nature, ultimately driving more accurate forecasts, improved budgeting, and increased accountability across teams.

By mixing these strategies into the fabric of your cloud financial management practice, your organization can achieve greater cost visibility, optimize resource utilization, and enhance overall financial health. Cloud cost allocation is not just a technical exercise; rather, it is a strategic advantage.

Personas impacting cost allocation

When it comes to cloud cost allocation, it is natural to think that finance holds the reins. After all, accurate reporting and tracking of revenue and expenses are the lifeblood of the finance function. Finance's ultimate responsibility is to ensure that expenses are properly attributed to the correct cost center or line of business, enabling accurate profitability measurement. Without this precision, decisions on pricing, investments in product enhancements, or even strategic exits would be like shooting in the dark.

In a RACI framework, finance is squarely in the responsible category when it comes to the accuracy and timeliness of cost allocation. Their job is to ensure that every dollar spent is mapped to the right business unit for a clear financial picture. Yet, finance cannot do it alone. It requires collaboration across the organization.

Engineering as the frontline of cloud cost attribution

While finance is responsible for allocating costs, engineering and development teams are the linchpin of accurate attribution. These teams are at the forefront, sourcing cloud services and making critical decisions about resource usage. They apply the hierarchy, account, and metadata (such as application ID tagging) that finance relies on for proper allocation. Engineers essentially set the stage for cost distribution by ensuring the right metadata is applied from the outset.

However, it is crucial to understand that cloud bills do not tell the full story. Bills are often high-level summaries, leaving finance in the dark about how specific resources are being used. This disconnect can lead to mistrust or misunderstandings if finance does not have visibility into the deeper layers of resource usage. Therefore, engineers play a key role, not only in applying the correct tags but also in consulting with finance to bridge this gap, ensuring that every cloud dollar is accounted for.

Business and product teams balancing direct and shared costs

Business and product teams are not only users of cost allocation but also influencers of the process. They deal with both direct costs tied to their specific product lines and shared costs that are allocated across the organization. For them, accurate allocation is a crucial input to inform product development, pricing strategies, and even the timing of new feature investments.

In the RACI model, these teams fall into the informed category, as they rely on allocation data for decision-making. However, their central role in managing and optimizing shared costs often moves them into the accountable category. They are well-positioned to spot inaccuracies and drive changes across resources, ensuring that costs are distributed fairly and effectively.

Decision-makers behind cost allocation strategy

Executives, while often removed from day-to-day cloud operations, are ultimately accountable for the profitability of their business units. They must have a deep understanding of the cost allocation strategy, working closely with product, engineering, and finance teams to ensure the accuracy and fairness of allocations.

The development of a robust cost allocation methodology often involves not just internal alignment but also decisions about investing in supporting applications, such as third-party cloud management tools. Executives are responsible for approving these investments and ensuring that the strategy aligns with the company's broader financial and operational goals.

In the end, a successful cloud cost allocation strategy requires not just accurate data, but active collaboration between finance, engineering, business teams, and executives. By working together, each function ensures that cloud spending aligns with business objectives, paving the way for better decision-making and more precise cost control.

Embracing other FinOps framework capabilities

A robust cloud cost allocation strategy is not an isolated mechanism; it serves as a foundation that integrates seamlessly with various other capabilities of the FinOps framework, amplifying their impact. By enabling better visibility, precision, and control over cloud spending, cost allocation becomes a vital enabler for core FinOps capabilities like anomaly management, budgeting, forecasting, invoicing, and reporting. The following is an exploration of how cost allocation enhances these capabilities to promote financial accountability and efficiency in cloud environments:

- **Anomaly management**: Strategic cost allocation plays a critical role in anomaly management by ensuring financial transparency and accountability at a granular level. By employing strategic tagging practices, such as assigning tags to workloads, departments, or projects, organizations can track cloud expenditures in real time. When anomalous spending occurs, cost allocation systems leverage these tags to trigger detailed anomaly alerts. For instance, if a specific team exceeds its allocated budget for storage due to unplanned scaling, the alerts provide granular insights about the anomaly, such as which tags (team, project, environment) contributed to the deviation. This detailed data empowers FinOps practitioners to:

  o Rapidly identify the root cause of anomalies.

  o Mitigate the anomaly with actionable insights.

  o This real-time feedback loop not only highlights anomalous events but also fosters a culture of shared accountability, where teams actively reflect on their spending behaviors and take corrective measures to prevent future occurrences.

- **Budgeting and forecasting**: Cost allocation is the cornerstone for precision in budgeting and forecasting, two distinct but interconnected FinOps capabilities. By accurately mapping cloud costs to business units, teams, or projects, enterprises gain clarity on where resources are consumed and how much budget should be allocated.

- **Budgeting**: Cost allocation strategy helps create realistic budgets by reflecting actual usage patterns and trends. By allocating costs dynamically based on accurate tagging and allocation models, organizations avoid over or under-budgeting, ensuring financial discipline.

- **Forecasting**: Cost allocation informs forward-looking financial models by offering historical cost data and current consumption patterns. For example:

  o Teams can forecast their future spend based on resource utilization trends.

  o Leadership can analyze seasonal workloads to make data-driven predictions about cloud expenditures.

Furthermore, integrating forecasting insights into the cost allocation model ensures that the strategy evolves to meet changing business requirements. This continuous feedback loop enables enterprises to stay agile and adjust their resource allocation models for maximum efficiency.

- **Invoicing and chargeback**: Cost allocation strategy underpins effective invoicing and chargeback mechanisms by ensuring that every expense is tied to the appropriate cost center. In a multi-cloud or hybrid-cloud environment, this becomes especially critical, as cloud bills often span multiple services and providers. With a well-implemented cost allocation model:

  o Invoicing becomes transparent, as every cost is tagged and linked to a specific team, department, or project. This eliminates ambiguity and prevents disputes over shared cloud costs.

  o Chargeback mechanisms leverage cost allocation to ensure that each team or department is accountable for its consumption. For example, if Team A consumes 30% of the compute resources and Team B consumes 70%, the invoice reflects this proportionate split. This alignment ensures fairness, promotes responsible spending, and fosters a culture of financial accountability.

- **Planning and estimating**: Cloud cost allocation strategy lays the groundwork for effective resource planning and cost estimation. By providing detailed insights into historical spending patterns and utilization metrics, it enables organizations to plan resource allocations strategically. For instance:

  o If a product team anticipates a spike in usage during a new feature rollout, cost allocation data from similar past events can guide the team in estimating and preparing for associated costs.

  o Similarly, planning for future workloads, such as expanding into new cloud regions or adopting emerging services, becomes more reliable when powered by cost allocation insights.

  o These insights enable organizations to align their cloud investments with business goals, minimizing the risk of overspending or underutilization.

- **Reporting and analytics**: Reporting and analytics are at the heart of FinOps, and cost allocation amplifies their value by providing actionable and precise data. A well-designed cost allocation model ensures that every dollar spent in the cloud can be tracked, categorized, and visualized in reports. The key benefits include:

  o **Granular insights**: Dashboards and reports can break down costs by team, department, application, or environment, providing clarity to stakeholders.

  o **Trend analysis**: Historical cost allocation data enables teams to identify trends, such as cost spikes during high-traffic periods or reductions after optimizing workloads.

o **Decision support**: Leadership can use analytics powered by cost allocation to make strategic decisions, such as renegotiating cloud provider contracts or adjusting budgets.

By transforming raw cloud expenditure data into actionable insights, cost allocation enables FinOps teams to effectively communicate the value of their efforts and drive informed decision-making throughout the organization.

A powerful cloud cost allocation strategy is the linchpin for enabling and enhancing other FinOps capabilities. It provides the structure and visibility necessary for effective anomaly management, precise budgeting, forward-looking forecasting, equitable chargeback systems, and impactful reporting. As organizations mature in their FinOps journey, leveraging cost allocation as a foundational strategy will ensure financial discipline, accountability, and scalability across multi-cloud environments. This integration of capabilities creates a virtuous cycle, where the strengths of one framework element reinforce and enhance the others, ultimately driving business success in the cloud.

Use cases of FOCUS with cost allocation models

Let us go over some use cases now of FOCUS with cost allocation models.

Report refunds by subaccount within a billing period

Use FOCUS data to identify refunds across multiple providers, billing accounts, and subaccounts.

FOCUS columns

The columns are:

- Provider
- Billing account ID
- Service category
- Billed cost
- Billing period start
- Sub account ID
- Sub account name
- Charge category

FOCUS SQL query

The query is as follows:

```
SELECT
        ProviderName,
        BillingAccountId,
        ServiceCategory,
        SubAccountId,
        SubAccountName,
SUM(BilledCost) AS TotalBilledCost
FROM focus_data_table
WHERE BillingPeriodStart >= ? AND BillingPeriodEnd < ?
        AND ChargeClass = 'Correction'
GROUP BY
        ProviderName,
        BillingAccountId,
        SubAccountId,
        SubAccountName,
        ServiceCategory
```

Allocate multi-currency charges per application

Finance needs to allocate costs and perform chargeback for charges for all applications that come from different geographic locations and are in different currencies.

FOCUS columns

The columns are:

- Provider
- Billing account ID
- Billing account name
- Billing currency
- Billed cost
- Tags
- Billing period start
- Billing period end

FOCUS SQL query

The query is as follows:

```
SELECT
        Tags["ApplicationId"],
        ProviderName,
        BillingAccountId,
        BillingAccountName,
        BillingCurrency,
SUM(BilledCost) AS TotalBilledCost
FROM focus_data_table
WHERE
        BillingPeriodStart >= ? AND BillingPeriodEnd < ?
GROUP BY
        Tags["ApplicationId"],
        ProviderName,
        BillingAccountId,
        BillingAccountName,
        BillingCurrency
```

Conclusion

The true power of FOCUS and cost allocation lies in its ability to adapt to various use cases, whether it is chargebacks, showbacks, or cost transparency across departments, teams, or business units. FOCUS ensures that every dollar spent is linked to the business value it drives, creating a culture where cost-consciousness and innovation coexist. By using this model, organizations not only optimize cloud spending but also empower decision-makers with actionable insights that guide product development, strategic investments, and operational efficiency.

Ultimately, these two together bridge the gap between technology and financial strategy, ensuring end-to-end accountability and fostering a FinOps culture where everyone, from engineers to executives, plays a critical role in managing and optimizing cloud costs. This is where cloud cost allocation transforms from a task to a competitive advantage, positioning organizations to thrive in an era of digital transformation.

Join our Discord space

Join our Discord workspace for latest updates, offers, tech happenings around the world, new releases, and sessions with the authors:

https://discord.bpbonline.com

CHAPTER 7

Cloud Cost Optimization Strategies

Introduction

The very frontline crashing element of today's cloud-centralized enterprises or the SMBs who have opted for cloud resource usage is exceeding costs. This we have already seen in the earlier chapters. However, what we have not yet questioned is how these costs can be saved. What are the ways to channel them in ways that help your enterprise? How can **cost optimization** strategies and techniques unlock more significant cloud and business potential?

Before going through each one in detail, let us peek into the cost optimization and the questions that you must reflect on as a FinOps adopting enterprise.

Defining cost optimization

As businesses embrace the cloud's scalability and flexibility to perform computing instances in a few minutes, most of the cloud resources remain underutilized or unused, adding unnecessary complexity and consuming a lot of IT budgets. Though enterprises choose the pay-as-you-go model, most of the cloud service providers charge for the resources whether they are used or not. This is where cloud optimization became crucial for enterprises with the goal of making cloud environments efficient and less complex.

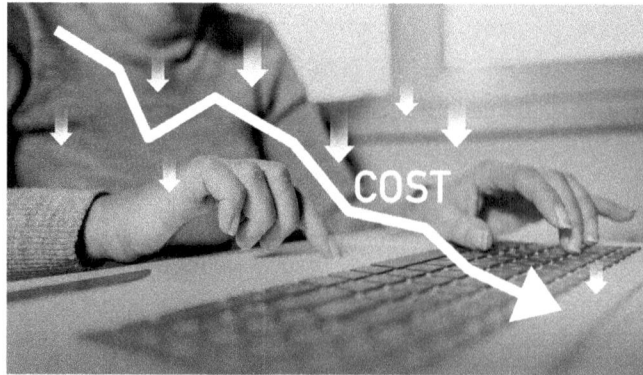

Figure 7.1: *Cloud cost optimization*

Cost optimization is more than just trimming expenses; it is about maximizing the value of your cloud investment while minimizing waste. The key to achieving this lies in the proactive management of cloud resources, ensuring that every dollar spent drives tangible business value. This involves identifying and eliminating idle or underutilized resources, optimizing workloads to match the right-sized infrastructure, and utilizing pricing models that align with your operational needs. Cost optimization is not a one-time effort; it is a continuous journey that evolves with your business and technology landscape, requiring ongoing monitoring and adjustments to prevent unnecessary overspending.

The most successful cloud optimization strategies not only focus on reducing costs but also enable greater agility and innovation. By optimizing cloud environments, enterprises can reinvest the savings into areas that foster growth, such as product development, customer experience, or digital transformation initiatives. Moreover, cloud optimization enhances financial transparency, enabling finance teams, engineers, and executives to better understand the origins of costs and how they can be managed more effectively. The goal is to establish a FinOps culture where every team takes ownership of their cloud spending and collaborates to ensure the business consistently achieves the best return on its cloud investment.

By adopting the right strategies and leveraging the appropriate tools, organizations can unlock new efficiencies, stay competitive, and make better data-driven decisions that enhance both the operational and financial health of the enterprise.

Critical need for cloud cost optimization

Cloud cost optimization is no longer a luxury; it is a business imperative. With organizations wasting an estimated 35% of their cloud spending, this inefficiency can drain financial resources, regardless of the organization's size. This is not just about reducing costs for the sake of it; it is about aligning cloud expenses with business objectives. Optimizing cloud costs allows businesses to identify unused resources, decommission obsolete tools, and ensure that every dollar spent is driving meaningful outcomes. Whether you are running a small business or managing multi-million-dollar cloud environments, cloud optimization can help maximize the value of your investment, turning cost efficiency into a competitive advantage.

Cloud optimization is also about strategic spending. There are times when paying more for a service makes sense, that is, if that additional spend directly contributes to revenue growth, higher productivity, or improved customer satisfaction. The goal is not just to slash costs but to spend intelligently, ensuring that cloud expenses are directly tied to the business outcomes you aim to achieve. By having a finely tuned cloud cost optimization strategy, organizations can rein in unnecessary expenses while still empowering teams with the cloud resources they need to innovate and operate efficiently.

Asking key questions for effective cloud cost optimization

The foundation of cloud optimization starts with asking the right questions before, during, and after cloud adoption. To effectively manage costs, organizations must first evaluate how cloud expenses are allocated across different teams and departments. This requires a clear understanding of cost visibility at every organizational level and ensuring that each team is accountable for its consumption.

Additionally, teams need to monitor and control cloud resource provisioning continuously, preventing overprovisioning and curbing overspending before it spirals out of control. Finally, establishing metrics beyond just the cloud bill, such as performance, utilization, and availability, enables teams to track and manage cloud consumption in real-time, ensuring that optimization efforts remain in lockstep with business objectives.

The questions include:

- How can our enterprise cloud costs be evaluated at all levels and manage cost allocation at the organization and team levels?

- How can we provision most of the cloud resources to manage and control overtime spending?

- How can we overcome overspending and overprovisioning?

- What metrics can be tracked?

By asking these critical questions and building a proactive optimization mindset, businesses can effectively navigate the complexity of multi-cloud environments while keeping costs under control and maximizing the cloud's value to the organization.

Importance of cloud cost optimization

Cloud cost optimization is not just about tightening the purse strings, it is about unlocking the full potential of your cloud investments. In a world where cloud services provide the foundation for modern business innovation and agility, an organization's ability to optimize cloud costs can have a direct impact on its profitability and long-term sustainability. Wasting 32% of cloud spend, as many companies do, represents not only financial leakage but also missed opportunities to reinvest in more strategic initiatives. Every dollar spent inefficiently on unused or underutilized cloud resources is a dollar that could have been invested in fueling growth, innovation, or enhancing customer experience.

The modern cloud landscape offers immense flexibility, but with that flexibility comes complexity. Without a clear strategy for cost optimization, businesses run the risk of cloud sprawl: over-provisioning, underutilizing, and losing control over their cloud expenses. Effective cloud cost optimization means ensuring that every investment in cloud infrastructure or services contributes to business outcomes, whether it is driving revenue, enhancing performance, or supporting innovation. It is a process of constant refinement, where the goal is not just to cut costs but to achieve a higher return on every cloud dollar spent. In today's competitive landscape, this level of financial discipline can be the difference between thriving and merely surviving.

Need for a cloud cost optimization strategy

A well-defined cloud cost optimization strategy is no longer a *nice to have*, it is mission-critical for any organization operating in the cloud. As businesses continue to expand their cloud footprints, the complexity of managing these environments grows exponentially. A cloud cost optimization strategy provides a structured roadmap for navigating this complexity, allowing organizations to proactively manage costs, improve efficiency, and ensure alignment with broader business objectives. It is not just about reacting to high bills, rather, it is about anticipating and preventing unnecessary expenses before they occur.

At its core, a cloud cost optimization strategy ensures that an organization has a comprehensive approach to managing its cloud spend across departments, regions, and services. Without a plan, cloud expenses can spiral out of control as different teams provision resources without a unified cost management framework. The need for visibility, governance, and accountability cannot be overstated. A robust strategy puts the right controls in place, enabling IT, finance, and engineering teams to collaborate effectively. It ensures that cloud resources are provisioned, utilized, and decommissioned based on real-time business needs and priorities, ultimately transforming cloud costs from a liability into a competitive advantage.

Difference between strategy and technique

While the terms *strategy* and *technique* are often used interchangeably, they represent distinct elements of cloud cost optimization, each playing a crucial role in driving effective outcomes. A strategy is the overarching plan, the guiding framework that outlines long-term goals and provides a vision for cost optimization. It encompasses the policies, governance structures, and cultural shifts required to manage cloud spending holistically.

In contrast, techniques are the specific actions or methods employed to execute that strategy. Techniques are the tactical steps, such as rightsizing, automation, and resource tagging, that bring the strategic vision to life.

Think of the strategy as the compass and the techniques as the tools used to navigate the journey. Without a clear plan, techniques become fragmented and reactive, leading to short-term fixes rather than long-term cost efficiencies. Conversely, a strategy without well-executed techniques lacks the practical application needed to drive results. A successful cloud cost optimization effort requires both a well-defined strategy to set the direction and precise techniques to achieve measurable outcomes. In this way, organizations can ensure that their cost management efforts are not just effective in the short term, but also sustainable and scalable as their cloud environments grow.

Strategies for cloud cost optimization

The old ways of managing IT infrastructure, like multi-year cycles of procuring, running, and decommissioning physical hardware, are becoming relics of the past. In the cloud, there is no room for long timelines or rigid change management strategies. Cloud estates require continuous optimization of capacity, consumption, cost, performance, and innovation. The speed at which hyperscalers release new features and updates is dizzying, and enterprises that continue to operate with a traditional mindset risk being left behind.

The key to thriving in this fast-paced environment is to embrace an agile, cloud-optimizing approach that keeps up with the relentless pace of change. Accenture refers to this as *Run Different*, a mindset that encourages continuous improvement and innovation rather than static, slow-moving processes. By breaking free from the shackles of outdated methodologies, companies can unlock the full potential of the cloud, delivering faster innovation, optimized costs, and greater value for their business.

Unlocking cloud value requires a multi-dimensional approach that goes beyond just managing costs. While cost is always a factor, the real power of cloud optimization lies in driving innovation, enhancing performance, and managing consumption intelligently. The ability to track, assess, and implement new services from hyperscalers is a critical component of this. When IT leaders can quickly evaluate and adopt new technologies, they do not just optimize their cloud estate; they can propel innovation and align with the company's broader growth agenda.

However, the constant release of new services can overwhelm even the most dedicated teams. This is where a cloud **center of excellence** (**CoE**) becomes invaluable. A CoE pools together the necessary business and technical expertise to ensure that each new cloud service is evaluated not just for its potential impact on the cloud estate but also for how it can drive innovation across the business. By setting up a dedicated CoE, organizations can systematically assess and adopt the right cloud capabilities while minimizing risk.

Consumption, cost, and performance

Achieving true cloud optimization means mastering the complex balance between consumption, cost, and performance. Cloud environments can be dynamic and complex, with usage patterns that fluctuate in unpredictable ways. That is where machine learning comes into play. By leveraging machine learning models, businesses can analyze historical usage data, predict future spikes, and adjust compute resources accordingly. This allows organizations to fine-tune their cloud consumption, maintaining the ideal balance between reserved and on-demand cloud instances while minimizing unnecessary costs.

Continuous monitoring is crucial; cloud optimization is not a one-time activity, but an ongoing process. Businesses must remain vigilant about the interplay between their cloud resources and business processes, constantly refining the way they provision resources to keep up with evolving user demands and workloads.

Power of FinOps transparency

FinOps, or financial operations for the cloud, introduces a new level of financial transparency into cloud management. One of the most significant pitfalls organizations face is losing track of workloads, resulting in excessive consumption and high costs. By implementing a FinOps model, organizations can shine a spotlight on cloud spending, revealing the true financial impact of each workload and resource. Chargeback mechanisms can assign cloud costs to the appropriate teams, giving them ownership of their own spending.

This is not just about cutting costs; it is about changing the culture. When teams are held accountable for their cloud usage, they are more likely to adopt a cost-conscious mindset. FinOps enables organizations to align their teams around the total cost of ownership for cloud resources, making everyone a stakeholder in the optimization process.

While cloud infrastructure is a critical piece of the puzzle, cloud management does not happen in isolation. Most enterprises operate a hybrid IT estate, combining on-premises systems, cloud environments, and edge computing. Successful cloud optimization means taking a holistic view of the entire technology landscape and understanding how each piece interacts with the others.

For example, managing data in the cloud is a complex challenge. With massive volumes of data, moving everything to the cloud may not be practical. In some cases, bringing compute power closer to the data or using smart data extracts may be the best solution. Similarly, optimizing edge computing is essential for minimizing latency and improving performance in mission-critical applications.

Networking services also play a crucial role in cloud optimization. As cloud providers continually expand their networking offerings, businesses must stay abreast of advancements in routing, switching, and network architecture. Let us not forget machine learning capabilities; these powerful tools offer insights that can help drive everything from customer segmentation to supply chain optimization.

Build optimization into your everyday operations

To fully reap the benefits of cloud transformation, businesses need to embed optimization, innovation, and agility into their daily operations. It is not enough to treat cloud optimization as a one-off project; it must become an integral part of how the organization operates. By adopting a *Run Different* mindset, businesses can turn cloud challenges into opportunities, maximizing the value of their cloud investments while staying ahead of the curve. The organizations that foster a culture of continuous cloud optimization are the ones that will thrive in today's fast-paced, digital-first world.

To make this happen, here are the top-recommended, well-researched strategies that help every enterprise manage their multi-cloud cost optimization simply:

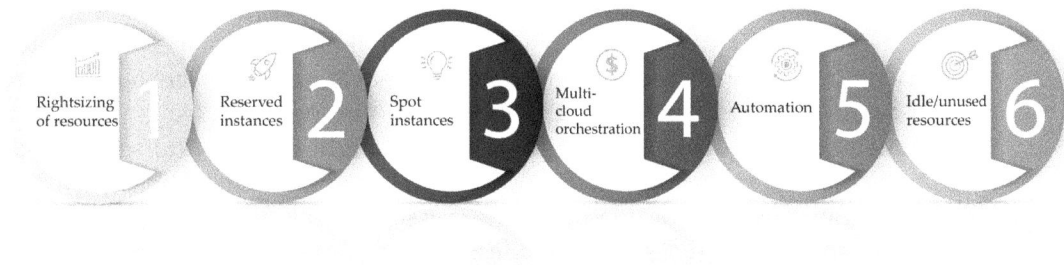

Figure 7.2: Strategies for cloud cost optimization

- Rightsizing of resources

- Reserved Instances

- Spot Instances

- Multi-cloud orchestration

- Automation

- Idle/unused resources

Let us explore each one in detail:

- **Rightsizing or tailoring cloud resources for maximum efficiency**: Right-sizing is the art of matching cloud resources to actual workload requirements, ensuring optimal performance without overspending. Think of it like fitting a custom suit; it needs to be the perfect size to be effective. In the cloud, this means analyzing your workloads and aligning them with the correct amount of compute, storage, and network capacity. The danger in over-provisioning is real: too much capacity, and you are burning money on unused resources, while with too little, you risk throttling performance. By consistently evaluating resource usage and fine-tuning capacity to match real-time demand, businesses can avoid the pitfalls of inefficiency. This proactive approach enables organizations to strike a balance between performance and cost, ensuring they maximize the value of their cloud spend while minimizing unnecessary waste. The key to rightsizing lies in continuous monitoring and adjustment, turning what may seem like a trivial tweak into a powerful optimization strategy.

- **Reserved Instances and lowering costs with commitment**: One of the most effective ways to slash cloud costs is by leveraging Reserved Instances; committing to a specific amount of cloud usage over a set period of time. By doing so, organizations can negotiate lower rates from cloud providers, taking advantage of long-term discounts. Reserved Instances offer predictability in costs, making them an ideal option for steady-state workloads that have a known and consistent demand. However, the trick is to ensure that these commitments are aligned with actual resource needs. Committing to more than you need can leave you paying for unused capacity, while committing too little might force you to scramble for expensive on-demand resources. To leverage Reserved Instances effectively, a deep understanding of your workload patterns is essential; it is about being smart with commitments to maximize savings while ensuring your cloud operations continue to run smoothly.

- **Spot Instances and saving costs by exploiting unused capacity**: When it comes to cost savings, Spot Instances are the ultimate opportunists. These instances enable organizations to leverage unused cloud capacity at a fraction of the cost of standard instances. Cloud providers eager to monetize their idle resources offer these instances at deeply discounted rates, allowing savvy users to run non-critical workloads at a reduced cost. However, the catch is that Spot Instances can be interrupted if the cloud provider needs to reclaim capacity, meaning they are best suited for fault-tolerant applications such as batch processing, big data workloads, or testing environments. To effectively use Spot Instances, organizations need robust systems that can handle potential interruptions without impacting operations. By balancing Spot Instances with other instance types, businesses can strategically optimize costs while maintaining operational resilience.

- **Multi-cloud orchestration and mastering flexibility across providers**: The era of single-cloud reliance is waning, and multi-cloud orchestration is emerging as a core strategy for cloud optimization. This approach involves dynamically distributing workloads across multiple cloud providers, ensuring optimal performance, cost-efficiency, and flexibility. By utilizing the strengths of different clouds, it price advantages, geographic distribution, or specific service offerings, organizations can create an environment that adapts to changing demands in real-time. Multi-cloud orchestration provides a layer of protection against vendor lock-in, allowing companies to optimize costs and mitigate risks by switching between providers as needed. However, to succeed in this strategy, seamless orchestration tools and governance policies are essential. With a well-implemented multi-cloud strategy, organizations can ensure they are always leveraging the most cost-effective and high-performing cloud resources for their unique business needs.

- **Automation or streamlining cloud operations for continuous optimization**: Automation is the cornerstone of modern cloud optimization. By automating tasks like scaling, scheduling, and provisioning, businesses can reduce manual intervention, minimize human error, and ensure continuous optimization of their cloud resources. Cloud environments are complex and dynamic, requiring constant attention to resource usage and cost management. Manual oversight, while possible, is both inefficient and prone to mistakes. Automation tools can dynamically adjust cloud resources in response to real-time demand, scaling applications up or down to meet performance requirements while keeping costs in check. From shutting down idle instances to optimizing storage, automation allows businesses to stay one step ahead in their cloud management journey. The beauty of automation lies in its ability to deliver consistent, predictable results without requiring manual effort, creating a cloud ecosystem that operates like a well-oiled machine. By embedding automation into cloud management practices, organizations can ensure that their cloud environment is continuously optimized for both performance and cost, allowing them to focus on innovation and business growth rather than routine operational tasks. These techniques provide the framework to not only control expenditure but also ensure that every dollar spent translates into tangible value for the business.

Conclusion

Ultimately, cloud cost optimization is about OpEx. It is a mindset shift that requires constant evaluation, agile decision-making, and the deployment of cutting-edge tools to achieve real-time efficiencies. With the right optimization strategies in place, businesses can ensure they are not only staying competitive in the cloud but also positioning themselves for sustainable growth and innovation. As we move deeper into the cloud-centric era, the ability to optimize costs will separate the businesses that thrive from those that merely survive. In essence, mastering cloud cost optimization is key to unlocking the full potential of the cloud, transforming it from a cost center into a strategic enabler of growth.

Join our Discord space

Join our Discord workspace for latest updates, offers, tech happenings around the world, new releases, and sessions with the authors:

https://discord.bpbonline.com

CHAPTER 8

Building a Multi-cloud Cost Optimization Plan

Introduction

The crest of multi-cloud adoption for quick scaling, operational efficiency, easy-to-manage resources, and speed deployments proves the way the cloud has been centralized across industries. The way enterprises design multi-cloud architectures and continue to advance their operations cycle is impressive as it paves the way for filling the marketplace with innovative products, making these enterprises future-ready, and embracing the change for the changing needs of the customers. All these are mighty gains and significant aspects, placing the industries on the top edge.

However, the other side of multi-cloud adoption is associated with costs. No matter how big the competition might be, one or the other industry is thriving by developing in-house solutions and by offering expert services such as cloud migration, edge computing, cloud generative AI services, and more. However, the blind spot of all these comes down to costs. The costs are ever-increasing, and industries do not understand how to slash their OpEx. That is why we are encouraging and drafting a roadmap for all these industries through FinOps adoption.

Although we have seen it in the previous chapters, here, our microscopic view is on multi-cloud cost optimization strategies. For all the innovation and game-changing technology you are building using multi-cloud as your core operational model, handling these costs and having a plan to save at least 50%-60% is needed. That is why we guide you here to create a blueprint for your multi-cloud cost optimization.

Architectural overview of multi-cloud

A multi-cloud model represents a transformative shift in how organizations architect their IT infrastructure, moving beyond reliance on a single cloud provider to embrace the capabilities of multiple **cloud service providers** (**CSP**). In this approach, enterprises leverage the unique strengths of leading CSPs, such as **Amazon Web Services** (**AWS**), **Google Cloud Platform** (**GCP**), and Microsoft Azure, to create a flexible, resilient, and optimized ecosystem. This strategic model empowers businesses to avoid vendor lock-in, achieve redundancy, and leverage the best-in-class offerings for specific workloads.

At its simplest, a multi-cloud setup can involve using different cloud providers for various SaaS applications, such as Webex for communication and Slack for team collaboration. These SaaS offerings, hosted on the public internet, provide accessible tools that enable teams to function efficiently, regardless of their location. However, this surface-level view of multi-cloud barely scratches the surface of its full potential. Multi-cloud is not just a tool for application diversity; it is a vehicle for achieving unparalleled operational agility, risk mitigation, and cost efficiency.

In more complex enterprise environments, a multi-cloud strategy enables businesses to assign different workloads to the most suitable cloud provider, based on performance, cost, or geographical requirements. For instance, an organization might utilize Microsoft Azure for its data storage needs, AWS for developing and testing new applications, and Google Cloud for backup and disaster recovery purposes. By leveraging each provider's strengths, organizations can refine their infrastructure to optimize performance while managing costs effectively. This strategic distribution not only improves operational efficiency but also minimizes the risks associated with relying on a single provider, such as outages or security breaches.

Rise of PaaS and IaaS

While SaaS plays a significant role in multi-cloud setups, modern enterprises are increasingly turning to PaaS and IaaS to power their core operations. PaaS solutions provide a comprehensive environment for developing, running, and managing applications, eliminating the cost and complexity of maintaining an on-premises platform. By delivering hardware, software, and infrastructure as a service, PaaS enables businesses to innovate more quickly and deploy applications more efficiently. For organizations looking to streamline their development processes, a PaaS approach can drastically reduce both time to market and the burden on IT resources.

Similarly, IaaS has revolutionized the way businesses scale their IT operations. Offering on-demand compute, storage, and networking resources, IaaS enables enterprises to dynamically adjust their infrastructure to match workload demands without the need for costly upfront investments in physical hardware. This elasticity allows businesses to rapidly scale up during periods of high demand and scale down when resources are no longer needed. The pay-as-you-go pricing model typical of IaaS also ensures that companies are only billed for the resources they use, driving significant cost savings compared to traditional IT environments.

However, before looking at a step-by-step cost optimization strategy, let us see how our research has led to land on the industry's most encountered challenges with multi-cloud adoption.

Biggest challenges with multi-cloud adoption

Let us go over some of the biggest challenges with multi-cloud adoption:

- **Partial visibility**: You cannot see your total spending on clouds. Though each cloud provider has their own dashboards to see your usage and spending, it is tough to know your spending on the cloud resources when you are switching to multi-cloud. As there is no unified dashboard for you to look at your spendings, hidden costs haunt your business, leaving you indecisive as to what to do.

- **Complex pricing models**: The pricing structure for each cloud environment varies. One cloud service provider may charge on an hourly basis, another by storage and usage, some offer discounts, some charge based on the geographical location, and some others provide flat pricing. These varying cloud costs can be confusing, leaving you unsure of how to utilize them to achieve maximum efficiency and leading to complications when trying to make multi-cloud budgeting decisions.

- **Evolving dependencies on multi-cloud**: Tracking and monitoring cloud costs based on organizational dependencies is the greatest need of the hour. One must track and monitor spending across multiple cloud environments. The enterprises must assign teams to do these activities and report across the board. Teams must also collaborate to maintain proper tags, policies, and alerts as well as rightly integrating third-party tools. Here, there are a lot of investments that keep on running: time, people, and cost.

- **Security and compliance concerns**: Many cloud providers implement a *shared responsibility model* when setting up cloud security. Here, the vendors will set up their own security posture, enabling users to secure their data and applications. As multiple cloud vendors must manage different dashboards at once, adhering to different security postures and compliance requirements gets time-intensive and complicated.

- **Increased operational and architectural complexity**: Monitoring, logging, troubleshooting, security postures, integrations, architectural design, automation, and data handling are the operational and architectural components that affect business line with multi-cloud. Managing these complexities either needs a well-versed roadmap and preplanning with in-house experts or a solution architect who can drive it for you.

- **Limited vendor tools**: Tracking, monitoring, and managing multi-cloud environments is possible when third-party tools are integrated into your accounts, where they track it for you. Out of the unlimited tools in the market, finding one potential tool that meets the needs of your business to make multi-cloud management simple and effective is an elephant-tusk task for enterprises.

- **Lack of expertise**: Our analysis has proved that more than 65% of companies lack skilled professionals. Though they exist, management is not ready to listen to them. This lack of skillset and ineffective collaboration is leading to failures. Moreover, multi-cloud adoption requires high levels of expertise, as it involves knowing every aspect of the cloud adoption process and migration as well. If not handled well, your entire business can be at stake.

- **Control or governance**: Multi-cloud adoption is like trying to herd cats; each cloud platform comes with its own rules, interfaces, and governance structures. Managing this diversity often leaves enterprises struggling to maintain control over their environments. The absence of a unified oversight system means that enforcing policies, ensuring security, and managing compliance across clouds becomes a juggling act. Without the proper governance framework, you are essentially trying to control a ship without a compass, leading to inefficiencies and potential risks.

- **Network latency and bandwidth**: When it comes to multi-cloud, the adage time is money takes on a literal meaning. Data transfers between clouds introduce latency and bandwidth constraints, which slow down processes and negatively impact user experience. These delays might seem like small hiccups at first, but over time, they snowball into significant productivity bottlenecks. The speed at which data travels and the quality of the connections between clouds often determine whether a company can keep pace with its demands or fall behind.

- **Interoperability**: Achieving seamless communication between multiple cloud platforms can feel like trying to make square pegs fit into round holes. Different platforms often speak different languages, requiring complex translation layers and integration efforts. The lack of interoperability creates friction, with enterprises having to invest in middleware solutions just to bridge the gaps. This challenge is a prime example of why multi-cloud strategies, while offering flexibility, can sometimes create more complexity than they solve.

- **Steep learning curve**: Multi-cloud adoption can be akin to climbing a mountain without a map. Each platform comes with its own set of tools, terminologies, and best practices. Teams accustomed to using a single cloud provider often face a steep learning curve when transitioning to new environments. The need for upskilling and cross-training becomes crucial, but it also slows down time to value. Without adequate training and preparation, the dream of multi-cloud can quickly turn into a nightmare, with teams struggling to stay on top of constantly evolving technologies.

Businesses must tackle these challenges head-on to avoid being sidetracked by the complexities. However, here is the multi-cloud cost optimization plan that helps industries to drive operational excellence via multi-cloud.

Roadmap for multi-cloud cost optimization strategy

Without a structured approach, organizations can find themselves facing a mountain of unforeseen expenses. As a FinOps practitioner, addressing these cost challenges begins with setting a clear direction, ensuring alignment with business goals, and utilizing the appropriate tools and frameworks. Let us dive deep into the essential components of multi-cloud cost optimization:

- **Cost optimization goals**: Effective cost optimization begins with clearly defined goals that resonate with the overall business objectives. It is not just about cutting costs for the sake of savings; but it is about aligning those savings with strategic priorities. Organizations need to ask themselves: what are the business-critical services that must remain fully optimized for performance? Where can we trim the fat without sacrificing quality? When cost optimization goals are tightly aligned with the business's growth strategies, every dollar saved serves a purpose, propelling the company closer to its desired outcomes. Think of it as sharpening your tools: cutting waste but keeping the edge strong for the tasks that matter most.

- **Cloud usage and cost analysis**: Before you can reduce costs, you must first understand them inside and out. A comprehensive analysis of cloud usage across all providers is crucial. This is the diagnostic stage, identifying how, where, and why cloud resources are being consumed. This exercise is like putting the multi-cloud environment under a microscope to reveal hidden inefficiencies, redundant resources, and usage patterns that do not align with actual business needs. A holistic view of all your cloud spending, including on-demand, reserved, and Spot Instances, provides the insights needed to target optimizations effectively. Only with this granular understanding can you make data-driven decisions.

- **Optimization strategies and techniques**: With clear goals and a detailed cost analysis in hand, the next step is to identify optimization strategies and techniques. These might include rightsizing instances, leveraging Spot Instances, and ensuring that you are only paying for what you use. Additionally, optimizing storage costs by selecting the appropriate storage tiers, autoscaling to prevent overprovisioning, and consolidating workloads on underutilized instances can yield significant savings. Every cloud platform has its nuances, and knowing how to exploit those quirks is what separates the leaders from the followers in multi-cloud cost optimization. This is where strategic finesse comes into play; you are not just turning dials, but you are orchestrating an efficient, dynamic cloud environment.

- **Optimization roadmap**: A great strategy without execution is nothing more than wishful thinking. That is why creating an optimization roadmap is critical. This roadmap must be detailed, outlining every step required to bring optimization strategies to life, from initial assessments to final implementations. Define clear timelines, milestones, and responsibilities to ensure accountability across teams. It is about translating the vision of optimized cloud costs into reality with structured, actionable steps that guide the journey, leaving no room for ambiguity. The roadmap serves as the backbone of the initiative, guiding teams through what can often feel like uncharted waters.

- **Performance metrics**: Tracking progress is the name of the game, and for that, you need robust performance metrics. Metrics such as cost savings, resource utilization, and service availability act as your compass, ensuring you are on course to meet your cost optimization goals. However, it is not just about measuring cost reductions in isolation. These metrics must also consider performance levels, ensuring that as costs decrease, service quality and availability remain high. It is a delicate balancing act: cutting costs without compromising the end-user experience. Regularly reviewing these metrics ensures continuous alignment with your overall business strategy.

- **Selecting the best cloud service providers**: Not all clouds are created equal. A fundamental part of your cost optimization strategy is ensuring you are selecting the best cloud service providers for your specific needs. This may mean leveraging the strengths of multiple providers, one for computing, another for storage, and yet another for advanced machine learning capabilities. The goal is to leverage the strengths of each provider while keeping costs under control. The key here is to remain vendor-agnostic; choose providers based on performance, pricing, and reliability, not just brand recognition.

- **Single pane of glass for enhanced visibility**: Managing costs across multiple cloud platforms can feel like trying to solve a puzzle without all the pieces in front of you. That is where a single pane of glass becomes invaluable, giving you a centralized view of your entire multi-cloud environment. This enhanced visibility is critical for identifying inefficiencies and ensuring transparency in your cloud costs. With a unified dashboard, decision-makers can monitor usage, performance, and spending in real time, enabling swift adjustments and fine-tuning of resources. After all, you cannot manage what you cannot see.

- **Leverage the power of automation tools**: In the realm of cloud cost optimization, automation is your best friend. Automated tools can manage repetitive tasks such as shutting down idle resources, scaling instances based on demand, and balancing workloads across regions or providers. This is the epitome of working smarter, not harder. By automating optimization processes, you eliminate human error, reduce manual effort, and ensure that your cost-saving measures are consistently applied across all platforms, day in and day out.

- **Zero Trust security approach**: While cost optimization is the focus, security can never be an afterthought. Embracing a Zero Trust security approach ensures that even as you optimize costs, your multi-cloud environment remains airtight. A breach can cost far more than any savings gained through optimization. Zero Trust means never assuming trust; every access request, whether from inside or outside the network, must be verified. This approach secures your cloud environment without compromising on performance or driving up costs.

- **Integrate compliance and regulatory requirements**: One area that can quickly escalate costs is non-compliance with regulations. Fines, penalties, and reputational damage can outweigh any potential savings. Therefore, it is essential to integrate compliance and regulatory requirements directly into your cost optimization strategy. This means not only adhering to global and industry standards but also ensuring that compliance tools and policies are integrated into your optimization roadmap from the outset. Proactive compliance management ensures that your organization remains compliant with regulations while keeping costs under control.

- **Adopting FinOps for cost optimization**: No multi-cloud cost optimization journey would be complete without FinOps at the core. FinOps brings financial accountability to the cloud, ensuring that your optimization efforts are continuously tracked and measured against financial performance goals. It is a collaborative effort, bringing together finance, operations, and engineering teams to strike the right balance between performance, cost, and speed. With FinOps, cost optimization becomes a dynamic process, allowing businesses to adapt in real-time to changing needs and market conditions.

- **Continuous improvement**: Finally, optimization is not a one-and-done exercise. The cloud is always evolving, and your cost optimization strategy must do the same. A commitment to continuous improvement ensures that your business stays competitive and efficient. Regular reviews, iterative updates, and ongoing monitoring of cloud usage and costs are essential to maintaining momentum. The goal is to create a feedback loop where optimizations are regularly assessed, refined, and re-implemented, ensuring that your multi-cloud environment remains optimized for both performance and cost efficiency.

In the ever-evolving world of multi-cloud, cost optimization is not just a box to tick; it is a strategic imperative that defines how organizations compete and thrive. The complexities of managing multiple cloud environments demand more than surface-level adjustments; they require a holistic, forward-thinking approach that aligns with broader business goals. A successful multi-cloud strategy is one where cost management becomes part of the organizational DNA, with every department, from IT to finance, playing an active role. This is not merely about reducing expenses; it is about reinvesting savings into innovation and growth, fueling your company's long-term success.

As multi-cloud ecosystems grow in scale and complexity, the businesses that will lead are those that view cost optimization as an ongoing, data-driven journey. By adopting a mindset of continuous improvement, leveraging the latest tools, and embracing cross-functional collaboration, organizations can transform what might seem like a daunting challenge into a sustainable competitive edge. In the end, mastering multi-cloud cost optimization is about more than achieving short-term savings, it is about building an adaptable, resilient, and future-ready infrastructure that drives innovation and value for years to come.

Cloud provider selection and management

To multiply value and accelerate innovation at scale, enterprises need cloud (as we have discussed so far). However, what if your enterprise enters into the dilemma of which cloud provider to choose? Vendor lock-ins, data safety and security, compliance standards, security posture, and data handling; each of these is crucial to evaluate before choosing a cloud provider. It follows a simple yet effective criteria for you to select the right cloud provider; either to tap the maximum cloud value or to accelerate FinOps adoption.

Moreover, choosing the right cloud service provider has a significant impact on your business operations. In-depth research on selecting the cloud service provider breeds clarity in addressing most of the organization's needs and support. Here is a breakdown of the criteria for choosing the right-fit provider:

Figure 8.1: Cost optimization

- **Analyze business needs**: Before embarking on the journey of selecting a cloud provider, take a step back and assess the core of your business operations. Every enterprise is unique, with distinct workloads, data requirements, and growth ambitions. Do you need a provider that supports high-performance computing, extensive AI capabilities, or cost-efficient storage? Will your cloud strategy prioritize agility, security, or compliance? Understanding your business goals upfront will ensure you choose a provider that aligns with your long-term vision rather than merely meeting short-term needs.

- **Research various cloud providers**: The cloud market is saturated with providers offering different service models, that is, IaaS, PaaS, SaaS, each with unique capabilities. You must conduct thorough research to compare Oracle Cloud, AWS, Microsoft Azure, Google Cloud, and niche providers based on performance, integration capabilities, and innovation roadmaps. A detailed comparison of cloud provider's strengths and weaknesses helps businesses select a provider that aligns best with their industry and workload needs.

- **Evaluate pricing models**: Cloud pricing is a labyrinth, often masked in layers of complexity. What seems like an affordable option at first glance may turn into an unpredictable cost sink due to hidden fees, egress charges, or suboptimal provisioning. Before signing on the dotted line, understand the cost implications of different models: pay-as-you-go, Reserved Instances, spot pricing, and enterprise agreements. Smart organizations do not just look at the price tag; they forecast long-term cloud expenditure and optimize costs before committing.

- **Assess data security and compliance**: With cyber threats growing in sophistication, cloud security cannot be an afterthought. Enterprises should evaluate a provider's security posture, including encryption standards, **identity and access management (IAM)**, and Zero Trust architecture. Additionally, compliance with industry-specific regulations like GDPR, HIPAA, PCI-DSS, and ISO 27001 ensures data governance and legal adherence. Selecting a provider with automated compliance management features helps mitigate security risks and reduce regulatory burdens.

- **Flexibility and scalability**: Cloud needs are rarely static. What serves your business today may not be enough tomorrow. The ideal provider offers on-demand scalability, allowing you to expand or contract resources as market conditions change. However, scalability is not just about infrastructure; it is about multi-cloud and hybrid capabilities, ensuring you are not locked into a single vendor and can adapt to new technologies without disruption.

- **Credibility of the vendor**: Trust is earned, not given. The credibility of your cloud provider is reflected in their market dominance and their track record of innovation, security, and customer support. Have they faced high-profile security breaches? How do they handle downtime? Do they invest in R&D to stay ahead of industry shifts? These are the questions that separate a long-term technology partner from just another service vendor.

- **SLAs and reliability**: A cloud provider's **service level agreement (SLA)** is a promise that defines how your business will be supported. Uptime guarantees, compensation clauses, and performance commitments should be scrutinized. A

99.9% uptime might sound impressive, but in mission-critical applications, even 0.1% downtime could mean millions in losses. Ensure your provider backs up their SLA with real-world reliability metrics, not just marketing claims.

- **Data privacy:** Data privacy is a matter of trust between your business and their service offering. The place where your data resides, is accessible, processed, and stored is essential in addition to handling geopolitical crises. Understanding a provider's data sovereignty policies, encryption standards, and regulatory alignment is critical in safeguarding not only your data but also your brand's reputation.

- **Service availability and disaster recovery**: The core potential trait of cloud is resiliency that offers global redundancy, automatic failovers, and rapid disaster recovery. Do they have multi-region replication, automated backups, and tested failover strategies? It is handling things when they go into unexpected disruptions proves how best the cloud provider can be.

- **Supported locations and infrastructure**: Cloud performance is often dictated by proximity. The provider's geographic coverage, availability zones, and edge computing capabilities determine latency, compliance feasibility, and scalability. If your customers are spread globally, but your provider's infrastructure is regionally constrained, you may encounter performance bottlenecks and regulatory roadblocks. Choose a provider that has data centers where you need them, not just where they exist.

Key takeaways for final decision

Let us now go over the key takeaways:

- **Align with business objectives**: Ensure the provider meets your operational, financial, and scalability goals rather than just offering generic cloud services.

- **Compare cloud providers thoroughly**: Evaluate AWS, Azure, GCP, and emerging players based on their strengths, limitations, and alignment with your industry needs.

- **Understand pricing models**: Assess **total cost of ownership (TCO)**, including hidden fees, egress costs, and optimization opportunities to prevent financial surprises.

- **Prioritize security and compliance**: Choose a provider with robust encryption, IAM controls, and regulatory compliance for frameworks like GDPR, HIPAA, and PCI-DSS.

- **Ensure scalability and flexibility**: Opt for a cloud partner that offers seamless scaling, hybrid cloud support, and multi-cloud interoperability.

- **Evaluate vendor credibility**: Research the provider's track record, customer support, and long-term innovation strategy to ensure reliability.

- **Scrutinize SLAs and performance guarantees**: Look for strong uptime commitments, compensation policies, and disaster recovery capabilities.

- **Assess data privacy and residency**: Understand how your provider handles data sovereignty, encryption, and legal compliance in different jurisdictions.

- **Verify disaster recovery and business continuity**: Choose a provider with automated failovers, backup solutions, and multi-region support for uninterrupted operations.

- **Analyze geographic coverage and latency**: Ensure the provider has data centers in regions that align with your business footprint for optimal performance.

All these aspects create a filter to pick the right service provider for your business operations and allow you to drive FinOps effectively in addition to the transformative initiatives you are looking for. When you take the time to reflect on each of these, your multi-cloud cost optimization strategy yields the following benefits.

Benefits of strategizing multi-cloud cost optimization with FinOps

In today's fast-paced, cloud-dependent business world, both **small and medium-sized businesses (SMB)** and large-scale enterprises must maintain agility while keeping costs in check. This delicate balancing act is where multi-cloud cost optimization, driven by FinOps, steps in to offer immense value. FinOps, or cloud financial operations, brings financial accountability and governance to the cloud ecosystem, empowering businesses to gain a firm grasp on cloud expenses while driving business growth. Let us explore the top five benefits of adopting a FinOps-driven multi-cloud cost optimization strategy:

- **Increased financial control and predictability**: A well-structured multi-cloud cost optimization strategy offers a bird's-eye view of your cloud spending across multiple providers, enabling both SMBs and large enterprises to gain increased financial control. In a multi-cloud environment, where businesses often juggle expenses from multiple CSP, it is easy for costs to spiral out of control. This is where FinOps adds value by bringing financial transparency to cloud operations.

    o FinOps helps to unmask hidden costs, giving organizations the insights needed to predict cloud expenditures more accurately. By establishing clear governance frameworks and cost monitoring tools, businesses can prevent unplanned expenses, allocate resources more effectively, and ensure that their cloud investments align with business priorities. The predictability FinOps provides enables both SMBs and large-scale enterprises to plan ahead, avoid financial surprises, and make data-driven decisions that keep budgets in check.

- **Optimized cloud usage and resource allocation**: In a multi-cloud environment, optimizing cloud usage is crucial to prevent resource waste and ensure efficiency.

Without a structured cost optimization strategy, organizations may end up with underutilized or idle resources, resulting in unnecessary cost increases. With FinOps at the helm, businesses can continuously monitor cloud usage patterns, rightsizing resources to match their real-time needs, and preventing the over-provisioning of services.

o   This approach is especially beneficial for SMBs, which often operate with limited IT budgets. By leveraging FinOps tools, small businesses can extract maximum value from every dollar spent, ensuring they only pay for what they use. On the other hand, large enterprises can benefit by scaling their cloud usage dynamically across multiple providers, thereby avoiding bottlenecks or unbalanced workloads that can lead to downtime or degraded performance. Whether it is autoscaling instances based on demand or utilizing Spot Instances for specific workloads, FinOps empowers businesses to fine-tune their cloud environments for both performance and cost efficiency.

- **Improved decision-making with real-time data**: One of the most significant advantages of a FinOps-driven strategy is the real-time visibility it provides into cloud spending. In the world of multi-cloud, where costs can be spread across multiple CSPs and cloud-based services, having access to real-time data is a game changer. FinOps platforms aggregate data from different providers into a single, easy-to-navigate interface, providing stakeholders with a clear view of how resources are being utilized.

o   This level of visibility empowers decision-makers to identify trends, pinpoint areas of cost inefficiency, and make adjustments on the fly. Whether you are scaling up resources during peak usage or scaling down after a project wraps up, having access to real-time data allows for proactive management rather than reactive troubleshooting. For large-scale enterprises, this means more effective budgeting and forecasting. For SMBs, it means staying agile and nimble in the face of fluctuating demands without compromising on cost management.

- **Enhanced scalability and flexibility**: In today's rapidly changing business landscape, scalability is not just a luxury; it is a necessity. A multi-cloud cost optimization strategy enables organizations to scale their cloud environments up or down seamlessly, depending on demand, while ensuring that they are not overpaying for unused resources. The integration of FinOps adds another layer to this scalability by tracking costs in real time and offering guidance on where and how resources should be allocated across multiple clouds.

o   For SMBs, this enhanced flexibility means they can compete with larger organizations by quickly scaling operations during peak periods without bearing the burden of high capital expenses. For large-scale enterprises, this means they can manage multiple cloud environments, distributing workloads based on performance, cost, and geography, without being locked into a single cloud provider. With FinOps, the flexibility of the multi-cloud environment is leveraged for cost-effective scalability, ensuring that organizations always pay the right price for the right number of resources.

- **Continuous improvement and innovation**: A FinOps-driven multi-cloud cost optimization strategy fosters a culture of continuous improvement and innovation. Rather than treating cloud cost management as a static, one-time exercise, FinOps encourages ongoing evaluation and optimization. This means regularly reviewing usage patterns, identifying inefficiencies, and implementing new optimization techniques. By embedding this process into the organization's fabric, businesses can continuously fine-tune their cloud environments to adapt to evolving business needs and technological advancements.

    o For SMBs, continuous improvement means staying lean and competitive, enabling them to quickly adopt new technologies and innovative cloud solutions without incurring unsustainable costs. For large enterprises, it means staying ahead of the curve in a rapidly evolving tech landscape, ensuring that they are always leveraging the most cost-effective and performance-driven cloud services available. This iterative process not only drives cost savings but also empowers businesses to innovate and future-proof their operations continuously.

Conclusion

Adopting a FinOps-driven multi-cloud cost optimization strategy is more than just a method for reducing cloud expenses; it is a powerful enabler for financial governance, scalability, and continuous innovation. Whether you are an SMB seeking to optimize limited resources or a large enterprise managing complex multi-cloud environments, the benefits of this approach are numerous. By combining the agility of multi-cloud with the financial rigor of FinOps, businesses can confidently navigate the cloud landscape, ensuring they remain competitive and cost-efficient in a rapidly changing world.

Join our Discord space

Join our Discord workspace for latest updates, offers, tech happenings around the world, new releases, and sessions with the authors:

https://discord.bpbonline.com

CHAPTER 9

FinOps Processes in a Multi-cloud Environment

Introduction

As organizations continue to embrace cloud computing, many are opting for multi-cloud environments, leveraging multiple cloud providers such as AWS, Microsoft Azure, Google Cloud, and **Oracle Cloud Infrastructure** (**OCI**) to meet their unique business needs. Multi-cloud strategies enable the use of the best cloud services for specific workloads, increase redundancy, and mitigate vendor lock-in. However, with this flexibility comes complexity, especially when it comes to managing cloud costs efficiently across diverse platforms.

Enter FinOps—a strategic approach to cloud financial management that ensures organizations can control, optimize, and govern their cloud expenditures without sacrificing performance or innovation. Implementing FinOps in a multi-cloud environment, as shown in the following figure, is particularly critical because the financial dynamics across different cloud providers can vary drastically. Organizations need to shift from just managing cloud costs to actively optimizing their cloud investments.

Figure 9.1: FinOps in multi-cloud environment

Core stages of FinOps processes

The FinOps framework is based on a set of processes that enable organizations to maintain financial accountability in the cloud while driving value and efficiency. These processes typically follow three core stages: inform, optimize, and govern. Let us go over them now.

Gaining visibility into cloud usage and costs in inform phase

In a multi-cloud environment, the Inform phase is the foundation of FinOps, providing the transparency necessary to manage cloud resources effectively. Cloud services are often abstract in terms of cost visibility, which can lead to overspending or underutilization if not monitored properly. This phase is about providing clear, actionable insights into cloud usage and spending, enabling organizations to maintain control over their financials.

The three pillars of inform: cost allocation, budgeting, and reporting, help create a single source of truth for cloud financials, regardless of how many providers an organization uses.

Cost allocation

Cost allocation is not just about assigning expenses to various teams or departments. It is about creating financial responsibility across the entire organization. For example, consider a retail company using AWS for backend services, Google Cloud for AI/ML workloads, and Azure for data storage. By allocating cloud costs based on which teams use which resources, the company can directly associate spending with business value. For instance, the AI/ML team may have a higher-than-expected cost due to their use of expensive machine learning instances on Google Cloud. With proper cost allocation, the team can be held accountable for those costs, making them more mindful of resource consumption.

The e-commerce platform running on AWS may experience spikes during seasonal shopping events, such as Black Friday. With real-time cost allocation, the IT team can anticipate such events and optimize their cloud spend accordingly.

In a software development company, the engineering team running Kubernetes clusters on Azure can be directly linked to their costs, prompting them to shut down unused environments after completing their projects.

Without proper cost allocation, cloud spending becomes a grey area where costs spiral out of control, and no one feels responsible for managing them. This accountability helps teams optimize their resource usage, which in turn reduces overall cloud costs.

Budgeting

Budgeting is the next critical element in the inform phase. In a multi-cloud environment, it is not enough to set a single cloud budget and hope it fits. Different providers have different pricing structures; AWS might offer Spot Instances that are highly cost-effective for short-term workloads, while Google Cloud might excel at data processing pricing for BigQuery.

Each team within an organization must understand how their portion of the cloud budget aligns with the services they consume. A technology company, for example, might need to allocate budgets for:

- The DevOps team, which requires compute resources for **continuous integration/ continuous deployment** (**CI/CD**) pipelines. Their budget needs to factor in on-demand compute services that auto-scale based on load.

- The marketing team, which might use Google Cloud's machine learning tools for personalized ad campaigns. Their cloud budget should reflect the high demand for data analytics tools during peak campaign periods.

By setting realistic and dynamic budgets, companies can forecast cloud spending more accurately. They can adjust for fluctuations in usage, like development projects ramping up or marketing campaigns running at full throttle, and ensure that financial constraints do not stifle innovation.

Reporting

The final component of the Inform phase is reporting. In a multi-cloud environment, real-time reporting becomes crucial for managing the fragmented nature of cloud spending. Each cloud provider has its native reporting tools, which can make it difficult to piece together a unified picture of overall spending. A holistic, customizable reporting solution enables an organization to see not only how much each cloud is costing but also how efficiently resources are being used.

Consider a global logistics company operating on AWS, Google Cloud, and Oracle Cloud for different purposes, such as:

- AWS handles its IoT systems that track fleet operations.
- Google Cloud processes big data for predictive analytics.
- Oracle Cloud runs its mission-critical database applications.

Without unified reporting, the company could struggle to pinpoint inefficiencies across these different clouds. Perhaps AWS's IoT costs are higher due to unoptimized data storage, or Google Cloud is underutilizing its expensive big data analytics capabilities. With consolidated, real-time reporting, the company can identify these patterns and take corrective action immediately.

Moreover, real-time reporting allows teams to identify outliers and avoid surprises. For instance, if a cloud service's usage unexpectedly spikes in the middle of the month, reporting tools can flag this to the responsible team. This gives decision-makers the power to nip cost overruns in the bud before they lead to budget blowouts.

Another example is in the healthcare industry, where HIPAA compliance and data sensitivity mean that cloud usage is tightly regulated. With effective reporting, healthcare providers can maintain compliance while ensuring that their cloud infrastructure remains cost-effective. Automated reports can alert finance teams to any anomalies, such as a sudden increase in data storage costs due to an influx of patient data, enabling them to quickly adjust storage policies or switch to more cost-effective archival storage options.

Optimizing stage with cost reduction and efficiency boosts

Once visibility is achieved, the focus shifts to optimization, which involves ensuring that cloud resources are used efficiently and at the lowest possible cost without compromising performance. The optimization phase of FinOps is where organizations can truly unlock the power of their multi-cloud strategy, fine-tuning their consumption to drive cost savings and maximize value. This phase includes several key components, each of which can dramatically impact a company's financial and operational performance. Let us go over them now.

Cost modelling

Cost modelling is the process of selecting the most cost-effective pricing structures based on an organization's specific workload needs. In a multi-cloud environment, where different cloud providers offer a range of pricing options, like on-demand instances, Reserved Instances, or spot pricing, the opportunity for optimization lies in understanding which pricing model best fits the nature of your workload.

For instance, an e-commerce company might rely heavily on on-demand instances during Black Friday or other sales events when traffic spikes are unpredictable. However, for steady, predictable workloads, such as running customer databases or processing payment information, Reserved Instances or committed-use contracts on Google Cloud or Azure could offer significant savings. By balancing flexibility with savings, cost modeling ensures that companies are paying for what they need, when they need it.

Take, for example, an AI/ML research lab that needs large amounts of compute power to train models. These workloads can be bursty and inconsistent, making Spot Instances an ideal choice because they are significantly cheaper than on-demand instances, albeit with a trade-off in availability. By utilizing Spot Instances for these non-critical workloads, the lab can significantly reduce costs without compromising the delivery of its research results. In contrast, for mission-critical services, the same lab could opt for Reserved Instances to ensure stability and predictability.

A media company that transcodes video content may find that Google Cloud's committed-use discounts for high-CPU-usage workloads offer the best balance between cost and performance for its large-scale video processing tasks. They can reserve compute resources for a full year, locking in a lower rate while ensuring that their heavy processing needs are consistently met.

Resource tagging

Resource tagging is another key element of cloud optimization. Without proper tagging, it becomes nearly impossible to keep track of who is using which resources, making optimization a blind process. Tagging ensures that each cloud resource, whether it is a virtual machine, storage volume, or network service, is assigned to the correct cost center, team, or department.

For example, in a financial services company, resource tagging can ensure that the costs associated with regulatory compliance workloads are differentiated from routine business processing. This allows the IT and finance teams to optimize resource usage based on the specific needs of each business unit.

Moreover, proper tagging helps identify and eliminate "zombie" resources, which are cloud services that are being paid for but no longer serve any purpose. For example, an automotive company might discover that several **virtual machines** (**VM**) that were spun up for testing purposes have been left running long after the project was completed. By implementing a rigorous tagging strategy, the company can identify and terminate these unnecessary virtual machines, resulting in immediate cost savings.

In the case of a global retail company, proper tagging might reveal that certain storage volumes used by the marketing team for a short-term campaign are still being billed even though the campaign has ended. By tagging and auditing resources effectively, the retail company can delete these storage volumes, reducing storage costs without impacting the business.

Automation

Automation is the ultimate tool for ensuring continuous optimization in the cloud. By automating key operational processes, companies can minimize waste, reduce human error, and make sure that cloud infrastructure is being used as efficiently as possible.

For example, an online gaming company can automate the scaling of its cloud infrastructure in response to player demand. During peak gaming hours, the infrastructure scales up to accommodate high traffic, and during off-peak hours, it automatically scales down, resulting in significant cost reductions. This approach ensures that the company is not paying for unused resources, while also preventing players from experiencing lag due to under-provisioning.

Moreover, automation can be used to enforce performance and cost thresholds. An energy company that uses machine learning to optimize energy consumption could set automated triggers that alert teams or scale resources when their cloud usage exceeds a specific budget or when performance drops below acceptable levels. This ensures both financial control and service reliability without the need for manual intervention.

While optimization often begins as an effort to reduce costs, it is really about finding the right balance between cost, performance, and scalability. For example, *Netflix*, a major player in the streaming industry, has a diverse multi-cloud strategy. To optimize their services, they leverage **Amazon Web Services** (**AWS**) for their global content delivery network, ensuring low latency for users around the world. However, they also use Google Cloud's AI capabilities for their recommendation algorithms, optimizing performance for different aspects of their service across clouds.

In another example, a pharmaceutical company running large-scale drug discovery simulations could choose to split workloads between Azure and IBM Cloud based on their performance requirements and geographical needs. Azure's global footprint may be optimal for running high-performance computing clusters in *Europe*, while IBM's specialized infrastructure may excel at running research workloads in Asia, allowing the company to strike a perfect balance between cost, performance, and latency.

Enforcing policies and controls in govern phase

The final step in the FinOps process is govern, which focuses on implementing and enforcing policies that keep the organization compliant with cost, security, and operational requirements. This step is crucial in a multi-cloud environment where the complexity increases with the diversity of cloud services and pricing structures. Without proper governance, companies risk overspending, security breaches, or failing to meet regulatory standards.

Governance in a multi-cloud strategy involves establishing a robust framework that aligns cloud usage with the organization's broader business objectives while also maintaining financial control. Key elements of the governance process include policy enforcement, monitoring, and compliance, and automation. These elements ensure consistency, security, and cost efficiency across multiple platforms. Let us go over them now.

Policy enforcement

At the heart of cloud governance is policy enforcement. Organizations must establish clear policies to define who can provision resources, how budgets are allocated, and what configurations are allowed. These policies act as guardrails to ensure that cloud resources are used responsibly and within financial limits.

For example, a large retail company operating in multiple regions may set a policy that prevents any one department from provisioning compute instances beyond a certain budget threshold. By enforcing these policies, the IT department can avoid overruns of cost caused by unnecessary scaling during seasonal sales events while still allowing teams to spin up additional resources when demand spikes.

In a healthcare organization, policies might be put in place to restrict the provisioning of cloud resources that do not meet HIPAA compliance standards. Here, governance ensures that sensitive patient data is stored only in certified cloud environments, thereby reducing the risk of regulatory violations and ensuring data security.

Another scenario is a global financial services firm that operates across various jurisdictions with differing regulatory requirements. Governance policies can ensure that cloud workloads containing financial data are only deployed in specific regions where data privacy laws, such as **General Data Protection Regulation** (**GDPR**) or **Central Consumer Protection Authority** (**CCPA**), are adhered to. These policies prevent the organization from facing hefty fines or reputational damage due to non-compliance.

Monitoring and compliance

Continuous monitoring is the cornerstone of cloud governance. Monitoring tools allow organizations to track cloud usage in real time, ensuring adherence to policies and detecting potential anomalies, such as cost spikes, unauthorized access, or security vulnerabilities.

For example, a media company that delivers content to a global audience might use monitoring tools to track bandwidth usage across multiple cloud providers. If usage spikes beyond budgeted thresholds in a specific region, the monitoring tool will alert the finance team to investigate and take corrective actions. This type of real-time visibility is crucial for maintaining control over cloud costs, particularly when streaming large amounts of data across a multi-cloud infrastructure.

Similarly, a telecommunications company might use monitoring to ensure that cloud services remain compliant with security policies. If an anomaly is detected, such as an attempt to access resources outside of approved regions, the monitoring tool will trigger an alert, enabling the security team to respond quickly. In a multi-cloud environment, the complexity of managing security across different providers increases the risk of security gaps, making continuous monitoring a critical governance tool.

In industries such as finance or defence, where compliance with stringent regulations is non-negotiable, continuous monitoring can ensure that cloud infrastructure complies with required security standards. For instance, an investment bank might use monitoring tools to ensure that all cloud workloads involving financial transactions meet the stringent requirements of **Sarbanes-Oxley** (**SOX**) or PCI-DSS.

Automating governance

Wherever possible, automating governance processes helps organizations enforce policies consistently and reduces the risk of human error. Automation is a powerful enabler in complex multi-cloud environments, ensuring that cost limits, security checks, and compliance measures are enforced uniformly across all cloud platforms.

For example, a technology startup working on AI research might automate the enforcement of cost limits by setting thresholds on the number of compute instances that can be spun up within each cloud provider. When these thresholds are reached, the automated system could automatically scale down or prevent additional instances from being created without managerial approval. This helps the startup manage costs effectively as their research needs fluctuate.

An international logistics company could also automate security compliance checks to ensure that no non-compliant configurations are deployed across any of their cloud environments. Automation tools can routinely audit infrastructure, flagging any misconfigurations or security vulnerabilities before they turn into expensive incidents or security breaches.

In the case of a global SaaS company, automation could be used to ensure that all cloud resources are tagged correctly. If a new server is deployed without the appropriate tags, which link the server to the right cost center or department, the system will automatically alert or rectify the issue. This helps with both cost allocation and resource tracking, ensuring that the financial responsibility for cloud usage is transparent.

Ultimately, effective governance ensures that cloud usage aligns with business objectives, financial constraints, and security requirements. This is particularly important in a multi-cloud environment where each provider may have different strengths and weaknesses.

Challenges of implementing FinOps in a multi-cloud environment

While the FinOps framework provides a robust approach to managing cloud financials, implementing FinOps in a multi-cloud environment presents unique challenges. The multi-cloud landscape, where multiple cloud providers, diverse pricing models, and a variety of services intersect, introduces a level of complexity that cannot be underestimated. Organizations may feel like they are navigating uncharted waters, with each cloud platform presenting its own intricacies. These hurdles can quickly snowball into bigger challenges if not addressed effectively. Let us now delve into the core challenges of implementing FinOps in a multi-cloud setup.

Figure 9.2: *Challenges of implementing FinOps in multi-cloud environments*

Lack of standardization

One of the most significant roadblocks in a multi-cloud environment is the lack of standardization across cloud providers. Each provider has its own billing structures, terminologies, and pricing models, making it a herculean task to create a unified financial strategy. What works on one cloud might fall short on another, leading to apples-to-oranges comparisons that obscure real cost insights.

Imagine trying to create a single budget for a household where each family member spends in a different currency. One pays in dollars, another in pounds, and a third in yen. This is akin to managing cloud costs when one provider charges by the hour, another by the minute, and yet another by the transaction. The lack of common ground in pricing models makes it difficult to compare costs and achieve clarity on where the financial leakage may be occurring.

The lack of alignment in billing and pricing schemes results in challenges when attempting to optimize cloud usage or negotiate contracts with vendors. Without a consistent framework for understanding the actual cost of services across clouds, organizations risk getting lost in translation between different billing formats and pricing models, leading to suboptimal financial decisions.

Data silos

In a multi-cloud environment, data silos are an inevitable consequence of the fragmented nature of cloud providers. Each provider has its own set of reporting tools, analytics capabilities, and cost breakdowns, which creates a fractured view of cloud usage and financials. With data spread across multiple platforms, consolidating this information into a single, coherent view becomes a game of hide and seek.

The inability to easily connect the dots across clouds can leave organizations flying blind, unable to see the big picture of their cloud spending and usage. This fragmented data leads to delayed decision-making, misaligned financial strategies, and missed opportunities for optimization. Gaining a holistic view of costs across multiple providers is like piecing together a jigsaw puzzle, except some pieces are missing or don't quite fit.

Bridging these silos requires organizations to adopt platforms or tools that can consolidate data from various cloud providers into a unified dashboard. However, stitching together this information takes time, resources, and expertise, and without the right approach, organizations risk missing vital insights that could drive cost efficiency and operational effectiveness.

Complexity in cost allocation

Allocating cloud costs in a multi-cloud environment is like trying to slice a pie with no clear boundaries; it is difficult to know where one slice ends and another begins. Each cloud provider categorizes resources in its own unique way, and without a standardized tagging strategy, it is easy to lose track of which team, project, or department is responsible for specific expenses.

Without proper cost allocation mechanisms, cloud costs can become a tangled web, leaving organizations unable to determine which parts of the business are driving up costs. A seemingly simple task of tracking who is using what becomes a logistical quagmire in a multi-cloud environment where resources and expenditures are scattered across platforms.

Implementing a consistent tagging and cost allocation strategy is critical to understanding cloud costs. When done correctly, it provides the visibility needed to assign costs accurately, hold departments accountable, and pinpoint areas for optimization. However, achieving this consistency across multiple cloud platforms requires significant effort and ongoing oversight. If not appropriately addressed, organizations risk becoming stuck in a cycle of trying to determine where cost overruns originate, often too late to take corrective action.

Security and compliance ·

The more cloud platforms an organization uses, the more challenging it becomes to maintain consistent security and compliance standards. Juggling multiple balls at once, each with its own set of security protocols and compliance frameworks, can quickly turn into a logistical nightmare. Every cloud provider operates with its own security features, and while they may offer robust protections individually, the lack of a unified approach across clouds can leave an organization vulnerable to gaps in its defenses.

For instance, ensuring compliance with security regulations and internal policies across a multi-cloud setup requires constant vigilance and cross-platform coordination. The risk of misconfigurations, non-compliant deployments, or security breaches rises exponentially with each additional cloud provider. Moreover, keeping all your ducks in a row when it comes to compliance can be an uphill battle, particularly when different clouds are subject to different governance requirements.

Without an overarching governance strategy that spans all clouds, security and compliance issues can slip through the cracks, resulting in costly fines or, worse, data breaches that erode trust and damage an organization's reputation. Ensuring consistent governance across multiple platforms is no small feat, but it is critical for safeguarding sensitive data and maintaining operational integrity.

Vendor-specific optimization tools

One of the double-edged swords of multi-cloud environments is that each cloud provider offers native optimization tools to help manage costs and improve efficiency. While these tools can be handy within the confines of a single cloud provider, they often lack compatibility with other platforms. This leads to fragmented optimization efforts where organizations must use multiple tools to manage different cloud environments.

The lack of a universal toolset can result in inefficiencies, as organizations are forced to use vendor-specific tools for each platform they operate on. The result is often more work with less clarity, as teams struggle to gain a unified view of their optimization efforts. The fragmented nature of vendor-specific tools creates a patchwork of solutions that can be difficult to integrate, leading to missed opportunities for optimization and higher overall cloud costs.

To overcome this challenge, organizations must seek out third-party tools that provide cross-cloud compatibility, enabling them to streamline optimization efforts across all platforms. However, finding a tool that works seamlessly with multiple cloud providers can be a challenge. Until the industry achieves greater standardization, organizations will need to adopt workarounds and creative solutions to ensure they optimize their cloud resources effectively.

Navigating the complexities of FinOps in a multi-cloud environment is no walk in the park, but with the right strategies, it is possible to overcome these challenges and achieve a high level of financial efficiency. Organizations must adopt a robust, flexible approach to FinOps that can adapt to the ever-changing dynamics of multi-cloud environments. This means creating a unified strategy for managing costs, breaking down data silos, implementing consistent tagging and tracking, and ensuring that governance and security standards are upheld across all platforms.

In the end, a one-size-fits-all approach simply will not cut it in a multi-cloud world. To truly master FinOps in this complex landscape, organizations must be prepared to roll with the punches, continuously refining their processes and tools to keep pace with the rapid evolution of cloud technologies. By embracing flexibility and innovation, organizations can turn these challenges into opportunities, ensuring they remain competitive and financially sound in the face of multi-cloud complexity.

Implementing FinOps processes in a multi-cloud environment

To implement FinOps in a multi-cloud environment, organizations must adopt a cohesive and cross-functional approach that brings together key stakeholders from finance, operations, and engineering. This is not a one-man job or a one-department show; it requires a holistic effort where every part of the organization plays its role in orchestrating the financial success of cloud operations. With multiple clouds in play, the complexity only grows, making collaboration and a unified strategy absolutely essential. Here are a few strategies that can serve as guiding principles to streamline the implementation of FinOps in a multi-cloud setup:

- **Centralized cost management**: One of the first steps to successful FinOps implementation in a multi-cloud environment is centralized cost management. With cloud usage spanning different platforms, each with its own pricing structures, billing cycles, and terminology, it can quickly become a tangled web of expenses that are hard to track. The solution? Implementing cloud management platforms or specialized FinOps tools that aggregate data from multiple providers into a unified dashboard. Having all your ducks in a row, in the form of a single interface that provides real-time insights into usage and costs across clouds, allows organizations to simplify the visibility and monitoring of cloud expenditures.

  o A unified dashboard helps cut through the noise of disparate billing and usage data, providing a clear line of sight into where costs are being incurred, which resources are being utilized, and who is responsible for them. This centralization does not just improve transparency; it enables accountability. Finance teams can easily track whether actual cloud spending aligns with budgets, while operations and engineering teams can assess whether resources are being used efficiently. Without a bird's-eye view of cloud operations, it is easy to lose track of where costs are spiraling out of control. Centralized cost management brings everything into focus.

- **Standardized tagging across platforms**: In a multi-cloud environment, consistency is king. This is especially true when it comes to tracking and managing cloud resources. Each cloud provider may use different terminologies, classifications, and resource categorization methods, which can make tracking costs a nightmare. The key to solving this problem is to implement standardized tagging conventions across all platforms. Tagging is not just a matter of organization; it is about creating a common language that allows teams to track, categorize, and manage cloud resources consistently.

  o Standardized tagging provides a framework for cost allocation, ensuring that every dollar spent is attributed to the correct team, project, or department. This simplifies the cost reporting process, making it easier for finance teams to allocate expenses accurately and for engineering teams to optimize resource utilization. It also lays the groundwork for better automation, as consistent tags enable automated systems to act on resources without confusion. Imagine trying to manage a warehouse without labels; chaos would reign. Similarly, without a standardized tagging system, cloud management can quickly become unmanageable.

   o   Additionally, standardized tagging facilitates cross-cloud transparency, giving organizations a clearer picture of where resources are being consumed and by whom. This helps identify resource sprawl, a common problem in multi-cloud environments, where unused or zombie resources can continue to incur costs without providing value. Tagging ensures that every resource is accounted for, tracked, and optimized.

- **Cross-functional collaboration**: At the heart of successful FinOps lies cross-functional collaboration. FinOps is not just a finance issue, nor is it solely an IT concern; it is a team effort that requires the alignment of finance, operations, and engineering. Each team brings its own expertise to the table. Finance focuses on budgeting, cost control, and ensuring that cloud expenditures align with the organization's bottom line. Operations are tasked with maintaining efficiency and uptime and ensuring the smooth functioning of cloud infrastructure. Engineering, on the other hand, is responsible for optimizing performance and scalability, making sure that the organization gets the most bang for its buck from its cloud investments.

   o   However, in a multi-cloud environment, silos will not cut it. If these teams operate in isolation, the result is often a disjointed strategy, where financial decisions are not aligned with technical needs, and technical efforts do not factor in budget constraints. Bridging these silos is crucial. Teams must be able to speak the same language, whether that is understanding the financial impact of technical choices or the technical feasibility of cost-saving measures.

   o   Regular cross-functional meetings where cloud usage, performance, and costs are reviewed keep everyone on the same page. It is in these discussions that the true power of FinOps comes to light, where finance learns how technical adjustments can lead to savings, and engineers grasp the financial implications of scaling decisions. When all hands are on deck, cloud investments align more closely with business goals, and the organization is better positioned to achieve financial agility in the cloud.

- **Automation of cost controls**: In a multi-cloud environment, the sheer volume of resources and complexity of billing structures make manual management a fool's errand. This is where automation becomes your best friend. Automating cost controls is not only about saving time; it is about ensuring consistency and accuracy in how resources are managed across cloud platforms. Automation takes the guesswork out of managing resources and spending, allowing organizations to focus on more strategic initiatives.

o   For instance, automating the scaling of resources, up or down, based on demand, can significantly reduce waste. If workloads spike, automation ensures that resources are increased to maintain performance. When demand falls, resources are scaled down automatically to minimize unnecessary expenses. Without automation, such adjustments would require constant vigilance and human intervention, which is not sustainable at scale.

o   Another critical area for automation is the enforcement of spending limits. In a multi-cloud environment, where costs can easily spiral out of control, automated spending controls serve as a safety net, preventing teams from exceeding their budgets. By setting predefined cost limits and automating notifications or even resource shutdowns when those limits are breached, organizations can maintain financial discipline without relying on manual checks.

o   Automation also helps with optimization, moving workloads between clouds based on cost-effectiveness, ensuring that resources are used efficiently, and reducing cloud sprawl. With automation, the FinOps process becomes a well-oiled machine, where resources are provisioned, optimized, and decommissioned in real-time, without delays or oversights.

Road to FinOps excellence in multi-cloud environments

Implementing FinOps in a multi-cloud environment is not a one-and-done process. It requires constant iteration, continuous monitoring, and an evolving strategy that adapts to the changing dynamics of cloud technologies and business needs. The preceding strategies outlined, centralized cost management, standardized tagging, cross-functional collaboration, and automation, are the building blocks that can set organizations on the path to FinOps excellence.

However, it is important to recognize that the journey does not end with implementation. The cloud is a moving target, pricing models change, new services are introduced, and business demands shift. Therefore, organizations must be nimble and adaptable, ready to pivot their FinOps strategies as needed. Keeping your ear to the ground in terms of new cloud developments, evolving financial models, and emerging automation technologies will help organizations stay ahead of the curve.

By adopting these strategies, organizations can achieve not only cost efficiency but also greater financial control in their multi-cloud environments. The ultimate goal of FinOps is to strike a balance between performance, scalability, and cost, getting more bang for your buck while ensuring that cloud investments drive real value for the business. The road to FinOps excellence may be winding, but with the right tools and approach, organizations can navigate the complexities of the multi-cloud world with confidence and clarity.

Best practices for cost allocation, budgeting, and reporting

Implementing effective cost allocation, budgeting, and reporting processes in a multi-cloud environment is non-negotiable for organizations striving to manage their cloud financials effectively. In a world where cloud expenses can quickly spiral out of control, having a structured and proactive approach ensures that businesses stay on a financially sound path. The complexities of multi-cloud environments, each provider with its own pricing models, billing cycles, and usage metrics, mean that organizations must be sharp as a tack when it comes to managing their cloud spend. Here are several best practices that can guide organizations toward financial discipline and optimal cloud expenditure management:

- **Granular cost allocation:** The principle of granular cost allocation is akin to the saying, *Take care of the pennies, and the dollars will take care of themselves*. In a multi-cloud environment, this means assigning costs to the smallest possible unit, whether it is a specific team, project, application, or even a particular resource type. Granularity creates visibility and accountability, allowing organizations to trace cloud expenses back to their source, and it gives teams skin in the game when it comes to managing their budgets.

  o When costs are broken down to this degree, organizations can pinpoint inefficiencies, cut the fat, and make informed decisions about where to tighten the purse strings. For example, by identifying which projects are consuming excessive resources without yielding proportionate value, companies can course-correct before costs spiral out of control. Granular allocation also makes it easier to track and manage shared resources. Instead of lumping costs into a vague, company-wide budget, businesses can assign precise costs to individual departments, fostering a culture of responsibility and enabling better financial forecasting.

- **Regular budgeting and forecasting**: Just as a ship needs constant adjustments to stay on course, managing cloud financials in a multi-cloud environment requires regular budgeting and forecasting. Cloud usage is not static; it fluctuates based on business demand, seasonality, or unexpected events. Therefore, it is essential for organizations to update their cloud budgets and financial forecasts continuously. Failing to do so is like flying blind, leaving businesses at the mercy of cost spikes that can wreak havoc on financial plans.

  o Frequent budgeting and forecasting allow organizations to stay ahead of the curve by anticipating usage trends and potential cost increases. The ability to course-correct in real-time means that organizations are not blindsided by surprises at the end of the billing cycle. When companies make a habit of revisiting and updating their budgets, they can adapt their spending in response to shifting business needs, ensuring they always have a firm grip on their cloud costs.

o   Moreover, this practice supports financial agility, that is, the ability to respond quickly to changes in market conditions, customer demands, or internal priorities. By regularly revisiting cloud forecasts, finance teams can fine-tune their financial models to align with real-time business objectives, providing a clear roadmap that keeps cloud expenses in check while enabling innovation and growth.

- **Automated reporting and alerting**: In the fast-paced world of cloud computing, knowledge is power, and real-time insights are worth their weight in gold. Manual reporting processes are often too slow and prone to human error to keep pace with the rapid evolution of cloud usage. This is where automated reporting and alerting come into play, providing teams with up-to-the-minute data on cloud usage, costs, and trends. Automated tools enable organizations to stay on top of their numbers, providing clear and actionable insights into where resources are being consumed and how they align with budgetary expectations. Automation is not just about making life easier, though that is certainly a benefit. It is about ensuring that financial decisions are data-driven, based on the most accurate and current information available. Real-time reporting removes the guesswork, empowering teams to make informed decisions that align with business goals. For instance, if cloud costs are trending upward unexpectedly, finance teams can respond immediately, rather than waiting until the end of the month to discover an unpleasant surprise on the invoice.

  o   However, reporting alone is not enough. Organizations must also implement alerting mechanisms to flag anomalies or red flags in cloud usage. Whether it is a sudden cost spike or unusual usage patterns, alerts can provide an early warning system that allows teams to take swift action and prevent budget overruns. In a multi-cloud environment, where costs can escalate quickly, these automated alerts serve as a safety net, ensuring that no spending goes unnoticed and that appropriate action can be taken before costs balloon out of control.

- **Encouraging financial accountability and transparency**: In a multi-cloud setup, effective financial management does not stop with the finance team; it is a company-wide responsibility. Financial accountability is crucial in ensuring that all departments, teams, and individuals are aware of the impact of their cloud usage on the company's bottom line. This is not just about setting budgets and hoping teams will follow them; it is about creating transparency and shared responsibility around cloud expenditures. By fostering an environment of financial transparency, organizations can ensure that cloud users, whether they be engineers, project managers, or IT staff, understand the financial implications of their actions. This involves educating teams about cloud pricing models, the importance of efficient resource utilization, and the direct impact of wasteful practices on the company's financial health. When teams are informed and empowered, they are more likely to act prudently, keeping costs in check and avoiding unnecessary expenditures.

  o   Transparency also paves the way for better collaboration between departments. For example, finance and IT teams can work together to establish spending limits or guardrails that ensure cloud usage remains aligned with budgetary goals. Open communication ensures that teams are not operating in silos but are instead rowing in the same direction, with everyone contributing to the overarching goal of financial efficiency.

- **Leveraging cloud cost management tools**: Organizations are often faced with an embarrassment of riches when it comes to cloud cost management tools. The key to success lies in leveraging these tools to their fullest potential. Modern cloud cost management platforms provide a wealth of features that enable organizations to track usage, allocate costs, forecast future expenses, and optimize their spending. These tools are not just for finance teams; they can be utilized across the organization to enhance visibility, streamline operations, and ensure financial clarity in every area of the business.

  o   By utilizing these platforms, organizations can stay one step ahead in managing their cloud financials. For instance, cost optimization features can recommend actions to reduce waste, such as identifying idle resources or suggesting more cost-effective pricing models. In a multi-cloud environment, where managing costs across multiple platforms can feel like juggling too many balls, cloud cost management tools offer a way to consolidate information and keep everything under control.

Importance of flexibility in financial planning

Finally, no discussion of cloud financial management would be complete without emphasizing the importance of flexibility. In a multi-cloud environment, where services, pricing models, and usage patterns can shift at a moment's notice, organizations must adopt a fluid approach to financial planning. Rigid financial structures are bound to crumble under the weight of constant change. Instead, organizations should embrace agility, building financial processes that can adapt to fluctuations in cloud usage, emerging technologies, and evolving business needs.

Flexibility is the cornerstone of future-proofing your financial strategy. By staying nimble, regularly revisiting budgets, and adjusting forecasts, organizations can navigate the ever-changing waters of cloud financial management without losing sight of their broader business objectives. Expecting the unexpected and building financial plans that can flex as needed ensures that organizations can continue to innovate and scale their cloud operations without being blindsided by unforeseen expenses.

Effective cost management in a multi-cloud environment

Effective cost management in a multi-cloud environment requires a combination of proactive monitoring, policy enforcement, and optimization strategies. By continuously monitoring cloud usage and costs, organizations can identify inefficiencies and adjust their cloud strategy in real-time. In addition to monitoring, automation plays a critical role in cost management by eliminating waste and ensuring that resources are scaled appropriately to meet demand.

A well-defined governance model is also crucial for maintaining control over cloud expenditures. Governance ensures that there are clear guidelines on spending limits, resource provisioning, and security compliance across all cloud platforms. This not only helps prevent overspending but also ensures that cloud investments are aligned with broader business goals.

Conclusion

Implementing FinOps in a multi-cloud environment is crucial for organizations seeking to optimize the value of their cloud investments. By following best practices, addressing common challenges, and leveraging automation and cross-functional collaboration, businesses can optimize their multi-cloud strategy and drive greater financial accountability in the cloud.

Join our Discord space

Join our Discord workspace for latest updates, offers, tech happenings around the world, new releases, and sessions with the authors:

https://discord.bpbonline.com

CHAPTER 10

Monitoring, Measuring and Reporting Cloud Costs and Savings

Introduction

As we move into the dynamic universe of cloud computing, where services and solutions scale seamlessly, costs also accrue rapidly. This is where the need for driving monitoring, measuring, and reporting cloud costs and savings has been prioritized for effective cloud financial management. The multi-cloud environment has its own pricing structures and consumption models, which we have understood till now. Therefore, now, acquiring complete control of cloud expenses becomes even more paramount.

We are in an endless loop of possibilities with the cloud infrastructure. For this infrastructure, one must carefully see through these possibilities to flip over financial pitfalls. The continuous monitoring of cloud usage revolves around paying for what you need. So-called unused or underutilized resources drain budgets, and if monitoring is taken care of, all inefficiencies become paralyzed, elevating your **return on investment (ROI)**.

Measuring is equally critical. Knowing how you are spending your money is great, but you also need to understand how you are spending it. Granular cost measurement enables organizations to break down their expenditures by department, project, or application, ensuring that every dollar spent is justified. Measuring provides the insights needed to make strategic decisions, such as identifying which workloads should remain on-demand and which could be better served with Reserved Instances or spot pricing.

Reporting takes the process a step further by delivering actionable insights to decision-makers. Reports consolidate complex data into understandable, meaningful narratives. When done correctly, reporting does not just tell you where your money is going; it highlights trends, reveals potential areas of waste, and provides a roadmap for cost optimization. It turns raw cloud usage data into a powerful tool for guiding both immediate action and long-term strategy.

Without these critical processes in place, organizations can quickly lose visibility into their cloud environment, making it nearly impossible to align cloud costs with business objectives.

Challenges of neglecting monitoring, measuring, and reporting

Failing to implement robust monitoring, measuring, and reporting practices can lead to a host of challenges that significantly impact both operational efficiency and financial health. Let us understand these challenges now.

Cost overruns

Cost overruns can be the proverbial iceberg lurking beneath the surface, waiting to sink your financial ship. Organizations that do not maintain a vigilant eye on their cloud usage risk overspending, often without a clue until it is too late. The situation is elevated in a multi-cloud environment, where the complexity multiplies exponentially with each additional provider. Here, different billing structures and pricing models can lead to a fog of confusion, making it nearly impossible for finance teams to track expenditures accurately.

When organizations overlook monitoring, they leave themselves vulnerable to the unexpected. Costs from various providers can spiral out of control, creating a perfect storm of financial chaos. It is not uncommon for finance teams to find themselves scrambling to make sense of the numbers, desperately trying to pinpoint where the budget has evaporated. Without real-time insights, companies risk becoming proverbial deer in headlights, unprepared for the financial impact that clouds bring. A proactive approach to monitoring is essential, allowing organizations to keep their fingers on the pulse of cloud spending and avoid the pitfall of unchecked costs.

Lack of accountability

In the absence of proper measurement and oversight, assigning accountability for cloud expenses becomes akin to trying to nail jelly to a wall. When expenses are not clearly defined or attributed, it creates a breeding ground for finger-pointing, which can quickly become the rallying cry when budgets exceed expectations, fostering a culture of blame rather than collaboration. This lack of accountability not only stifles initiative but also fosters an environment where inefficiencies can thrive unchecked.

When teams are not held accountable for their cloud usage, they may feel less inclined to manage resources wisely, leading to a *let someone else handle it* mentality. Without clear ownership, the responsibility for optimizing cloud resources becomes diluted, and costs can spiral out of control. Ultimately, this lack of accountability can undermine the organization's financial health and strategic objectives, making it imperative to establish clear metrics and ownership structures that promote financial responsibility across all departments.

Missed optimization opportunities

Regular monitoring and measuring are crucial to revealing areas where cost savings can be realized. Whether it is pinpointing underutilized resources that quietly drain budgets or identifying more cost-effective service tiers, organizations that lack a clear picture of their cloud resource usage risk sailing blind.

Optimizing cloud resources is not a one-time effort; it requires ongoing vigilance and a commitment to uncovering new opportunities for improvement. Without a culture that values continuous measurement and monitoring, businesses may miss out on significant savings that could bolster their bottom line and improve overall performance.

Unpredictable financial forecasting

When it comes to financial forecasting in the cloud, failing to measure and report accurately can turn the process into a game of chance. The highly variable nature of cloud consumption can be influenced by a myriad of factors, such as seasonal demand spikes, unexpected product launches, or even shifts in market dynamics. Without precise measurement, organizations find themselves navigating through murky waters, unable to predict future expenditures with any degree of confidence.

This unpredictability can lead to unexpected financial shortfalls, forcing organizations to scramble for budget cuts in other critical areas. The inability to forecast accurately not only undermines financial stability but also erodes stakeholder trust. Leadership teams need reliable data to make informed decisions about resource allocation and strategic investments. In this landscape, organizations must prioritize accurate measures to maintain financial agility and ensure they can adapt to changing market conditions.

Difficulty in cost allocation

Cost allocation in a multi-cloud environment can feel like trying to solve a Rubik's Cube, which is complex and frustrating, especially when each cloud provider operates under its own set of rules. Without detailed reports and a standardized approach to tagging and reporting, organizations face the monumental task of reconciling costs across different platforms. It is easy for teams to become overwhelmed, leading to inefficiencies and confusion that can derail even the best-laid budgeting plans.

Without effective measurement and reporting, identifying which teams or projects are responsible for specific costs can become an insurmountable challenge. This lack of clarity not only hampers budgeting efforts but also stifles innovation, as teams hesitate to invest in new initiatives without a clear understanding of their financial implications. To overcome this hurdle, organizations must implement robust tracking mechanisms that provide transparency and accountability, paving the way for informed decision-making and effective cost management.

Inability to demonstrate savings

When organizations fail to establish consistent reporting mechanisms, they find themselves unable to demonstrate the value of their cost-saving efforts. This inability to showcase success can undermine the credibility of FinOps initiatives and erode leadership support for ongoing optimization efforts.

Leadership teams are seeking evidence that their investments in cloud optimization are yielding results. Without solid data to back up claims of savings, the time and resources spent may go unrecognized, resulting in a lack of motivation to continue pursuing cloud financial management strategies. Demonstrating savings requires a commitment to transparency and a willingness to share both successes and areas for improvement. When organizations prioritize clear reporting, they not only strengthen their FinOps initiatives but also build trust with stakeholders, ensuring continued support for financial stewardship.

Compliance and governance risks

In today's fast-paced regulatory landscape, organizations cannot afford to overlook the importance of compliance and governance. Failure to monitor, measure, and report cloud usage accurately can expose organizations to significant risks, such as, financial penalties, reputational damage, and legal ramifications. The stakes are high, and the consequences of non-compliance can be far-reaching.

Navigating the complexities of multiple cloud providers further complicates governance efforts, as each may have different security standards and compliance requirements. Without a systematic approach to monitoring and reporting, organizations risk falling out of compliance, which can lead to costly fines and erode stakeholder confidence. To mitigate these risks, organizations must establish robust governance frameworks that prioritize transparency and accountability in their cloud operations. By embedding compliance into the fabric of their FinOps strategy, organizations can safeguard against potential pitfalls and ensure that their cloud investments align with broader regulatory and operational objectives.

These challenges clearly highlight the critical need for organizations to embrace the three ground pillars, that is, monitoring, measuring, and reporting. While planning a futuristic roadmap, companies can establish sustained success in ever-evolving complex cloud ecosystems. It is a way to harness the full potential of cloud investments that helps you to drive long-term growth.

As we deeply dive into how each of these embraces the enterprises to adopt FinOps, let us also look at the best practices to raise the foundation for each of these pillars that lead to huge cost savings.

Cost monitoring and a comprehensive view of cloud costs

Real-time visibility, tracking cloud service usage, costs, and performance around the clock: this is the foundation of effective cloud cost monitoring. In today's cloud-driven business landscape, cloud cost monitoring has evolved far beyond basic reporting. It now blends cutting-edge automation, advanced analytics, and deep operational checks to provide enterprises with a granular, real-time understanding of their cloud financials. This level of oversight is no longer a luxury; it is a necessity. The complexities of multi-cloud environments, with their varied pricing models and ever-changing resource demands, necessitate that organizations be vigilant, agile, and proactive in managing cloud expenditures.

At its core, cloud cost monitoring enables organizations to pinpoint inefficiencies such as cost overruns, identify unused or underutilized resources, and detect anomalies before they spiral into budgetary nightmares. With automation at the helm, this process is no longer about manual intervention or retrospective analysis. Instead, automated tools continuously scan cloud environments, flagging potential issues in real time. Whether it is a sudden spike in resource consumption, untagged resources draining the budget, or workloads running in low-efficiency modes, the platform itself raises red flags. It is like having a financial watchdog on duty 24/7, ensuring that every dollar spent on cloud services is accounted for and justified.

The true power of modern cloud cost monitoring lies in its ability to send automated alerts the moment irregularities are detected. These real-time notifications empower businesses to act swiftly, ensuring optimal resource utilization and budget adherence. Imagine a scenario where a department inadvertently over-provisions resources or forgets to decommission a testing environment; without real-time monitoring, these costly oversights can remain hidden until the end of the billing cycle. By then, the damage is done. However, with intelligent monitoring systems in place, alerts are triggered immediately, allowing teams to course-correct before budgets spiral out of control.

This proactive approach not only saves money but also aligns cloud consumption with broader business goals. Enterprises today are expected to be nimble, responsive, and cost-conscious—traits that are only possible when there is complete transparency and control over cloud costs. Automated monitoring ensures that financial and operational teams are always one step ahead, with insights that allow them to optimize usage patterns, predict future spending trends, and maintain fiscal discipline.

Moreover, the integration of anomaly detection capabilities takes cloud cost monitoring to a whole new level. These systems do not just look for the obvious; they delve deeper, analyzing patterns and flagging subtle yet significant anomalies. It is not just about identifying an unused server or storage bucket; it is about understanding shifts in consumption patterns that may signal inefficiencies or misaligned resource allocation. These subtle irregularities, if left unchecked, can lead to a significant financial drain over time.

The benefits of cloud cost monitoring extend beyond mere cost control. By bringing real-time visibility into cloud operations, organizations can foster a culture of accountability and transparency. Different teams and departments can be empowered with the data they need to manage their cloud spending. At the same time, leadership retains the ability to maintain a bird's-eye view of overall cloud expenditures. This cross-functional collaboration is essential in a multi-cloud environment, where cloud resources are shared across various teams and projects.

Standardizing cloud cost monitoring for enterprises

As we establish standards across the enterprise, where cost monitoring is no longer a challenge but a clear and concise way to balance multi-cloud environments, we recommend implementing flawless practices for effective monitoring. Each one of these practices can be scaled up as per your business needs and FinOps adoption phases. These include:

- **Establishing clear ownership and accountability**: Cloud usage cannot be left idle when every team member is using it. Every team and department must remain accountable for what they are using through a governance framework, by assigning ownership to individuals and teams. Moreover, transparency plays a crucial role in this regard as it enables seamless communication between stakeholders and teams so that they can see how the cloud consumption is impacting the overall budget.

- **Integrate real-time monitoring tools**: Cloud moves businesses quick, and cost overruns happen because of extreme cloud usage. Gaining real-time visibility into cloud usage through tools that have automated features gives you a comprehensive view of insights whenever there are spikes in consumption, idle resources, or unexpected behaviors. Cloud-native, third-party tools, such as Heeddata, CoreStack, and IBM's Cloudability, offer real-time dashboards, alerts, and reports in instances. These tools send immediate notifications of potential issues, enabling teams to respond quickly and avoid the pitfalls of unnecessary spending, underutilized resources, and undisciplined budgets.

- **Automation to alerts and notifications**: Automation is the game-changer in multi-cloud environments. As soon as the usage exceeds the predefined thresholds, enterprises can get notifications once automated alerts are in action. For example, if a virtual machine is left running over the weekend, an alert can notify the responsible team to shut it down, preventing unnecessary waste. Similarly, alerts can flag unexpected increases in data transfer, storage consumption, or other cloud services, enabling teams to address the issue before it becomes an expensive surprise. Ensure these alerts are configured based on business priorities and fine-tune them regularly for accuracy.

- **Maintain consistency in tagging strategy**: In our observation, enterprises do not tag the resources in a proper way, leading to thousands of resources remaining unnoticed. Categorizing the cloud resources by project, department, or cost center helps businesses offer clarity on which resources are used by whom. One of the elephant-tusk challenges in multi-cloud environments is maintaining consistency across platforms, but if it is lacking, the accuracy of cost tracking becomes miserable. Defining a company-wide tagging policy and enabling every resource to follow the same brings better financial reporting, budgeting, and accountability.

Frequently audit and review cloud costs

Cost monitoring demands ongoing focus and periodic audits to ensure everything is in order. This allows you to identify any inefficiencies in resource utilization, ensuring that your cost-saving initiatives align with the expected outcomes. Deep-rooted audits identify misconfigurations or abandoned resources that contribute to unnecessary expenses, providing an opportunity to restructure budgets and forecasts based on actual usage patterns. Let us go over the following points now:

- **Optimize resource utilization continuously**: More than identifying current expenses, considering the future optimization is also essential. Evaluate continuously how resources are being utilized and identify opportunities to right-size or decommission unused resources. For example, ensure that virtual machines are correctly sized to match workloads, and consider implementing auto-scaling to ensure that resources are provisioned dynamically based on demand. Additionally, review storage costs regularly; sometimes, large volumes of unused or cold data are sitting in expensive tiers when they could be moved to more cost-efficient storage solutions.

- **Employ multi-cloud cost management tools**: In a multi-cloud environment, monitoring costs across multiple platforms can become complex. Relying on disparate cost-tracking methods from each provider can lead to confusion and inefficiency. To simplify this, invest in multi-cloud cost management tools that aggregate data from all providers into a single dashboard. These tools provide a unified view of cloud spending, making it easier to manage costs holistically. They also facilitate comparisons between cloud providers, enabling teams to identify cost-saving opportunities or optimize workload distribution.

- **Use Reserved and Spot Instances wisely**: Cloud providers offer various pricing models to accommodate different usage patterns. For workloads with predictable demand, consider using Reserved Instances or Savings Plans, which can significantly reduce costs compared to on-demand pricing. Conversely, for workloads that are flexible or non-time-critical, using Spot Instances (or preemptible instances) can offer substantial savings. Regularly monitor these opportunities and balance them against your operational needs to maximize cost efficiency.

- **Conduct regular forecasting and budgeting exercises**: Monitoring cloud costs in real-time is essential, but it must be paired with long-term financial planning. Develop a culture of regular forecasting and budgeting, ensuring that your cloud spend aligns with the organization's overall financial goals. This helps prevent budget overruns and provides a framework for making strategic decisions about resource allocation. Use historical data, business forecasts, and seasonality trends to anticipate future cloud spending. Tie these forecasts back to your monitoring practices so you can adjust them if actual usage deviates from predictions.

- **Monitor for cost anomalies and fraud**: With multiple teams accessing cloud resources, there is always a risk of unauthorized usage or fraud. Cost anomalies may arise from unapproved projects, misconfigurations, or even malicious behavior. Monitoring cost anomalies is crucial to safeguard against financial risks. Implement machine learning-powered tools that detect abnormal usage patterns, unauthorized access, or unusual spikes in cloud consumption. This helps mitigate risks early and allows for rapid response before costs escalate beyond control.

- **Foster a culture of cost awareness**: Beyond the technical tools and processes, one of the most effective practices for cloud cost monitoring is fostering a culture of cost awareness across the organization. Cloud spending should not be seen as solely the responsibility of the finance department. Engineering, operations, and leadership teams must all be engaged in cost management efforts. Provide training on cloud cost monitoring tools, encourage accountability, and make cost efficiency a key performance metric across teams. When everyone in the organization understands the importance of cloud cost management, they are more likely to take proactive steps to manage and optimize their usage.

- **Focus on performance versus cost trade-offs**: Cloud cost monitoring is not just about cutting expenses; it is about ensuring value for money. Sometimes, the cheapest option may not deliver the performance needed for critical applications. Conversely, high-performance options may be overkill for less mission-critical workloads. Cloud monitoring tools can provide valuable insights into these trade-offs, enabling teams to strike the optimal balance between cost and performance.

Regularly assess workloads to ensure that they are running on the most cost-efficient services without compromising on quality or service levels.

Implementing cloud cost monitoring is an ongoing journey, one that requires constant vigilance, collaboration, and a proactive approach to optimization. By adopting these best practices, organizations can ensure that they maintain tight control over cloud expenditures while continuing to drive innovation and value from their cloud investments. With real-time insights, automation, and a culture of accountability, businesses can transform cloud cost management into a strategic advantage.

Multi-cloud cost measuring

In today's complex multi-cloud environments, *what gets measured gets managed*. While many organizations focus on monitoring cloud usage, the real value lies in measuring it with precision. Measuring is not merely about knowing you are spending money; it is about understanding *how*, *where*, and *why* you are spending it. This insight lays the foundation for strategic decisions, accountability, and optimization, ensuring that every dollar spent aligns with business objectives and drives value.

Power of granular cost measurement

Granular cost measurement is the cornerstone of effective multi-cloud FinOps. Unlike surface-level tracking, granular visibility enables organizations to dive deep into their cloud expenditures. By dissecting costs at the department, project, or application level, organizations can uncover inefficiencies, identify waste, and make informed decisions. This approach shifts the narrative from *We are spending too much on cloud* to *Here is exactly where our money is going and how we can optimize it*.

Imagine your cloud expenditure as a complex jigsaw puzzle. Without granular visibility, you are left staring at a blurry picture, unable to see the details that make up the whole. Granular measurement sharpens this picture, providing clarity on which teams or applications are consuming resources and whether those resources are truly necessary. For example, a detailed breakdown might reveal that one department's overprovisioned virtual machines are driving up costs, or that an application's inefficient architecture is causing unnecessary data transfers.

Measuring unit economics

Beyond granular visibility, unit economics offers a lens to evaluate cloud spending in terms of value. Unit economics measures the cost of delivering a single unit of a product or service, whether it is a user session, a transaction, or a gigabyte of storage. This metric provides a tangible way to tie cloud expenditures to business outcomes, ensuring that the investment in cloud resources is justified by the value they deliver.

For instance, understanding the unit economics of an e-commerce application might involve calculating the cloud cost per customer transaction. If the cost is disproportionately high, it signals inefficiencies that need addressing, perhaps through resource optimization or workload migration to a more cost-effective cloud provider. By measuring unit economics, organizations can benchmark their performance, set cost efficiency targets, and make data-driven decisions that boost profitability.

Strategic insights through measuring

Granular cost measurement and unit economics unlock actionable insights that drive smarter decisions:

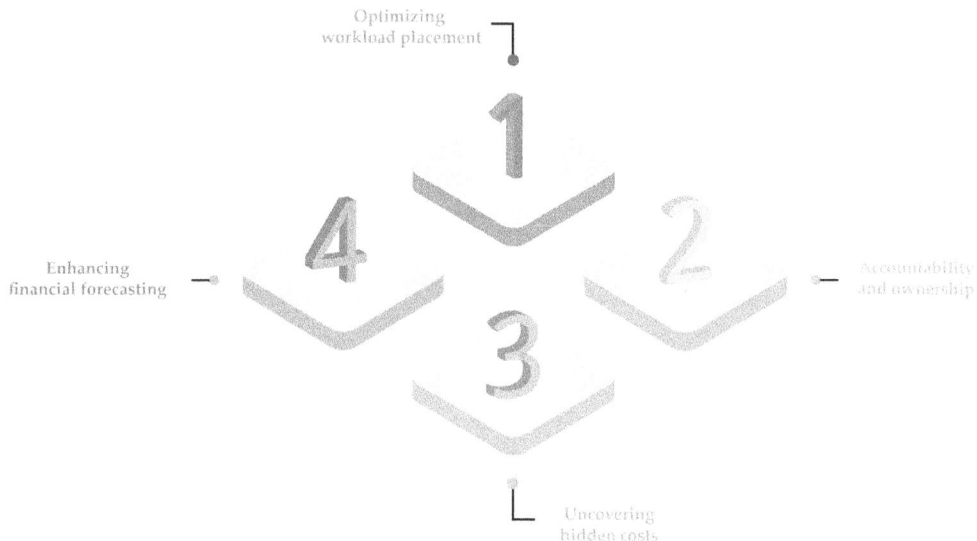

Figure 10.1: Strategic insights through measuring cloud environment

Let us look at the details for the insights mentioned in the preceding figure:

- **Optimizing workload placement**: Not all workloads are created equal. Some demand the scalability and flexibility of on-demand instances, while others can thrive on the cost-efficiency of Reserved Instances or spot pricing. By measuring costs at a granular level, organizations can identify which workloads to prioritize for cost-saving measures. For example, seasonal applications might benefit from Spot Instances, while mission-critical workloads may require reserved capacity to balance cost and performance.

- **Accountability and ownership**: Detailed measurement ensures accountability across teams and departments. When each unit is measured for its specific cloud usage and costs, it is easier to assign ownership and hold teams responsible for their spending. This fosters a culture of cost consciousness, encouraging teams to actively participate in cost-saving initiatives.

- **Uncovering hidden costs**: Multi-cloud environments often mask hidden costs, such as data transfer fees, idle resources, or misconfigured services. Granular measurement shines a light on these inefficiencies, allowing organizations to eliminate waste and optimize their cloud strategies.

- **Enhancing financial forecasting**: Accurate measurement feeds directly into better financial forecasting. With granular data, organizations can predict future spending more reliably, allocate budgets effectively, and align cloud investments with business goals. This prevents surprises and ensures that cloud costs remain predictable and manageable.

Challenges in measuring multi-cloud costs

Measuring in a multi-cloud environment comes with its own set of challenges, such as:

- **Data fragmentation**: Each cloud provider offers its own billing structures, metrics, and reporting tools. Consolidating this data into a single source of truth requires advanced tools and standardized processes.

- **Complexity of cost structures**: Multi-cloud environments involve diverse pricing models, such as, on-demand, Reserved, Spot Instances, making it difficult to compare costs across platforms without granular measurement.

- **Resource tagging inconsistencies**: Measuring costs at the application or department level often relies on consistent tagging. Without a standardized tagging policy, it is nearly impossible to achieve accurate measurements.

Overcoming these challenges requires a strategic mindset. Organizations must invest in platforms like Heeddata that provide unified visibility across multi-cloud environments and foster collaboration between finance, engineering, and operations teams to ensure accurate measurement.

Role of automation in measuring costs

Data is not the new oil—it is the new soil. Measuring cloud costs enriches this soil, enabling organizations to grow smarter, leaner, and more competitive in the digital age. With the right tools, processes, and mindset, organizations can transform cost measurement from a reactive chore into a proactive strategy for success.

With the sheer volume of data generated in multi-cloud environments, manual measurement is both impractical and error-prone. Advanced automation tools can aggregate cost data from multiple providers, apply business-specific tags, and generate real-time reports. These tools also facilitate anomaly detection, alerting teams to irregular spending patterns before they escalate into budget crises.

For example, automated measurement tools can identify unused or underutilized resources, calculate cost-per-unit metrics, and even recommend optimization strategies.

By automating these processes, organizations can focus their energy on strategic decision-making rather than administrative tasks.

True success in multi-cloud FinOps requires more than tools and processes; it demands a cultural shift toward measurement-driven decision-making. Leaders must emphasize the importance of granular visibility and unit economics, ensuring that every team understands its role in managing cloud costs effectively. Regular training, transparent reporting, and clear communication of goals can foster a culture where measurement is not just a task but a mindset.

Measuring multi-cloud costs is not about getting lost in numbers; it is about turning those numbers into actionable strategies. Granular visibility and unit economics provide the clarity needed to optimize spending, enhance accountability, and drive value from cloud investments.

Multi-cloud cost reporting

In the world of multi-cloud FinOps, reporting serves as the bridge between raw data and actionable strategy. While monitoring and measuring cloud costs provide the foundation, cost reporting elevates these efforts by translating complex data into clear, meaningful narratives that guide decision-making. It is not just about listing where money is spent; it is about uncovering patterns, identifying inefficiencies, and charting a course for optimization. Reporting transforms cloud usage data into a strategic compass, enabling organizations to steer their cloud investments with precision and confidence.

Importance of reporting in multi-cloud FinOps

Reporting is where strategy meets insight. In the absence of effective reporting, even the most comprehensive monitoring efforts can lose their value. Decision-makers need more than a deluge of metrics; they need context, clarity, and actionable insights. A robust reporting framework ensures that cloud cost data is presented in a way that drives informed decisions at every level of the organization, from engineering teams to the C-suite. Let us go over the following now:

- **Clarity in complexity**: The multi-cloud landscape is inherently complex, with different providers offering varied billing models, pricing structures, and usage metrics. Reporting simplifies this complexity by consolidating data from all platforms into a unified narrative.

- **Actionable insights**: Effective reporting does not just highlight how much you are spending; it reveals why and how those costs are incurred. It identifies areas of inefficiency, potential savings opportunities, and trends that might otherwise go unnoticed.

- **Enabling strategic decision-making**: With the right reports, organizations can balance short-term actions, like reducing waste, with long-term strategies, such as reallocating workloads to more cost-efficient platforms.

Best practices for multi-cloud cost reporting

To ensure that cost reporting is impactful, organizations should adhere to the following best practices:

- **Customize for stakeholders**: Reporting is not one-size-fits-all. Engineers, financial analysts, and executives have different priorities and need reports tailored to their unique perspectives. While an engineering team might need granular cost breakdowns by application, executives may prefer high-level dashboards showing overall spend and ROI.

- **Utilize real-time data**: Cloud costs can fluctuate rapidly, making real-time reporting crucial for staying current. By leveraging automated reporting tools that update continuously, organizations can respond to changes proactively instead of retroactively.

- **Focus on trends, not just on snapshots**: Static reports provide a momentary glimpse but fail to show the bigger picture. Reports should emphasize trends over time, whether it is seasonal cost spikes, gradual increases in data transfer fees, or improvements in cost optimization efforts.

- **Incorporate anomaly detection**: An effective reporting framework includes mechanisms for identifying anomalies. Sudden cost surges, unexpected resource usage, or deviations from forecasted budgets should trigger alerts, ensuring rapid response to potential issues.

- **Integrate cost attribution and benchmarking**: Reports should clearly show which teams, projects, or departments are responsible for specific costs. This fosters accountability and enables benchmarking against industry standards or organizational goals.

- **Simplify visualizations**: Reports are most impactful when they present data visually. Clear charts, graphs, and dashboards make it easier to understand trends and patterns briefly, empowering quicker decision-making.

Use cases for multi-cloud cost reporting

The following *Table 10.1* features some use cases and their impacts:

Cost reporting aspects	Use case	Impact
Resource optimization	An organization with applications running on multiple clouds can use reports to identify underutilized virtual machines or storage instances. For example, a report might highlight a server with less than 10% utilization, prompting the team to downsize or decommission it.	Reduces waste and ensure that resources are aligned with actual business needs.

Cost reporting aspects	Use case	Impact
Budget tracking and adherence	A financial team receives weekly reports that show spending by department and the variance from the budget. If one department is consistently overspending, the report provides the data needed to investigate and rectify the issue.	Prevent budget overruns and ensure financial accountability across the organization.
Migration planning	A cost report reveals that data transfer fees between two clouds are significantly higher than anticipated. Based on this data, the organization decides to migrate interconnected workloads to the same provider to reduce costs.	Enable smarter workload placement and minimize unnecessary expenditures.
Long-term trend analysis	Over a year, an executive-level report shows a consistent upward trend in cloud spending despite efforts to optimize. The trend analysis reveals that increased demand during product launches is the primary driver. This insight prompts the organization to explore Reserved Instances for predictable demand periods.	Strategic changes reduce long-term costs while maintaining performance.
Compliance and governance	A compliance report consolidates data on cloud usage, spending, and tagging adherence, ensuring the organization meets governance standards. Any deviations from policies, such as untagged resources, are flagged for correction.	Mitigate compliance risks and avoid potential penalties or reputational damage.

Table 10.1: Use cases for multi-cloud cost reporting

Challenges in multi-cloud cost reporting

Despite its importance, reporting in a multi-cloud environment comes with hurdles:

- **Data silos**: Consolidating data from multiple cloud providers, each with its own format, can be a logistical nightmare.

- **Overwhelming volume**: With vast amounts of cloud data generated daily, distilling it into meaningful insights requires sophisticated tools and processes.

- **Inconsistent tagging**: Reports rely on consistent tagging across platforms. Without standardization, it is challenging to attribute costs accurately or gain a holistic view.

Organizations must tackle these challenges head-on, leveraging automation, standardized processes, and cross-functional collaboration to build effective reporting frameworks.

Turning reports into results

As the saying goes, Knowledge is power, but applied knowledge is transformation. With robust reporting practices, organizations can not only understand their cloud costs but actively shape their cloud strategy, ensuring that every dollar invested delivers maximum value. When done right, reporting becomes the backbone of informed decision-making and the catalyst for continuous improvement in multi-cloud environments.

In the realm of multi-cloud FinOps, reporting is more than a back-office function; it is a strategic enabler. By translating raw cloud usage data into actionable insights, reports empower organizations to optimize their resources, align spending with business goals, and build a culture of financial accountability.

Conclusion

The ability to monitor, measure, and report cloud costs and savings is both an operational necessity and a strategic imperative. These processes collectively form the foundation upon which financial accountability, cost optimization, and long-term cloud success are built. Without them, organizations risk navigating the turbulent waters of cloud expenditure blindfolded, leaving their investments at the mercy of inefficiencies, misaligned priorities, and unforeseen financial pitfalls. Monitoring ensures visibility, measurement provides actionable insights, and reporting translates those insights into clear directives that guide both immediate actions and strategic decisions.

When implemented effectively, these practices empower organizations to not only identify inefficiencies and cost overruns but also capitalize on optimization opportunities that might otherwise remain hidden. They foster a culture of accountability, where every team, project, or department takes ownership of their cloud spend, aligning resource usage with business objectives.

More importantly, they enable businesses to anticipate future challenges, adapt to dynamic workloads, and make data-driven decisions that ensure sustainable growth. Multi-cloud FinOps is not merely about managing costs; it is about harnessing the power of data to transform how organizations operate, innovate, and compete in a cloud-centric world.

By embracing robust monitoring, precise measurement, and insightful reporting, businesses gain the clarity and control needed to steer their cloud journey with confidence. These practices not only mitigate risks but also unlock opportunities, driving value creation at every turn. In a world where agility and efficiency define success, the organizations that excel in mastering their cloud costs will not only survive but they will thrive, setting benchmarks for innovation, scalability, and financial discipline in the multi-cloud era.

Join our Discord space

Join our Discord workspace for latest updates, offers, tech happenings around the world, new releases, and sessions with the authors:

https://discord.bpbonline.com

CHAPTER 11
Cloud Security, Governance, and Compliance

Introduction

As enterprises scale their cloud adoption across multiple platforms, the need for robust cloud security, governance, and compliance has never been more critical. In an era where cloud FinOps drives efficiency and cost optimization, security remains the cornerstone of trust, resilience, and financial sustainability. A secure cloud environment not only protects business-critical assets but also ensures compliance with evolving regulatory frameworks while keeping FinOps initiatives aligned with financial and operational objectives.

Cloud security

Cloud security serves as the first line of defense against cyber threats, data breaches, and financial risks within an organization's cloud ecosystem. Unlike traditional on-premises security, cloud security requires a dynamic approach, one that adapts to shared responsibility models, evolving attack vectors, and regulatory requirements across AWS, Azure, GCP, and hybrid environments.

With data, applications, and workloads distributed across multiple clouds, security concerns expand beyond perimeter defenses to **identity and access management (IAM)**, encryption, workload security, compliance auditing, and real-time threat detection. As businesses transition to a cloud-first model, implementing a security-by-design approach ensures that security vulnerabilities do not compromise financial and operational efficiencies in FinOps.

Principles of cloud security

Cloud security is built on fundamental principles that establish a resilient, scalable, and cost-effective security framework. The following six guiding principles lay the foundation for securing cloud environments:

- **Shared responsibility model**: Every cloud provider follows a shared security model, where the provider secures the underlying infrastructure, while organizations are responsible for securing applications, data, and user access. Misconfigurations due to a misunderstanding of this model are one of the leading causes of security breaches in the cloud.

- **Zero Trust Architecture (ZTA)**: The traditional *trust but verify* approach is no longer viable in multi-cloud environments. Zero Trust Security operates on the principle of *never trust, always verify*, which requires strict authentication, least-privileged access controls, and continuous monitoring.

- **Data protection and encryption**: Data is the lifeblood of cloud computing, making encryption, tokenization, and access controls essential for securing sensitive information. Organizations must encrypt data at rest, in transit, and in use while enforcing **data loss prevention** (**DLP**) policies.

- **Identity and access management (IAM)**: IAM ensures that only authorized users and services can access cloud resources. Implementing **role-based access control** (**RBAC**), **multi-factor authentication** (**MFA**), and just-in-time access provisioning minimizes the risk of privilege escalation attacks.

- **Continuous monitoring and threat detection**: Cloud environments demand real-time visibility into security threats and anomalies. Security teams should leverage **Security Information and Event Management** (**SIEM**) tools, AI-driven threat detection, and cloud-native monitoring solutions to proactively detect and mitigate security risks.

- **Compliance and regulatory alignment**: Regulatory compliance is non-negotiable for cloud security. Organizations must ensure adherence to industry-specific frameworks like GDPR, HIPAA, PCI-DSS, and SOC 2, integrating security controls into FinOps processes to maintain regulatory alignment while optimizing costs.

Cloud security architecture considerations

We have seen many organizations that fail to develop a future-proof security architecture because designing a cloud security architecture is not a one-size-fits-all approach. Depending on the enterprise's operating methods, it must consider the unique risks, compliance requirements, and operational needs of a multi-cloud ecosystem. Hence, we have identified the following architectural elements that are crucial for robust security:

- **Multi-layered security model**: A defense-in-depth strategy ensures that security is not reliant on a single layer but is distributed across multiple controls, including:

o **Network security**: Firewalls, **Virtual Private Clouds (VPC)**, **intrusion detection/prevention systems (IDS/IPS)**.

o **Application security**: API gateways, secure coding practices, DevSecOps integration.

o **Data security**: End-to-end encryption, backup and recovery strategies, access policies.

- **Secure DevOps (DevSecOps)**: Security must be embedded from code to deployment. Shift-left security integrates security checks early in the **software development lifecycle (SDLC)**, preventing misconfigurations before they reach production.

- **Cloud-native security solutions**: Public cloud providers offer built-in security tools, such as:

o AWS Security Hub, Azure Security Center, and Google Security Command Center for compliance management.

o Cloud-native **Web Application Firewalls (WAF)** to mitigate DDoS attacks.

o Identity and key management solutions for enforcing least-privilege access.

- **Automated security remediation**: Automation reduces human error and strengthens security posture. Tools like **Cloud Security Posture Management (CSPM)** and **Cloud Workload Protection Platforms (CWPP)** automate threat detection and remediation.

Role of cloud security in FinOps

Many organizations consider security as an integral pillar of FinOps success, and when security lapses arise, financial consequences are no exception. Breaches, compliance failures, and downtime can lead to crippling fines, revenue loss, and reputational damage. Here is why cloud security is indispensable to FinOps:

- **Security breaches lead to uncontrolled costs**: A data breach or ransomware attack can incur millions in damages, including regulatory fines, legal fees, and reputational losses. Effective cloud security mitigates financial exposure by preventing security incidents before they escalate.

- **Compliance violations impact cost governance**: Organizations that fail to comply with data privacy laws, such as GDPR, HIPAA, and SOC 2, face substantial penalties. Embedding security within FinOps ensures that cost governance aligns with compliance requirements, preventing financial and legal setbacks.

- **Secure cost optimization without compromise**: FinOps teams often focus on reducing cloud costs, but security cannot be sacrificed in the process. Secure cost optimization ensures that:

o　Cloud resources are right-sized without exposing workloads to vulnerabilities.

o　Reserved Instances are managed securely to prevent unauthorized access.

o　Cost-saving automation does not create security blind spots.

- **Real-time security monitoring for financial insights**: Security monitoring tools provide real-time visibility into cloud usage patterns, which also aids in FinOps cost tracking. By analyzing anomalous activity, shadow IT expenses, and unexpected data transfers, organizations can prevent both security threats and cost overruns.

- **Role of AI-driven security in FinOps**: **Artificial intelligence** (**AI**) plays a dual role in cloud security and FinOps by:

o　Identifying cost inefficiencies through intelligent security log analysis.

o　Detecting fraudulent cloud activities that could result in financial loss.

o　Enhancing proactive governance by predicting security and cost anomalies.

Aligning security, governance, and FinOps

In the multi-cloud era, security and FinOps are not competing priorities; they are two sides of the same coin. Organizations that embed security best practices into their FinOps strategy will fortify their cloud infrastructure against evolving cyber threats.

By ensuring proactive risk management, automated compliance enforcement, and secure cost optimization, enterprises can drive sustainable growth while safeguarding their cloud investments. In the world of FinOps, security becomes a strategic advantage.

Cloud governance

Great governance with best methods is the hallmark of FinOps centralized enterprises. Driving the implementation with integrity is our core passion.

The dynamic nature of cloud environments and their most promising benefits have unlocked the potential for many industries and enterprises by bringing digital and business transformations along with empowering innovation and scalability. As third-party vendors are involved in managing cloud environments alongside in-house teams, unexpected complexities arise, demanding a fine-tuned management approach. For industries based on geopolitical standards, they must align to those regulations so that their operations remain smooth and flexible. This is where cloud governance expands its reach to encompass all the complexities and guides cloud operations smoothly.

Cloud governance is defined as the set of rules, policies, and frameworks designed and implemented to enhance system integration, data security, and proper management of cloud deployments. The need for balancing resource utilization and risk management along with accountability increases the spin; cloud governance strategy drives organizations to manage all these aspects efficiently. Gauging the challenges due to the dynamic nature of cloud environments and cloud decentralization demands cloud governance, which is an ability for enterprises to rely on. If the robustness of cloud governance is compromised, organizations face risks such as poor integration of cloud infrastructure, misaligned business goals, and potential security vulnerabilities.

Importance of cloud governance

Cloud is known for offering extreme flexibility and scalability for enterprises and hybrid cloud models extend their support for enterprises in driving these aspects. When the cloud is decentralized, IT teams face a new set of complexities in managing these resources, and cloud computing traps the enterprises into infrastructure and resource limitations, increasing costs with an increase in resource usage, greater security risks, and ineffective policies. Therefore, a governance framework with stringent processes for enforcement and monitoring drives most of the cloud operations, aligning with business requirements. A standard and comprehensive cloud governance strategy is needed because of the following reasons:

- **Optimizes management of cloud resources**: Cloud governance slices the cloud systems into individual accounts referring to departments, projects, or cost centers within the organization, which is indeed a best practice recommended by many cloud experts and providers. This type of segregating cloud workloads into individual components can enhance cost control and visibility.

- **Downsizes shadow IT**: Many organizations are unaware of information about the existence of systems and data, and employees immediately shift their heads to shadowed IT systems when they do not receive an instant response from traditional systems. This problem can be addressed through effective cloud governance. Employees have the flexibility to request cloud resources securely, enabling enterprises to control and see through clearly. Rather than shadow IT, employees can have access to cloud systems, pertaining to compliance standards and aligning within budgets.

- **Scale down administrative overhead**: Manual processes run in the organizations for tracking cloud accounts, accrued costs, compliance issues, or while handling access controls, and budget planning, which is inefficient, error-led, and collapses at large scale. When cloud governance falls in place, policies become centralized, and most of these aspects can be automated, reducing manual efforts and saving time.

- **Resolves cloud security challenges**: Through governing the cloud, one can drive an authentication strategy to secure confidentiality, integrity, and availability. Regardless of where the data resides, organizations will have complete control over critical deployments while ensuring security sophistication.

- **Safeguards against vendor lock-ins**: Organizations often depend on vendors for their cloud purchases and capabilities. However, establishing the governance model expands the cloud environment bringing freedom to the organization.

- **Promotes data portability and interoperability**: Connecting with other apps, products, and software is a crucial component of a cloud environment, and that is what governance leads to, decreasing the impact of chaos in the cloud due to inefficient system designs.

- **Enables business continuity**: All the business units are visible to drive action plans and plan forehead in case of downtimes or data breaches.

- **Increase compliance with policies and standards**: Organizations will tend to follow applicable regulations along with stringent compliance monitoring that improves operational effectiveness, eliminates bottlenecks, and simplified management processes.

Governing the cloud effectively

Governing the cloud is a continuous process that demands relentless monitoring, evaluation, and adjustments as they must cope with new, cutting-edge technologies, risks, and compliance standards. However, the **Cloud Adoption Framework** (**CAF**) segregates the cloud governance into the following five steps:

1. **Governance team**: Build a potential team that can define and maintain the cloud governance policies while reporting on the overall functioning of cloud governance.

2. **Cloud risk assessment**: The use of the cloud always wakes up the underlying potential risks. Evaluate and prioritize them through a unique risk assessment that includes regulatory compliance, security, cost, data, operations, AI, and resource management.

3. **Document policies**: Set the rules and guidelines, that is, the cloud governance policies on cloud usage as they will minimize the identified risks.

4. **Implement policies**: Bring cloud governance policies and compliance in action with the help of automated tools or manual processes. The goal is to ensure that cloud resource usage aligns with the defined cloud governance policies.

5. **Continuous monitoring.** Monitor cloud usage across the enterprise and identify the teams responsible for governance to ensure they are compliant with cloud governance policies.

Cloud governance checklist

Crafting an effective cloud governance framework is a task that requires both strategic insight and operational rigor. Much like the foundation of a towering structure, a governance framework must be meticulously planned and firmly grounded in key principles. Before diving headfirst into its design, having a comprehensive checklist is indispensable. The checklist, as depicted in *Table 11.1*, serves as a compass, ensuring that every aspect of cloud governance aligns with organizational goals, financial discipline, and compliance requirements:

Cloud governance aspect	Tasks	Functions
Cloud governance team	Define functions	<ul><li>Engaging stakeholders</li><li>Cloud risk assessment</li><li>Develop and update governance policies</li><li>Review</li></ul>
	Define the authority of the teams selected	<ul><li>Align cloud governance with business goals</li><li>Define authority levels</li><li>Communicate authority across teams</li></ul>
	Define the scope	<ul><li>Establish cross-collaboration</li><li>Use a **Responsibility, Accountability, Consulted, and Informed (RACI)** matrix</li></ul>
Assessing cloud risks	**Identify risks:** <ul><li>Regulatory compliance risks</li><li>Security risks</li><li>Cost risks</li><li>Operation risks</li><li>Data risks</li><li>Resource management risks</li><li>AI risks</li></ul>	1. List all the cloud assets 2. Find cloud risks 3. Loop key stakeholders 4. Validate risks
	Analyze cloud risks: Define qualitative and quantitative ranking to each risk and prioritize them by severity.	**Evaluate probability of risks:** <ul><li>Use common benchmarks</li><li>Scan historical data</li><li>Assess the effectiveness of risk-mitigation controls</li></ul>**Determination of risk impact:** <ul><li>Perform financial analysis</li><li>Reputational impact assessment</li><li>Analyze operational disruption</li><li>Consider legal implications</li></ul>**Calculate priority of risks:** Define probability vs impact matrix for qualitative and quantitative assessments **Risk level assessment:** Categorize the risks into major (Level 1), Subrisks (Level 2), and Risk Drivers (level 3)

Cloud governance aspect	Tasks	Functions
Assessing cloud risks	Strategize and standardize risk management across the enterprise	Every risk has its own set of resolving options, including avoidance, mitigation, transfer, or acceptance • Authorize risk owners • Document possible cloud risks • Review them with the help of regular assessments
Documentation of cloud governance	Defining the approach to standardize cloud governance	• Define a standard governance language • Identify the various scopes involved in governance • Evaluate the effects of governance in the larger scope
	Develop cloud governance policies	• **Policy ID** to uniquely define each policy • Define the **policy statement** that addresses identified risks • Match the policy with **risk ID** • Define the purpose of the policy • Define the scope of the policy • Define policy remediation strategies
	Distribute the policies across the enterprise	• Have a centralized repository for policies • Create a checklist of compliances
	Review cloud governance policies	• Drive feedback mechanisms • Consider event-based reviews • Conduct regular reviews • Embrace change control • Track inefficiencies

Cloud governance aspect	Tasks	Functions
Approach for integrating cloud governance policies	Enforce policies across the enterprise	• Drive governance accountability • Inheritance model adoption • Open the stage for implementation specifics • Monitor the policies • Have a small list of services • Implement a tagging and naming strategy
	Automate policies	• Begin with a minimal set of automated policies • Take the help of cloud governance tools • Integrate the policies when the right scope is identified • Set up policy enforcement aspects • Run policy as code • Develop custom solutions as per business needs
	Manual implementation of policies	• Define checklists • Conduct regular training sessions • Monitor manually
	Review policy enforcement	• Involve stakeholders to evaluate the enforcement mechanisms that align with business objectives and compliance requirements • Monitor the requirements continuously

Cloud governance aspect	Tasks	Functions
Monitoring cloud governance	Configuration involves security, cost management, operations, data, resource management, and AI governance	• Choose monitoring tools • Monitor manually when needed • Document monitoring solution • Centralize monitoring of governance • Work on top of a governance baseline • Audit the effectiveness of monitoring
	Alert configuration	• Alerting mechanisms for cloud-native • Thresholds for noncompliance • Send alerts about noncompliance information
	Remediation plan to address noncompliance events so that it corrects the deviations, minimizing risk and impact	• Have a remediation timeline • Remediate high-risk violations quickly • Create follow-ups on low-risk violations • Automate when possible • Update policies and enforcement mechanisms
	Audit governance regularly	• Internal auditing to assess compliance with governing policies • External auditing to validate compliance with regulatory and legal requirements based on the region you operate from

Table 11.1: Cloud governance checklist

Principles for effective multi-cloud management

Governance fosters financial discipline and operational efficiency in the realm of dynamic multi-cloud environments. It balances innovation and control while gearing up the accountability, transparency, and optimization. Among these, anomaly management, budgeting, forecasting, and tag policy management emerge as the critical pillars. Let us go over them now.

Anomaly management

Anomalies in cloud spending can often be the silent culprits that derail financial strategies. Whether it is a sudden spike in resource consumption or an unnoticed misconfiguration, these deviations can snowball into significant cost overruns. An effective anomaly management system acts as the organization's early warning mechanism, flagging irregularities in real-time.

Sophisticated monitoring tools equipped with machine learning capabilities can identify outliers and trigger alerts for immediate action. However, beyond technology, anomaly management requires a proactive mindset. Teams must establish clear protocols to investigate and resolve anomalies swiftly, ensuring that corrective actions are both timely and effective. By treating anomalies not as disruptions but as opportunities to refine governance, organizations foster a culture of continuous improvement.

Budgets

A well-structured budgeting process serves as the bedrock of cloud cost governance. Budgets are not just financial plans; they are strategic enablers that align cloud investments with business priorities. Establishing budgets at granular levels, by teams, projects, or applications, ensures accountability and empowers decision-makers to manage their resources with precision.

Dynamic cloud environments demand dynamic budgets. Organizations must regularly review and adjust budgets to reflect changes in business goals, market conditions, or workload demands. Additionally, integrating budget tracking with real-time monitoring tools provides a unified view of spending, enabling stakeholders to act decisively and avoid end-of-quarter surprises.

Forecasting

Forecasting is the art and science of predicting future cloud costs based on historical data and anticipated needs. It provides organizations with the foresight to prepare for upcoming expenditures, avoiding the financial shockwaves of unexpected demands. Effective forecasting combines robust data analytics with cross-functional collaboration, ensuring that predictions align with both technical realities and business ambitions.

Forecasting should never be a static exercise. Regular updates, driven by new insights and emerging trends, keep forecasts relevant and actionable. Moreover, organizations that embrace scenario planning can simulate various outcomes, equipping themselves with strategies to navigate uncertainties. In essence, forecasting transforms cloud cost governance from a reactive process into a proactive strategy.

Tag policy management

Tags are the unsung heroes of cloud governance, providing the metadata needed to categorize, track, and manage resources effectively. However, without a consistent and enforceable tag policy, the benefits of tagging can quickly unravel. Tag policy management involves defining standardized naming conventions and ensuring they are applied uniformly across all cloud platforms.

The power of tags lies in their versatility. They enable granular cost allocation, facilitate compliance audits, and enhance reporting accuracy. To maximize these benefits, organizations should adopt automated tagging tools that ensure adherence to policies and minimize the risk of human error. Regular audits of tagging practices can further enhance consistency, driving better outcomes across governance initiatives.

Cloud cost governance is more than a checklist of principles. It is a holistic approach to managing resources with intention and foresight. Anomaly management ensures no deviation goes unnoticed, budgets create a disciplined framework for spending, forecasting provides the strategic lens to anticipate the future, and tag policy management builds the foundation for accountability. Together, these principles empower organizations to govern their multi-cloud environments with confidence and clarity, turning challenges into opportunities for innovation and growth.

Key components in cloud governance framework

In the intricate maze of multi-cloud ecosystems, governance, compliance, and management take center stage, each intricately woven into the operational fabric to ensure efficiency, security, and accountability. To navigate this terrain effectively, organizations must adopt comprehensive strategies across asset management, data stewardship, financial oversight, operations handling, performance tuning, and security frameworks. Refer to the following figure:

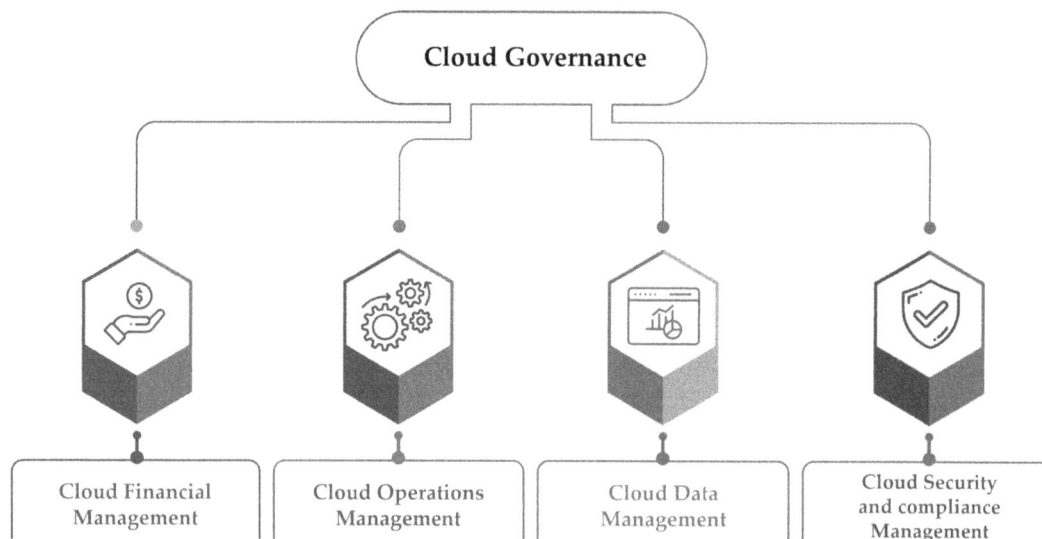

Figure 11.1: *Key components of cloud governance framework*

Let us now delve deeper into each dimension to see how they underpin operational excellence.

Achieving stability through asset and configuration management

Effective asset and configuration management is akin to having a well-oiled engine driving the cloud journey. Controlled processes for deploying clusters or utilizing cloud services provide a blueprint for operational consistency. These practices are pivotal for determining what applications and services to deploy in specific environments, ensuring every resource serves a defined purpose.

In an era of heightened sensitivity around data security, directives for managing sensitive information such as credentials and encryption keys are paramount. By maintaining tight control over how such assets are deployed and stored, organizations can mitigate risks and foster trust. After all, it is not just about what is deployed but ensuring it is done in a secure, efficient, and cost-effective manner. Let us go over the following now:

- **Data security**: Data is the currency of the digital economy, and managing it effectively is non-negotiable. With data access controls and policies, organizations establish guardrails that ensure only the right individuals have access to sensitive information. This is complemented by a lifecycle management strategy that oversees retention, archiving, and disposal, adhering to both operational needs and regulatory requirements. Data security measures, such as encryption and stringent access controls, serve as a fortress, while data quality assurance ensures that decisions are made on reliable and consistent information. Equally critical are the roles of data stewards, who champion the cause of data integrity and compliance. Their stewardship ensures that organizations do not just manage data but wield it as a strategic advantage.

- **Financial management where costs align with business goals**: In the realm of cloud financial management, every dollar counts, and transparency is the name of the game. From allocating and tracking costs to precise budgeting and forecasting, financial management serves as the bridge between cloud operations and business strategy. By keeping a keen eye on license management and cost optimization, organizations can eliminate unnecessary expenditures and ensure resources are utilized to their fullest potential. Resource utilization monitoring serves as an invaluable compass, providing actionable insights into how cloud investments are performing. It is about more than just saving costs; it is about maximizing value and aligning every expense with organizational objectives, ensuring financial resilience.

- **Seamlessly execute and run operations**: A well-structured operations management framework is the linchpin for successful multi-cloud deployment. Rules for creating new applications or workloads provide clarity, while robust monitoring, logging, and incident response mechanisms ensure that no issue slips through the cracks. Deployment processes, capacity planning, and resource allocation strategies further enhance operational readiness. These steps not only streamline workflows but also set the stage for scalability, ensuring that organizations can pivot and adapt as business demands evolve.

- **Turning metrics into mastery to manage performance**: Performance management is where operational metrics meet actionable insights. Monitoring application performance metrics, be it latency, user counts, or database transaction volumes, provides a real-time pulse on system health. Such monitoring is not merely diagnostic; it is strategic, enabling organizations to preempt potential issues and ensure seamless user experiences. By optimizing these metrics, organizations gain the agility to meet user demands without compromising performance. In the digital age, where milliseconds can define user satisfaction, performance management becomes a key differentiator.

- **Security and compliance management**: Security and compliance are no longer optional; they are foundational. From vulnerability testing to disaster recovery planning, these practices are designed to fortify the organization against threats while ensuring business continuity. Identity and access controls, encryption protocols, and compliance reporting form the backbone of a secure multi-cloud environment.

Privacy policies that align with evolving regulations are not just a regulatory checkbox but a commitment to users and stakeholders. Meanwhile, risk assessment and management ensure that organizations remain prepared for the unpredictable, turning potential vulnerabilities into areas of strength.

In the dynamic realm of multi-cloud ecosystems, a robust framework across these critical management areas is indispensable. It is not just about managing assets, data, or finances in silos; it is about creating a cohesive strategy that aligns all facets of cloud governance with organizational goals. When executed effectively, these practices enable organizations to fully leverage the cloud's potential, driving innovation while ensuring resilience, compliance, and strategic foresight.

Roadmap to implementing a comprehensive cloud governance framework

In most cases, a cloud governance framework is developed by using the existing IT practices, but in some instances, organizations unfold new developments, architected for the cloud. Implementing and monitoring this framework enables organizations to develop foresight and enable control over crucial cloud operations, including data security and management, risk management, legal procedures, cost management, and more, ensuring each of these aspects meets business goals.

Creating an effective cloud governance framework is not merely a box-ticking exercise; it is a strategic journey that requires foresight, collaboration, and adaptability. For industries of all types and sizes, establishing a governance framework is crucial for building a solid foundation that supports growth, aligns cloud operations with business objectives, and mitigates risks. Here is a detailed roadmap that serves as a blueprint for success:

1. **Define objectives and vision**: The first step in this journey is to clearly articulate the objectives that the governance framework aims to achieve. Whether the focus is on cost control, regulatory compliance, or operational efficiency, understanding the *why* behind the framework is paramount. This vision acts as the *North Star*, ensuring every subsequent decision aligns with the organization's broader goals. Engage stakeholders across departments to define these objectives collaboratively. From finance to IT and operations, each team brings valuable perspectives that help create a governance model that is holistic and robust. When objectives are shared and understood across the organization, the framework gains the buy-in and commitment needed for its successful implementation.

2. **Conduct a comprehensive cloud audit**: An effective framework is built on a clear understanding of the current state of cloud usage. Conduct a thorough audit of all cloud resources, spanning multiple providers, workloads, and environments. This audit should answer critical questions:

   a. What resources are currently in use?

   b. Are there underutilized or redundant resources?

   c. How are costs distributed across departments, teams, or projects?

   This exercise provides the data needed to design a governance structure tailored to the organization's unique cloud landscape. Moreover, it sets the stage for identifying inefficiencies and opportunities for optimization that the governance framework will address.

3. **Establish clear policies and standards**: At the heart of any governance framework lies a well-defined set of policies and standards. These rules establish the boundaries within which teams operate, ensuring consistency and compliance across the organization. Policies should cover critical areas such as:

   a. **Cost management**: Guidelines for budget creation, resource provisioning, and cost allocation.

   b. **Compliance**: Adherence to industry regulations and internal security protocols.

   c. **Tagging conventions**: Standardized naming and tagging to ensure accurate resource tracking and reporting.

   Avoid the pitfall of over-complicating policies; they should be stringent enough to provide structure yet flexible enough to adapt to changing business needs. Clear documentation and accessible communication channels ensure that these policies are understood and followed organization-wide.

4. **Implement governance tools and automation**: No governance framework can thrive on manual processes alone. Leverage governance tools and automation to streamline the enforcement of policies and improve operational efficiency. Tools should enable:

   a. Real-time monitoring of resource usage and costs.

   b. Automated alerts for anomalies or policy violations.

   c. Dashboards that provide granular visibility into cloud operations.

   Automation reduces human error and frees up valuable time for strategic tasks, turning governance into a proactive rather than reactive process.

5. **Foster collaboration and accountability**: Governance is not the responsibility of a single team; it is a shared endeavor that spans finance, IT, security, and operations. Create a structure that clearly defines roles and responsibilities, ensuring that every stakeholder understands their part in maintaining the governance framework. Encourage cross-functional collaboration through regular meetings, workshops, or dedicated FinOps committees. Accountability fosters a culture of ownership, where teams are motivated to adhere to governance principles not out of obligation, but because they see the value it delivers.

6. **Build metrics for continuous monitoring and improvement**: What gets measured gets managed. Establish **key performance indicators** (**KPI**) that reflect the effectiveness of the governance framework. Metrics might include:

   a. Percentage of resources tagged correctly.

   b. Cost savings are achieved through optimization efforts.

   c. Number of compliance violations detected and resolved.

   Regularly review these metrics to identify areas for improvement. Governance is not a one-time implementation, but an evolving process that should grow in tandem with the organization's needs.

7. **Communicate and train**: Even the most well-designed framework will falter without proper communication and training. Develop a robust training program that educates employees on governance policies, tools, and best practices. Use workshops, documentation, and e-learning modules to ensure everyone is equipped to contribute to the framework's success. Equally important is ongoing communication. Create channels where employees can provide feedback, report issues, or seek clarification about governance policies. This fosters an open dialogue that strengthens the framework's effectiveness.

8. **Scale and adapt**: As the organization grows, its cloud operations will inevitably become more complex. A successful governance framework is one that scales with this growth while remaining agile enough to adapt to new challenges and opportunities. Periodically review the framework to ensure it continues to align

with the organization's strategic goals. Incorporate feedback from stakeholders, embrace advancements in cloud technology, and stay ahead of regulatory changes. This iterative approach ensures that the governance framework remains a strategic enabler rather than a restrictive burden.

Implementing a cloud governance framework is not just about setting rules; it is about creating a culture of accountability, efficiency, and innovation. By following this roadmap, industries of all sizes can establish a governance structure that not only manages risk but also unlocks the full potential of cloud technology. With clarity, collaboration, and a commitment to continuous improvement, organizations can ensure that their cloud operations are not only controlled but also strategically aligned to drive long-term success.

Best practices for effective cloud governance

Implementing centralized monitoring tools is akin to placing a lighthouse in the vast sea of your cloud infrastructure. These tools provide interactive dashboards that illuminate key performance indicators, data correlation capabilities to connect the dots between disparate data points, and comprehensive activity logs to track every action. Security metrics collection ensures vulnerabilities are identified early, while automated severity-based alerting acts as a vigilant watchdog, alerting teams to potential breaches or inefficiencies.

By centralizing monitoring, organizations gain the foresight to proactively identify and resolve issues, streamline resource utilization, and ensure unwavering compliance with governance policies, that is, a trifecta of operational excellence. Let us go over the best practices now:

- **Automate workflows for precision and efficiency**: In the fast-paced realm of cloud governance, manual processes are a relic of the past. Automation is the backbone of efficiency and error reduction. By leveraging CI/CD pipelines, **infrastructure as code (IaC)**, configuration management tools, and orchestration platforms, organizations can automate repetitive workflows with precision. These practices not only save time but also fortify operational consistency, making governance tasks smoother and less prone to human error. Automation paves the way for scalability and agility, two critical pillars for navigating a dynamic multi-cloud environment.

- **Foster accountability with robust IAM**: Accountability is the cornerstone of a resilient cloud governance framework. Enforcing access controls ensures that only authorized individuals can access sensitive resources, reducing the risk of data breaches. Strengthen this foundation with robust IAM solutions and standardized provisioning processes to instill clarity and responsibility across teams. A culture of accountability empowers stakeholders to take ownership of their roles, creating an environment where governance becomes a shared responsibility rather than a top-down directive.

- **Dynamic governance through policy evolution**: Cloud governance is not a *set it and forget it* initiative; it requires continuous refinement. Regularly review and update governance policies to address emerging threats, vulnerabilities, and evolving regulatory landscapes. Treat your policies as a living document, adapting them to the ever-changing digital frontier. This proactive approach ensures compliance along with fortifying the organization's defenses against unforeseen risks.

- **Minimize external exposure with advanced security measures**: Reducing your attack surface is non-negotiable in a multi-cloud setup. Implement security measures such as VPC, firewalls, and intrusion detection/prevention systems to limit external exposure. These safeguards serve as barriers, ensuring that sensitive data and critical systems remain protected from external threats. A layered security approach, complemented by rigorous monitoring, creates a robust shield against cyberattacks, securing the integrity of cloud operations.

- **Building the future of cloud governance**: Incorporating these practices transforms cloud governance from a reactive necessity into a proactive advantage. Centralized monitoring, automation, accountability, education, dynamic policy management, and fortified security measures converge to create a governance framework that is not only robust but also future proof. By embedding these principles into their operational DNA, organizations can turn the complexities of multi-cloud management into a competitive edge, navigating the digital landscape with confidence and precision.

Enterprise-wide automation of cloud governance

Cloud environments scale rapidly beyond the manual control capabilities, and automation can be the game-changer that drives cloud governance efficiency. However, there are many solutions where they automate a specific set of processes, such as infrastructure provisioning, cloud security, compliance, network management, workload management, and more, but managing all these together is a complex job, and all the enterprises will be left with are inconsistencies and redundancies.

A unified multi-cloud governance automation platform like Heeddata adjoins these elements, allowing IT teams to implement the governance approach across their cloud environments. Here, IT teams can have consistency over monitoring and controlling every aspect of cloud usage and strategy. Hence, automation with tools allows organizations to:

- Accurately understand cloud usage to plan investments and budgets in best ways possible.

- Schedule workflows for continuous cloud auditing and gain granular visibility into current infrastructure and usage, so that automation can optimize most of these workflows.

- Automate the implementation of governance policies at scale, along with enforcement actions and resource allocation across clouds.

- Create, manage, and enforce backend policies for securing business operations.

Unraveling the intricacies of cloud cost management

Cloud costs are constantly shifting, and decision-making is often decentralized in large organizations, making visibility into expenses difficult. Rapid scalability is one of cloud computing's major strengths, but it also makes it easy for IT staff to spin up services without considering the cost. Implementing a cloud cost management strategy can help an organization plan for future costs and consumption.

For companies that use multi-cloud combinations, it is also important to practice effective multi-cloud cost management that takes the costs of several different public cloud providers into account. With a better understanding of costs and usage, a business can more effectively enforce accountability across the company and improve the performance and efficiency of its cloud technology.

Cloud spending is increasing, and a lack of insight into costs can have considerable financial consequences. The potential results of a lack of proper cloud cost management can include an unexpected spike in costs, overpaying for unused resources, or even inadequate performance.

Strategies for multi-cloud cost management

In the era of multi-cloud adoption, managing cloud costs is not merely about crunching numbers; it is about cultivating clarity, control, and confidence in how resources are used and optimized. Enterprises are increasingly realizing the importance of implementing well-defined strategies to navigate the complexities of cloud expenses. Let us delve into three critical strategies that can transform how organizations manage their cloud investments.

Single pane of visibility

The phrase *single pane of glass* perfectly encapsulates the goal of a unified dashboard that consolidates data across multiple clouds and platforms. In today's sprawling IT landscapes, achieving visibility is like trying to see the forest for the trees. With each cloud provider offering its own set of tools, enterprises often end up with fragmented data and siloed insights.

A single pane of visibility brings everything together; offering a centralized view of usage, costs, performance, and compliance metrics. It serves as the nerve center for cloud operations, empowering businesses to:

- **Identify inefficiencies**: Quickly spot underutilized or idle resources.
- **Track spending trends**: Monitor costs by team, project, or geography.
- **Enhance governance**: Enforce policies and ensure compliance across the board.

Moreover, it enables real-time decision-making, equipping leaders to respond to anomalies or cost spikes with agility. When all your data is at your fingertips, you gain the ability to steer your cloud strategy with precision.

Handling multicurrency at the organizational level

In today's interconnected world, businesses often operate across borders, leveraging cloud services in multiple regions. This introduces a unique challenge: managing costs in multiple currencies. Without a robust strategy, fluctuating exchange rates and localized pricing models can muddle financial planning and distort budget forecasts.

A well-structured multicurrency approach allows organizations to:

- **Simplify financial reporting**: Consolidate expenses into a single currency for consistent reporting.

- **Mitigate exchange rate risks**: Use forward contracts or hedging strategies to stabilize costs.

- **Optimize regional costs**: Take advantage of region-specific discounts and pricing.

By centralizing multicurrency management at the organizational level, businesses can ensure transparency and fairness in cost allocation across teams or departments. This approach also helps maintain budget discipline while supporting global growth initiatives.

Granularity at the resource level

When it comes to cloud cost management, granularity is your greatest ally. Knowing how much a project costs is not enough; organizations need to drill down to the individual resource level to truly understand where their money is going.

Granularity means having the tools and processes to:

- **Break down costs**: Attribute expenses to specific virtual machines, storage buckets, or network traffic.

- **Pinpoint inefficiencies**: Identify over-provisioned resources or unnecessary services.

- **Support chargebacks**: Enable accurate cost allocation to business units or teams.

This level of detail is essential for fostering accountability and driving informed decision-making. For example, understanding the cost of a particular workload or application allows teams to fine-tune configurations, implement right-sizing practices, or adopt cost-saving measures like Reserved Instances.

Granularity also plays a pivotal role in aligning IT spending with business outcomes, ensuring that every dollar contributes to organizational goals rather than being lost in the shuffle.

Strategic benefits of combining these approaches

While each strategy offers unique advantages, their true power lies in integration. A single pane of visibility provides the oversight needed to manage costs effectively across regions, while multicurrency handling ensures global operations do not derail budgets. Granularity at the resource level complements both, offering actionable insights that fuel optimization.

Together, these strategies form a holistic framework for cloud cost governance, helping enterprises:

- **Stay competitive**: By minimizing waste and maximizing efficiency.

- **Drive accountability**: Empowering teams to take ownership of their spending.

- **Future-proof operations**: Building resilience against market volatility and cost fluctuations.

The other common ground strategies include:

- **Right-sizing**: Ensure that the public cloud instances you choose are the right fit for your organization's needs.

- **Automatic scaling**: This allows organizations to scale up resources when needed and scale down the rest of the time, rather than planning for maximum utilization at all times (which can be needlessly expensive).

- **Power scheduling**: Not all instances need to be used 24/7. Scheduling non-essential instances to shut down overnight or on weekends is more cost-effective than keeping them running constantly.

- **Removing unused instances**: If you are not using an instance, there is no need to keep it around (or pay for it). Removing unused instances is also important for security, since unused resources can create vulnerabilities.

- **Discount instances**: Since discount instances usually do not guarantee availability, they are not appropriate for business-critical workloads that must run constantly, but for occasional use, they can result in a significant cost savings.

- **Organizational strategies**: In addition to the IT strategies outlined above, creating budgets and setting policies around cloud usage is also important to cloud cost management.

Cloud cost management is not a one-and-done exercise; it is an ongoing journey that requires vigilance, adaptability, and the right tools. By adopting these strategies, organizations can turn complexity into clarity, chaos into control, and costs into a competitive advantage.

Remember, the cloud is only as powerful as your ability to manage it. The question is not whether you can afford to invest in cost management strategies; it is whether you can afford not to.

Issues with cloud cost in businesses

In today's cloud-driven economy, managing costs effectively is not just about balancing the books; it is about empowering businesses to unlock the full potential of their cloud investments while steering clear of financial pitfalls. The rapid rise in cloud spending across industries has created both opportunities and challenges. Without a robust cloud cost management strategy, businesses risk leaving money on the table or worse, finding themselves in a fiscal bind due to unchecked expenses. Here is why cloud cost management is a non-negotiable cornerstone for modern enterprises:

Ripple effects of neglected cloud cost management

The effects are as follows:

- **Lack of visibility**: Imagine trying to navigate a dense forest without a map or compass. That is what cloud operations can feel without proper visibility. Businesses often struggle to gain a clear view of their resource utilization and cost breakdowns. This opacity can lead to blind spots in budgeting and missed opportunities to optimize spending. Without detailed visibility, the organization's cloud ecosystem becomes a black hole of uncertainty, draining financial resources without offering actionable insights. Visibility is more than just a luxury; it is the bedrock of cost control and governance.

- **Lack of accountability**: Who owns the costs? Without clearly defined ownership and accountability, cloud spending can spiral out of control. Decentralized decision-making often results in individuals or teams provisioning resources without oversight or alignment with organizational goals. Accountability is not just about assigning blame; it is about creating a culture of stewardship. By ensuring everyone knows their role in managing costs, organizations can reduce cloud expenses by up to 20%, redirecting those savings to fuel innovation and growth.

- **Inability to automate visibility and accountability**: In a world where automation drives efficiency, relying on manual processes to manage cloud costs is like using a bucket to bail out a sinking ship. Without automation, organizations face bottlenecks in tracking usage, monitoring compliance, and enforcing accountability. Automation tools enable real-time insights and seamless governance, ensuring that visibility and accountability do not fall through the cracks. They turn data into actionable intelligence, helping teams make faster, smarter decisions.

- **Lack of expertise**: Managing cloud costs is not a task you can approach with a *wing it* mentality. Cloud ecosystems are complex, with intricate pricing models, dynamic resource needs, and evolving governance standards. The lack of internal expertise often leads to inefficient provisioning, unnecessary expenses, and security vulnerabilities. Building or hiring a skilled FinOps team is essential. These professionals serve as the compass for navigating cloud complexities, ensuring businesses stay on course toward their financial and operational objectives.

- **Insufficient tools for holistic management**: You cannot fix what you cannot measure. Businesses often lack the necessary tools to tackle all aspects of cloud cost management, from visibility and accountability to automation and governance. Relying on native cloud provider tools alone can create gaps in multi-cloud environments. Comprehensive third-party solutions offer the depth, breadth, and flexibility necessary to address the unique challenges of multi-cloud environments, providing a unified approach to cost management.

Financial and strategic consequences of neglect

The absence of effective cloud cost management can create a domino effect of negative outcomes:

- **Unexpected cost surges**: Unmonitored usage can lead to surprise invoices that wreak havoc on budgets.

- **Wasted resources**: Overprovisioned or idle instances drain resources without delivering value.

- **Performance bottlenecks**: Mismanaged resources can result in under-provisioning, hampering application performance.

- **Lost competitive edge**: Money wasted on inefficient cloud operations could be invested in innovation and growth.

These consequences underscore the strategic importance of proactive cost governance.

Turning challenges into opportunities

Let us understand these points:

- **Visibility + Accountability = Impactful cost management:**

  o Investing in visibility tools and fostering accountability are the twin pillars of effective cloud cost management. They provide the clarity and control needed to optimize spending and improve decision-making.

- **Empower teams with expertise and automation:**

  o Training your workforce and implementing automated tools create a synergistic approach to cost management. Together, they reduce human error, streamline processes, and ensure consistent governance.

- **Adopt a holistic approach:**

  o Effective cost management is not just about cutting costs; it is about aligning cloud spending with business objectives, improving agility, and fostering innovation. A holistic strategy enables businesses to weather fluctuations in demand while staying within budget.

Bridging the cap between technology and finance

Cloud cost management is as much about fostering collaboration as it is about controlling costs. Bridging the gap between technical teams and financial stakeholders is essential for crafting strategies that are not only technically sound but also economically viable. This shared understanding enables enterprises to align their technical capabilities with financial objectives, ensuring sustainable growth.

Mindset of continuous improvement

In the ever-evolving cloud landscape, resting on laurels is not an option. Enterprises must cultivate a mindset of continuous optimization, revisiting their strategies regularly to adapt to emerging technologies, shifting usage patterns, and evolving business needs. Cloud cost management is not a one-time project; it is a perpetual journey toward efficiency, visibility, and performance excellence.

By anchoring their efforts in strong cost management principles, businesses can navigate the complexities of cloud technology with clarity, confidence, and purpose, turning potential pitfalls into pathways for innovation and growth.

Conclusion

Cloud cost management enables businesses to effectively control their cloud service spending while maximizing their resource utilization. Most cloud providers offer basic cloud cost management tools to help achieve this, and there are also more specialized third-party solutions that provide additional visibility and insight into cloud costs. By making cloud cost management a priority, an enterprise can control its costs and practice good governance while also ensuring that it has the cloud resources it needs to stay competitive.

In addition, cloud cost management best practices also support other business objectives and cloud best practices, such as security, visibility, organization, and accountability. Thus, cloud cost management is important for reasons beyond simple cost control. Effective cloud cost management enables businesses to plan, minimize waste, and accurately forecast both their costs and resource requirements.

With the right strategies, enterprises can achieve a harmonious balance between cost-efficiency and operational excellence, ensuring their cloud investments deliver consistent and sustainable value.

By making cloud cost management a cornerstone of their operations, organizations not only safeguard their bottom line but also unlock the full potential of cloud technology, driving innovation and competitive advantage in equal measure while laying the roadmap for adopting the evolutionary FinOps practices and trends.

CHAPTER 12

Case Studies and Real-world Examples of Multi-cloud FinOps

Introduction

Understanding how diverse enterprises, from startups to global organizations, are implementing FinOps sheds light on its transformative potential. The real-world examples that we will go through in this chapter highlight the tangible benefits FinOps brings to businesses across industries, scaling their cloud operations efficiently and sustainably.

FinOps adoption across small, mid, and large enterprises

Let us now learn about FinOps adoption across small, mid, and large enterprises.

Driving operational efficiency with small-scale retailer

Startups operate in a high-stakes environment where every dollar spent must deliver measurable value. A promising technology startup, experiencing rapid growth, encountered soaring cloud expenses that threatened to derail its expansion plans. Through FinOps, the company achieved the following milestones:

- **40% reduction in cloud costs**: Automated rightsizing of virtual machines and optimized storage allocations.

- **Streamlined team collaboration**: Implemented cost accountability measures, bridging the gap between engineering and finance teams.

- **Enhanced agility**: Leveraged predictive analytics to proactively allocate resources for expected spikes during product launches.

The startup's success showcases how FinOps lays a robust foundation for scaling cloud operations without compromising financial discipline.

Enhancing financial discipline with mid-scale manufacturer

A mid-scale manufacturer faced escalating costs due to inefficient resource utilization across AWS and Azure. The lack of visibility into multi-cloud spending created challenges in budgeting and forecasting. With FinOps practices, they achieved:

- **25% savings**: Identified redundant storage and optimized compute usage.

- **Improved cross-team collaboration**: Bridged the gap between engineering and finance teams for unified decision-making.

- **Governance compliance**: Enforced policies to ensure adherence to stringent industry standards.

Here, we highlight the FinOps enablement to tame the complexities of multi-cloud ecosystems while promoting operational efficiencies.

Precision scaling with large-scale financial institution

A global financial institution leveraged FinOps to regain control over its sprawling cloud infrastructure spanning AWS, GCP, and Azure. The organization was struggling with unpredictable cloud costs and underutilized resources, which affected profit margins. FinOps turned the tide by delivering:

- **30% reduction in cloud spending**: Rightsized resources and eliminated redundant instances.

- **Forecasting Accuracy**: Predictive analytics enabled the finance team to anticipate cloud costs with over 90% accuracy.

- **Cultural shift**: Cross-functional collaboration between IT, finance, and operations teams ensured cost-conscious decisions became the norm.

For this financial giant, FinOps was not just about cost savings, it became the catalyst for strategic realignment, aligning cloud spending with business objectives.

Let us now go over a scenario where a major insurance pioneer saved 40% with a FinOps Tool.

In the fiercely competitive insurance industry, a prominent player faced spiraling cloud costs due to increasing reliance on multi-cloud platforms for underwriting, claims processing, and customer analytics. The adoption of a robust FinOps tool led to the following remarkable results:

- **Cost reduction**: By optimizing workloads and eliminating underutilized resources, the company achieved a staggering 40% reduction in cloud spending.

- **Improved accountability**: The tool's advanced tagging features enabled cost allocation across teams, ensuring better accountability and ownership of expenses.

- **Enhanced decision-making**: Granular visibility into costs empowered leadership to align cloud spending with strategic business goals.

- **Governance at scale**: Automated policy enforcement ensured compliance with internal financial and operational guidelines.

Key enablers of success

The key enablers of success are:

- Early integration of FinOps practices into their digital transformation strategy.

- Regular optimization cycles that ensured continuous cost savings.

- Strong collaboration between engineering, finance, and operations teams.

FinOps adoption by a leading sustainable energy enterprise

As a global leader in renewable energy solutions, this organization faced challenges in managing a hybrid cloud environment essential for powering real-time energy monitoring systems and analytics. Adopting FinOps revolutionized their approach by enabling:

- **Operational sustainability**: Streamlined resource allocation reduced costs while maintaining green energy objectives.

- **Predictive analytics**: Sophisticated cost forecasting tools ensured budgets aligned with market demand fluctuations.

- **Scalability**: The flexibility to scale operations across AWS, Azure, and GCP supported the growth of new energy projects globally.

Best practices implemented

The best practices that were implemented are as follows:

- Automation of cost controls to prevent wasteful spending.

- Development of FinOps champions within key teams to drive cultural adoption.

- Real-time dashboards providing unified cost visibility across multi-cloud platforms.

Strategic interventions

Some strategic interventions were as follows:

- Comprehensive tagging strategies for clear resource identification.

- Regular audits and optimization reviews to ensure continuous improvement.

- Integration of FinOps into DevOps pipelines to enhance collaboration.

Conclusion

From established global enterprises to nimble start-ups, FinOps has proven to be the cornerstone of effective multi-cloud management. By combining transparency, governance, and optimization, organizations can tame the complexities of multi-cloud environments, turning potential liabilities into strategic assets. Heeddata is another accelerator to drive most of the success stories.

Whether you are a small retailer, a mid-size manufacturer, or a global energy leader, adopting FinOps practices is not just about cost savings; it is about driving innovation, aligning cloud strategy with business goals, and setting the stage for long-term growth.

Join our Discord space

Join our Discord workspace for latest updates, offers, tech happenings around the world, new releases, and sessions with the authors:

https://discord.bpbonline.com

CHAPTER 13

Future Scopes and Trends in Multi-cloud FinOps

Introduction

The world of cloud FinOps is on the cusp of remarkable transformations, poised to evolve into a cornerstone for enterprise-wide cost management strategies. As cloud adoption becomes ubiquitous, FinOps will transcend its current boundaries to integrate deeply into every aspect of enterprise operations, shaping how businesses optimize, automate, and sustain their financial practices in an increasingly digital world.

We have seen and observed that FinOps is known for cloud entirely, thanks to the board of FinOps organization, that is catering the FinOps into SaaS and data center as well. This scope of FinOps proves how strongly its culture could resemble across the enterprises for efficient management of costs and accelerate business value for the resources used. Let us understand the scope of FinOps in these two wings and how they can be potent powerhouses to drive overall value.

Scopes of FinOps

The scope of FinOps highlights the integration of its best practices for organizations across all business units, processes, and departments within an organization. These determine the potential application of FinOps and the extent to which it supports the enterprise-grade cost-saving mechanisms.

Software as a service

Enterprises adopt SaaS platforms to streamline operations, and FinOps becomes the crux of tracking and optimizing SaaS expenditures across departments. Unlike traditional cloud infrastructure, SaaS costs often lie hidden in subscription fees, user licenses, and feature tiers, making visibility a challenge. FinOps provides transparency into these spending patterns, ensuring organizations only pay for what they truly use. It empowers teams to right-size SaaS subscriptions, eliminate shadow IT, and consolidate redundant tools. Moreover, with FinOps automation and chargeback mechanisms, companies can foster accountability and align SaaS usage with business outcomes. This drives cost efficiency while maximizing the value of every SaaS investment.

Data center

As the cloud ecosystem evolves, FinOps will be a driving force in integrating technological advances with financial sustainability. The transformative trends of spatial computing, edge computing, and AI-powered cloud search engines exemplify the next frontier where FinOps will thrive, enabling enterprises to achieve operational excellence without overspending:

Figure 13.1: Future scope and trends in FinOps

Future trends in FinOps

Here is how FinOps will synergize with these evolutionary technologies.

FinOps and spatial computing

Let us look at the following points in detail:

- **Optimizing resources for virtual worlds**: Spatial computing, the convergence of AR, VR, and IoT, presents extraordinary computational demands. From rendering immersive 3D environments to managing real-time sensor data, these applications consume significant cloud resources. FinOps will enable precise resource allocation, balancing computational power with cost efficiency. This approach ensures enterprises can meet the escalating demands of spatial computing without unnecessary overprovisioning.

- **Real-time cost monitoring**: Spatial computing applications are inherently dynamic, with fluctuating workloads. Real-time cost monitoring, powered by FinOps, will allow organizations to track expenses on the fly, adjusting budgets in tandem with resource utilization. This agility ensures financial viability for even the most resource-intensive projects.

- **Collaborative accountability**: Developing immersive experiences requires collaboration across multiple teams: designers, developers, and financial strategists. FinOps will act as the common ground, fostering transparency in resource usage and aligning all stakeholders with shared financial and technical goals.

FinOps and edge computing

Let us go over the following:

- **Granular cost visibility at the edge**: The decentralized nature of edge computing, where processing occurs closer to the source (for example, IoT devices), introduces new challenges to cost governance. FinOps will provide granular visibility into resource usage at the micro-level, helping enterprises pinpoint inefficiencies and optimize resource allocation.

- **Streamlining operations across distributed systems**: Managing thousands of edge locations requires robust orchestration. FinOps frameworks will integrate with edge orchestration tools to dynamically adjust workloads, ensuring cost-efficient operations while maintaining performance standards across distributed systems.

- **Reducing latency without overspending**: Edge computing prioritizes low latency but can inadvertently increase costs. FinOps will play a critical role in finding the sweet spot: minimizing latency while keeping costs in check by optimizing resource utilization and avoiding over-engineered solutions.

FinOps and AI-powered cloud search engines

Let us go over the following:

- **Cost efficiency for AI model training**: AI search engines rely on extensive resources to train and fine-tune models. FinOps will streamline these processes, leveraging discount instances, efficient workload scheduling, and resource pooling to reduce expenses during computationally intensive operations.

- **Predictive cost analytics**: AI's integration into FinOps will elevate predictive cost analytics, offering insights into the financial impact of scaling AI-driven search engines. This foresight will empower enterprises to make proactive adjustments, ensuring that resource consumption aligns with business objectives.

- **Enhanced budgeting for intelligent insights**: With the growth of user-driven interactions, FinOps will optimize the pay-as-you-go models of AI-powered search platforms. These strategies will ensure minimal waste while enabling enterprises to meet user demands effectively, enhancing both ROI and user experience.

Integration across business units

In the coming years, FinOps will no longer be confined to IT departments. Its principles will permeate all business units, embedding cost-consciousness into core strategies. This democratization of financial accountability will drive data-driven decision-making at all organizational levels, ensuring operational and financial alignment. Cross-functional teams will access real-time insights into their resource utilization, fostering a collaborative approach to cost optimization.

AI and automation in FinOps

Artificial intelligence (**AI**) will revolutionize FinOps by enabling predictive analytics, anomaly detection, and real-time optimization. AI-driven automation will allow organizations to proactively manage costs, adjusting workloads dynamically and mitigating inefficiencies before they escalate. Personalization powered by machine learning will provide actionable recommendations tailored to each business unit, making FinOps more intuitive and impactful.

Sustainability-focused evolution with GreenOps

The rising emphasis on environmental responsibility will lead to the emergence of GreenOps, a fusion of cost optimization and sustainability. Organizations will integrate FinOps practices with carbon-reduction strategies, minimizing energy consumption and leveraging renewable energy sources. GreenOps will not only enhance cost efficiency but also serve as a competitive differentiator in markets where environmental compliance is a priority.

Superclouds and industry-specific clouds

The complexity of managing multi-cloud environments will drive the development of supercloud platforms: solutions that unify governance, visibility, and interoperability across cloud providers. Additionally, the rise of industry-specific clouds will provide tailored solutions for verticals such as healthcare, finance, and manufacturing, necessitating FinOps strategies that adapt to unique cost structures and compliance requirements.

Decentralized and edge-driven FinOps

As edge computing becomes mainstream, FinOps will address the challenges of managing costs in decentralized infrastructures. This includes tracking granular resource consumption across geographically dispersed systems while ensuring cost efficiency. Tools tailored for edge architectures will enable precise budgeting and governance at micro-locations, enhancing the performance of edge-driven ecosystems.

Multicurrency and globalized governance

The global nature of modern enterprises will necessitate FinOps tools capable of handling multicurrency transactions and regional cost variations. These tools will provide comprehensive visibility into global operations while maintaining localized control, empowering organizations to balance regional compliance with overarching financial strategies.

Enhanced tooling and collaboration

The next decade will witness the evolution of FinOps platforms, offering seamless integration with **enterprise resource planning** (**ERP**) systems and other financial tools. These platforms will feature user-friendly interfaces, real-time dashboards, and automated reporting, enabling finance, operations, and development teams to collaborate effortlessly. Simplified workflows will democratize FinOps practices, making them accessible across organizational silos.

Focus on FinOps maturity models

Organizations will benchmark their cost management practices against FinOps maturity models, driving continuous improvement. These frameworks will guide enterprises in enhancing visibility, accountability, and optimization, fostering a culture of excellence in financial operations. Structured assessments will help identify gaps and implement strategies to achieve higher maturity levels.

Customizable governance frameworks

The future of FinOps will prioritize flexible governance frameworks that cater to diverse business needs while maintaining compliance. Policy-driven automation will enforce cost controls across multi-cloud environments, enabling enterprises to strike a balance between agility and oversight.

Cultural transformation

The success of FinOps hinges on more than just technology: it requires a cultural shift. Organizations will invest in upskilling employees, fostering cross-functional collaboration, and embedding a cost-conscious mindset into their DNA. Leadership will champion this transformation, aligning financial strategies with organizational goals.

Enabling synergies with evolutionary trends

FinOps will be at the helm, ensuring these technologies deliver sustainable value. Key contributions include:

- **Integrating AI for proactive management**: The use of AI within FinOps itself will enable actionable insights, helping businesses navigate the complex financial landscapes of cutting-edge technologies like spatial and edge computing.

- **Promoting sustainability**: As technologies like spatial and edge computing evolve, FinOps will integrate sustainable practices to reduce energy footprints. By encouraging optimized workloads and waste reduction, FinOps will align cost efficiency with environmental goals.

- **Driving business agility**: FinOps will provide businesses with the agility to adapt to technological shifts quickly. Enterprises will leverage FinOps to implement cost-effective solutions that fuel innovation without compromising financial health.

Conclusion

As enterprises adapt to technological shifts, FinOps will become a strategic pillar, ensuring innovation is financially sustainable. By integrating advanced tooling, fostering collaboration, and embracing emerging trends, FinOps will redefine cost management, driving business agility and resilience. Over the next decade, it will not just be a function; it will be a philosophy that empowers enterprises to thrive in a competitive, cloud-driven world.

The integration of FinOps with cutting-edge cloud trends like spatial computing, edge computing, and AI-powered cloud search engines will revolutionize how enterprises leverage the cloud, ensuring not just cost efficiency but also alignment with emerging technologies.

The next ten years will see FinOps maturing into a pivotal discipline that not only manages costs but also propels innovation. By weaving advanced tools, AI-driven insights, and collaborative cultures into FinOps strategies, enterprises will thrive in an era defined by agility, sustainability, and technological excellence.

In this future, FinOps will transcend its current role as a cost management practice, becoming the bedrock of enterprise cloud strategies. It will empower organizations to achieve scalable innovation, enabling them to stay ahead of the curve in an increasingly digital and interconnected world.

APPENDIX A
Multi-cloud FinOps Platform

Overview of Heeddata

This appendix covers the best-in-class, a FinOps driving platform for enterprises where overprovisioning of resources, increasing cloud costs, and anomaly risks become challenging. This is where Heeddata serves its purpose.

In the fast-paced realm of multi-cloud ecosystems, **Heeddata** emerges as a beacon of clarity and control. The product is purpose-built to address the complexities of cloud cost management, governance, and optimization, enabling businesses to fully leverage the potential of their multi-cloud investments without compromising financial discipline.

Why Heeddata?

Let us look at its **Dashboard**:

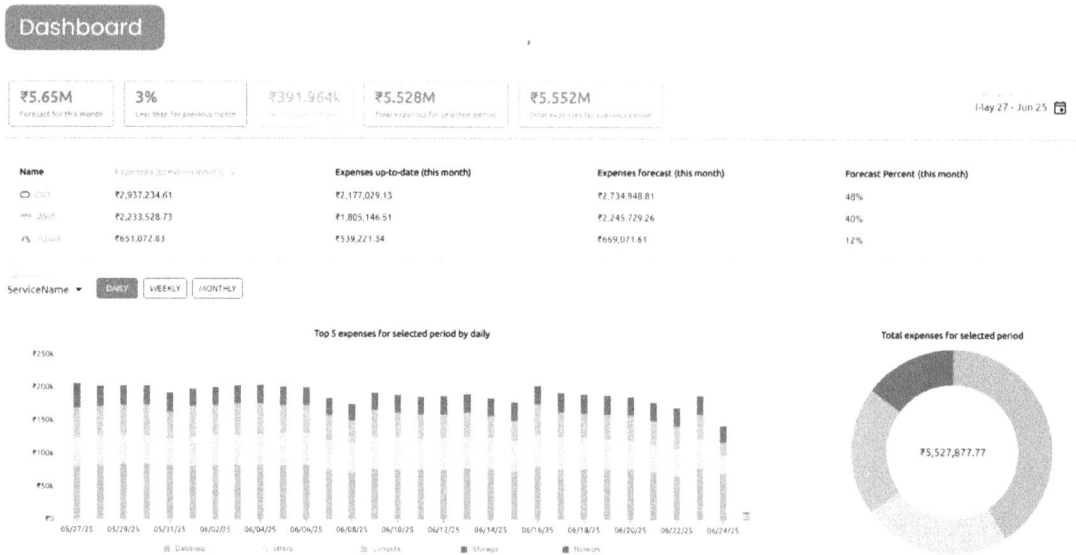

Figure 14.1: Heeddata Dashbaord

Modern enterprises face an uphill battle managing cloud resources spread across multiple providers. Challenges such as a lack of visibility, inefficient resource utilization, and adherence to governance policies are pervasive. **Heeddata** addresses these issues directly, providing a centralized, intelligent platform that automates cloud financial management, streamlines governance, and enables informed strategic decision-making.

Heeddata differentiators and key features

Let us now go through the Heeddata differentiators and key features:

- **Unified visibility and control**: Heeddata consolidates cloud data from multiple providers into a single pane of glass, offering unparalleled visibility into costs, trends, and resource utilization.

- **AI-powered cost optimization**: Harnessing the power of advanced analytics, Heeddata provides actionable recommendations for rightsizing resources, identifying wastage, and implementing cost-saving measures.

- **Comprehensive governance tools**: Heeddata's governance features enforce cost policies, monitor tagging compliance, and ensure that cloud expenses align with corporate financial goals.

- **Granular insights**: With its resource-level drill-down capabilities, Heeddata offers deep insights into individual workloads, helping teams pinpoint inefficiencies and optimize their usage.

- **Seamless integrations**: The platform integrates effortlessly with existing workflows and tools, ensuring businesses can adopt Heeddata without disrupting their operational ecosystems.

Let us look at the Heeddata **Dashboard** overview for multi-cloud FinOps:

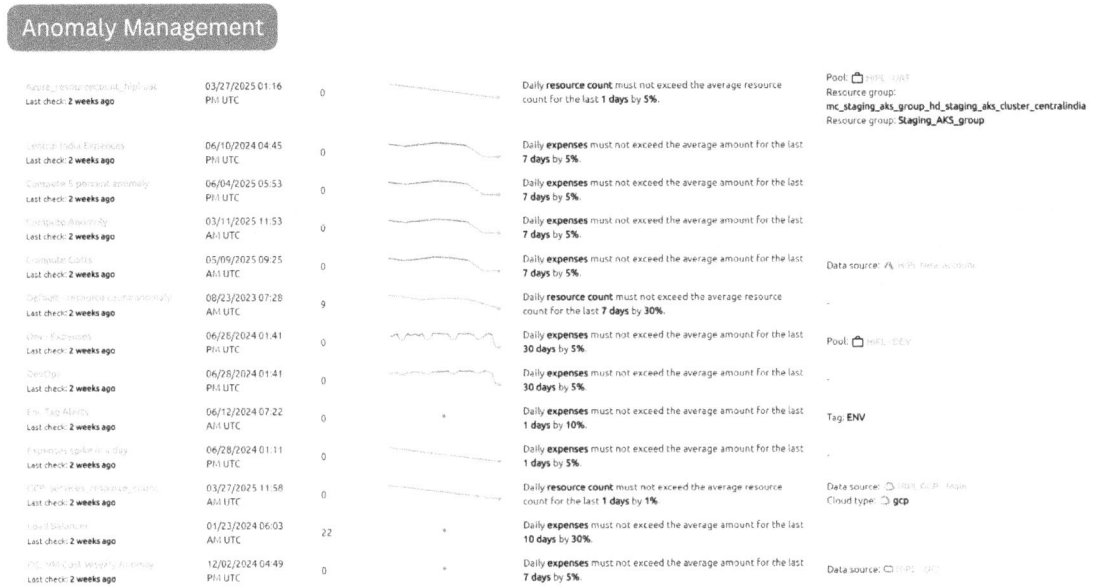

Figure 14.2: Anomaly Management

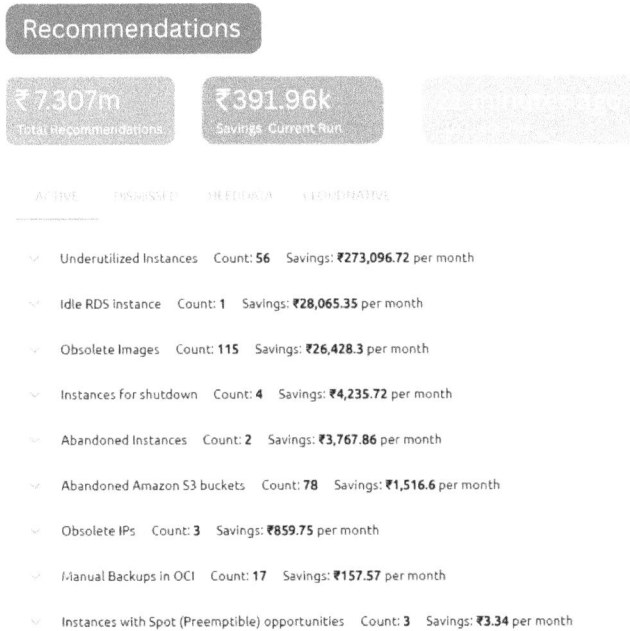

Figure 14.3: Recommendations

Let us look at some more dashboards shown in *Figures 14.4, 14.5:*

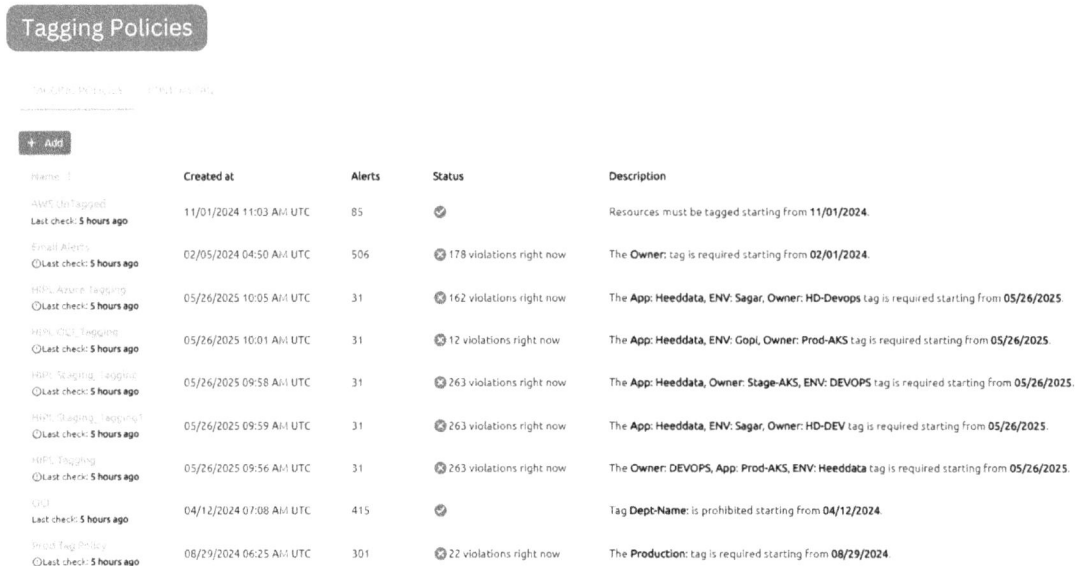

Tagging Policies

+ Add

Name	Created at	Alerts	Status	Description
AWS Untagged Last check: **5 hours ago**	11/01/2024 11:03 AM UTC	85	✓	Resources must be tagged starting from **11/01/2024**.
Email Alerts Last check: **5 hours ago**	02/05/2024 04:50 AM UTC	506	✗ 178 violations right now	The **Owner:** tag is required starting from **02/01/2024**.
HDPL Azure Tagging Last check: **5 hours ago**	05/26/2025 10:05 AM UTC	31	✗ 162 violations right now	The **App: Heeddata, ENV: Sagar, Owner: HD-Devops** tag is required starting from **05/26/2025**.
HDPL GCL Tagging Last check: **5 hours ago**	05/26/2025 10:01 AM UTC	31	✗ 12 violations right now	The **App: Heeddata, ENV: Gopi, Owner: Prod-AKS** tag is required starting from **05/26/2025**.
HDPL Staging, Tagging Last check: **5 hours ago**	05/26/2025 09:58 AM UTC	31	✗ 263 violations right now	The **App: Heeddata, Owner: Stage-AKS, ENV: DEVOPS** tag is required starting from **05/26/2025**.
HDPL Staging, Tagging1 Last check: **5 hours ago**	05/26/2025 09:59 AM UTC	31	✗ 263 violations right now	The **App: Heeddata, ENV: Sagar, Owner: HD-DEV** tag is required starting from **05/26/2025**.
HDPL Tagging Last check: **5 hours ago**	05/26/2025 09:56 AM UTC	31	✗ 263 violations right now	The **Owner: DEVOPS, App: Prod-AKS, ENV: Heeddata** tag is required starting from **05/26/2025**.
GCU Last check: **5 hours ago**	04/12/2024 07:08 AM UTC	415	✓	Tag **Dept-Name:** is prohibited starting from **04/12/2024**.
Prod Tag Policy Last check: **5 hours ago**	08/29/2024 06:25 AM UTC	301	✗ 22 violations right now	The **Production:** tag is required starting from **08/29/2024**.

Figure 14.4: Tagging Policies

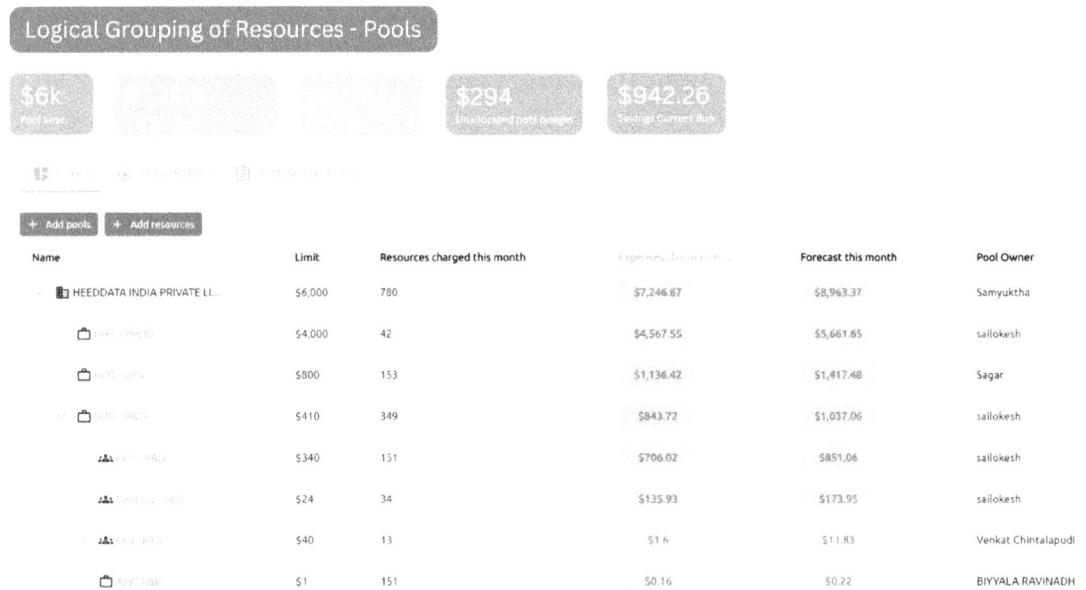

Logical Grouping of Resources - Pools

$6k
Pool limit

$294
Unallocated pool budget

$942.26
Savings Current Run

+ Add pools   + Add resources

Name	Limit	Resources charged this month	Expenses this month	Forecast this month	Pool Owner
▸ 🗂 HEEDDATA INDIA PRIVATE LI...	$6,000	780	$7,246.67	$8,963.37	Samyuktha
🗁 HDPL GROUP	$4,000	42	$4,567.55	$5,661.65	sailokesh
🗁 HDPL APPS	$800	153	$1,136.42	$1,417.48	Sagar
▾ 🗁 HDPL APPS	$410	349	$843.72	$1,037.06	sailokesh
👥 HDPL APPS	$340	151	$706.02	$851.06	sailokesh
👥 HDPL APPS	$24	34	$135.93	$173.95	sailokesh
▸ 👥 HDPL APPS	$40	13	$1.6	$11.83	Venkat Chintalapudi
🗁 HDPL APPS	$1	151	$0.16	$0.22	BIYYALA RAVINADH

Figure 14.5: Resource Grouping

The **Quotas and Budgets** dashboard is as follows:

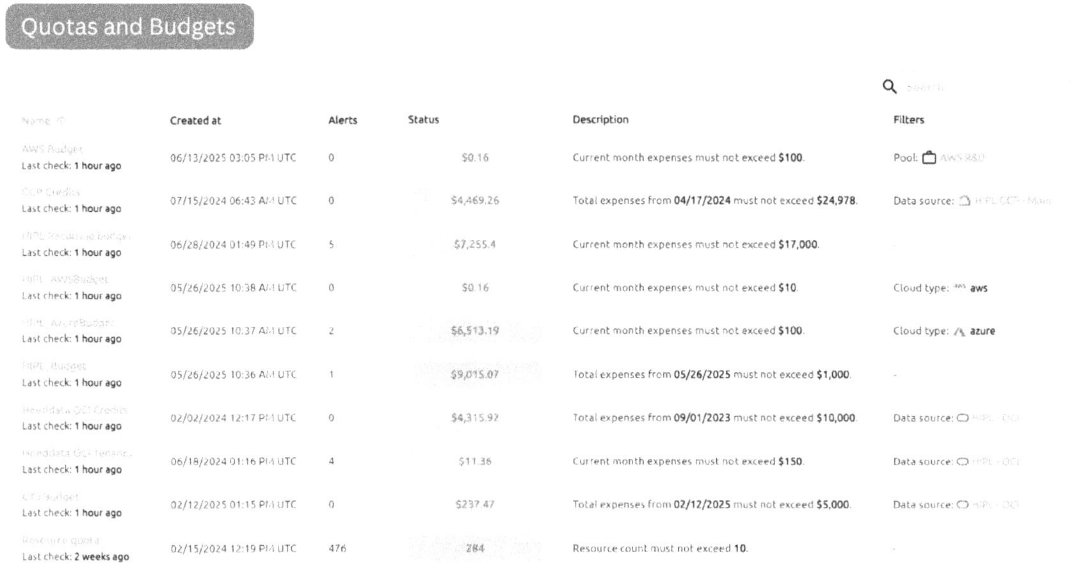

Figure 14.6: Quotas and Budgets

Heeddata benefits for multi-cloud FinOps

Let us go over the benefits now:

- **Enhanced cloud governance**: Heeddata establishes a robust governance framework that ensures compliance with financial and operational policies, reducing risks associated with unchecked cloud spending.

- **Streamlined cloud financial management**: From budget enforcement to real-time cost monitoring, Heeddata simplifies cloud financial management, making it accessible and actionable for all stakeholders.

- **Accelerated digital transformation**: By eliminating inefficiencies and optimizing resource usage, Heeddata accelerates enterprises' ability to innovate and adapt to new market dynamics.

- **Cross-team collaboration**: The platform fosters collaboration between finance, operations, and engineering teams, ensuring all stakeholders work toward unified financial and operational objectives.

Key features driving FinOps excellence

Let us understand the key features now:

- **Dashboards for unified insights**: Intuitive dashboards provide a real-time view of cloud expenses, enabling businesses to track top services, analyze cost drivers, and forecast spending trends.

- **Cost explorer**: This feature enables teams to drill down into details, identify cost outliers, and compare expenditures across time periods, empowering strategic budgeting.

- **Anomaly detection**: Proactively flags unusual cost spikes, allowing teams to address potential overruns before they spiral out of control.

- **Tagging governance**: Ensures consistent tagging of resources, improving cost allocation and enhancing reporting accuracy.

- **Optimization engine**: AI-driven insights guide organizations in maximizing their cloud ROI by automating rightsizing and workload distribution.

- **Unified currency support**: Simplifies financial reporting by consolidating cloud expenses into a single currency, regardless of the cloud provider.

Challenges Heeddata solves

Heeddata can solve the following challenges:

- **Lack of cloud visibility**: Heeddata provides a unified view of cloud costs, breaking silos across providers and offering actionable insights into resource utilization.

- **Inefficient resource utilization**: The platform identifies overprovisioned or underutilized resources, recommending measures like rightsizing to reduce wastage and optimize spending.

- **Policy enforcement**: Heeddata ensures adherence to governance policies by setting budgets, monitoring compliance, and providing real-time alerts for anomalies.

- **Slow FinOps adoption**: By simplifying FinOps principles and automating key processes, Heeddata accelerates the adoption of FinOps practices across teams.

Heeddata and the FinOps journey

Let us understand the stages in the Heeddata and FinOps journey:

- **Crawl stage: Establishing a foundation**
  - o   **Visibility**: Heeddata provides granular insights into cloud spending, creating awareness of cost drivers and inefficiencies.

- o **Accountability**: Teams can collaborate effectively, ensuring clear ownership of financial outcomes.

- **Walk stage**: **Implementing optimization**

  - o **Automation**: Automates cost-saving actions like rightsizing and resource scheduling.

  - o **Predictive planning**: Leverages analytics to forecast costs and align budgets with future needs.

- **Run stage**: **Continuous improvement**

  - o **Iterative optimization**: Continuously monitors and fine-tunes cloud environments for efficiency.

  - o **Strategic decisions**: Empowers leaders with actionable data to drive innovation and maximize ROI.

Heeddata is not just a tool but a transformative platform that addresses the pain points of managing multi-cloud environments. By bridging the gaps between financial discipline, operational efficiency, and innovation, it enables businesses to navigate the complexities of the cloud with confidence.

With Heeddata at the helm, organizations can achieve unparalleled transparency, optimize resource allocation, and enforce governance, all while accelerating their FinOps journey toward sustained growth and digital excellence.

Join our Discord space

Join our Discord workspace for latest updates, offers, tech happenings around the world, new releases, and sessions with the authors:

https://discord.bpbonline.com

APPENDIX B

Cloud FinOps in Nutshell

FinOps personas

FinOps is never for one team; it necessitates the involvement of many stakeholders or personas across the enterprise, promoting collaboration with the FinOps team. All the FinOps personnel involved in taking advantage of the cloud, that is, managing, tracking, or directing, will gain the maximum from the FinOps framework, which is chosen and implemented as an operating model.

In our research with mid and large-scale enterprises to track cloud utilization, we have clearly observed that defined personas bring more accountability while expanding FinOps discipline to broad stakeholders, who must collaborate and work together.

If this is not prioritized before establishing or at the time of planning, the whole advantage of FinOps goes in vain. Though personas may vary from one enterprise to another, there is the possibility of a single person playing the role of multiple personas so that FinOps stays effective and streamlined.

However, based on the responsibilities defined, these FinOps personas are of two kinds.

Core personas

Whenever a cultural practice comes into the foreground, there are core personas who define all the organizational disciplines so that there is a maximum of cloud utilization. These personas must:

- Aim at perceiving and accepting FinOps in various angles, spreading awareness and mighty vision about what to achieve and how to achieve the respective goals.

- Align these goals to higher objectives and estimate the challenges or risks that can halt during the implementation across teams or enterprises.

- Derive metrics at the team level to understand how the cloud resources are being used with the help of tools like Heeddata and understand a comprehensive view of cloud costs.

- Inspire teams to optimize cloud resources and validate the cloud resources to be used in business hours based on cloud dependencies and operations being performed.

- Outcomes that the individual persona has to deliver by focusing and driving their teams towards a shared goal.

Ensuring all these are taken care of, each persona has a set of responsibilities based on their profile. We will explore and determine how our enterprise can define a persona in reality, enabling us to streamline the FinOps framework across the organization.

FinOps practitioner

The primary duty of a FinOps practitioner is to enable standardization of FinOps culture across enterprises by establishing a bridge between engineering, business, and finance teams. Additionally, enabling business-based decisions in near real-time optimizes cloud usage and accelerates business value. Focused on involving all the stakeholders for FinOps framework pitching, they induce principles and capabilities of the framework along with industry-led best practices.

Though FinOps practitioner seems to be superlative of all the functions, the path is not always filled with petals of roses as they encounter with:

- Lack of data accessibility.

- Distributed accountability.

- Driving enterprise-wide FinOps adoption.

- Tools that have not emerged with capabilities needed.

To navigate the cultural change smoothly, enable business decisions more intelligently, and create benchmarks for teams, the abovementioned challenges need to be addressed. Moreover, the right expertise and tool can release you from the challenges.

Single solution for all

After crisscrossing across many tools, we have ended up at Heeddata, a multi-cloud FinOps platform. The promising advantages this platform brings, allows FinOps practitioner to access data instantly from anywhere without depending on anyone else, knowing the accountability of individual business teams where tracking made simpler, FinOps adoption at scale seems to be seamless, and it is embedded with all the capabilities that you need for effective establishment of FinOps culture.

This will enable the FinOps practitioner to derive key insights on:

- Accurate budget tracking.
- Flawless forecasting of costs and cloud resources.
- Unit cost economics.
- Discount/reservation coverage.
- Percentage of untagged resources.
- Leveraging the opportunities to enhance efficiency.

Leadership

> *Culture from leadership creates more leaders, fosters discipline, and stands for centuries.*
>
> *-Anirudh Sharma*

Without leadership initiatives, nothing works, and if it works, the results will not align with business objectives. The involvement of Executives such as vice president/head of infrastructure, head of cloud operations, CTOs, or CIOs, makes your FinOps culture work for the enterprise. Their primary focus is to ensure accountability and transparency, productivity, and not overrunning the budgets across the teams.

The executive board, known as the **leadership persona**, is greatly involved in collaboratively serving the organizational needs in whatever ways possible, owing to their objectives, challenges, metrics, and outcomes.

The evolution of FinOps drives these personas to facilitate approvals, buy-in options, and streamlining FinOps as a way to accelerate cloud transformation.

The motivation behind each leadership personal unleashes maximum value that FinOps brings for an enterprise. CEOs, CTOs, CFOs, and CIOs play a mighty tusk role in implementing FinOps and fostering financial discipline among all the other teams. However, CIOs and CEOs think in the direction of growth and strategic advantage that this framework brings; CTOs work on the technological landscape to ensure FinOps has all the resources in place to run smoothly across the enterprise; and CFOs investigate financial aspects, as this is a single source of business continuity. In this process, each of the roles has its own challenges considering their objectives. Let us demystify each one of them in detail:

CEOs and CIOs/CTOs role in FinOps implementation

Pressing huge on staying competitive and embedding next-gen technologies being cloud-centralized, all these leadership personas dream to thrive in the evolving market while sustaining through various challenges that include:

- Unpredictable or chaotic cloud spend.
- Unable to match the synergy between engineering efforts and business objectives.
- Not sure of ROI on cloud investments.
- Facing the stress of reducing cloud costs.
- Difficulty of choosing guardrails on spend.
- Unable to foster accountability.
- Business continuity and reliability.

CFOs involvement

The only difference from higher leadership personas to CFOs is that these act as a bridge between technology adoption and higher personas adoption by calculating the costs. Managing the cloud cost utilization and ensuring that money becomes advantageous for the enterprise is what a CFO mainly stresses. Amidst the challenges such as ROI fluctuations, cloud costs moving out of budgeting cycles, and inability of cost tracking going in vain poses risk not only to their commitment to role but also to the organization.

Calculated risks are extremely great but what about an increase in cloud costs and continuous overruns in budgets? 75% of organizations that face these challenges either lack of expertise or awareness in these areas. The solution is a multi-cloud FinOps platform, Heeddata.

Addressing all the preceding challenges and scenarios, this FinOps platform (as far as we have explored and considered the best) excels, navigating your business through its complexities. Here is how the above challenges can be ditched through:

- Out of hundreds of thousands of cloud resources, the platform enables get a clear view of cloud spend, giving the cost map views at the most granular levels, leaving you organized and eliminating chaotic cloud spend.

- Cloud-centralized enterprise, along with aligning to business objectives, is a maze for many, but establishing the accountability between engineering teams and business objectives becomes simpler because of Heeddata. Heeddata enables engineering teams to derive actionable insights and act on them as soon as possible, so that ultimate objectives are being met.

- More than 30% ROI has been achieved for enterprises that trusted and integrated Heeddata into their cloud platforms, as reported in our research. Saving 30%, according to *Venkat Chintalapudi*, is huge, and it drives leadership personas to operate on the cloud without even worrying about cost overruns.

- With this platform, it is quite promising that manual efforts are not needed any further, as the platform handles optimization techniques and recommendations to redefine cloud costs.

- Though many businesses rely on cloud and only a few succeed in complete implementation and management, this single platform is all you need to bolster your bottom line. Being in the leadership arena and serving at your best, your commitment to one single choice differentiates you from the rest as you optimize your cloud spending, gaining business momentum.

- For CFOs, from cost tracking mechanisms to optimizing cloud costs, everything is efficiently and advancingly managed by this unified platform.

For this, all the C-suite leadership personas can rely on this tool to enhance cloud optimization while streamlining FinOps within every business unit across the enterprise.

Product

The impact product teams create is massive, and there is no necessity to drive high-performing teams because they take ownership of every element that comes under their portfolio. The primary role of product teams is to innovate products and add new features or customizations as needed, aligning with business requirements and competitive market pricing. However, the same objective aligns with FinOps culture when it comes to product teams. However, it is not always slicing the bread's way.

Most of the product teams are extremely focused on the value they create by leveraging evolving technologies for their customers. Product owners work collaboratively with IT teams to accelerate and deliver the digital value of the cloud. In FinOps, product personas include business operations, product and program managers, systems analysts, and product owners who share common objectives, goals, and encounter similar challenges while developing cloud-native apps.

Challenging scenario with cloud

Product teams are highly focused and motivated to develop and deploy new features and bring new products to the limelight, following agile methodologies as part of software development lifecycle. But this would keep them occupied, leaving the edge of tracking cloud costs when releasing these into new markets, or whenever pricing misuses happen.

How FinOps help

The FinOps framework enables risk management, connects business decisions with product outcomes, and forecasts the use of cloud infrastructure and the corresponding costs involved when new features or products are released. It is location-specific and enables the product teams to view cloud resources so that they have access to modify and optimize. This leads to significant savings and reduces cloud cost consumption.

Engineering

Nowhere do the engineering teams consider cost as a metric when adding digital value through innovation within enterprises. In FinOps, the engineering personas build, run, and support organizations in delivering services as-is without any change in the processes or workflows. However, the only additional metric they work on is using cost and resources as a metric and objective that enables efficient use of resources as they architect, design, and run apps on the cloud.

Engineering personas are major ones who use maximum cloud resources to perform activities such as choosing the appropriate resource locations, resizing the cloud resources to be in sync with workload requirements, running cloud resources only when needed, eliminating unused/underutilized resources, and continuously monitoring the spend anomalies.

Though the engineering persona is vast and includes cloud architects, engineering leads and teams, software engineers, developers, or platform engineering people, enabling cloud resources as metrics into their day-to-day activities helps your enterprise to save huge on cloud spend.

The most challenging scenarios in this process are:

- Engineers find it uninteresting as workloads keep on rising.

- Delivery cycles prolong over time.

- Unpredictable impact on budgets.

- Involved difficulties in identifying service or application ownership.

- As new features or products are developed, the cost prediction cannot be tracked.

Finance

Typically falling under the CFO's purview, finance teams manage corporate finance, strategic planning, financial analysis, budget analysis, and accounting seamlessly. As these finance teams collaboratively work with FinOps practitioners and gain access to historic billing data, these agile teams focus on creating on-the-fit forecasting models, planning and budgeting on entire cloud resources becomes optimized. Finance will become a key player in FinOps reporting, show back, chargeback, commitment, discounting the purchases, and invoice management with cloud providers.

All the preceding finance roles collaborate and report their forecasting plans to corporate finance, C-suite leaders, including CFOs, and advisors as well. However, the teams must ensure cost performance, keep budgets in line with organizational objectives, report current running investments and trends versus predicted investments, and find ways to normalize recurring spending.

In this process of planning and forecasting, the significant roadblocks include:

- Unpredictable cloud spending, leading to chaotic losses and operational failure.

- Distributed cloud cost accountability creates confusion, and a lot of work is involved as teams need to collaborate seamlessly to ensure forecasting and budget planning is agreed by everyone.

- OpEx versus CapEx challenges co-exist for longer time.

Procurement

More than cloud resource optimization, the key of FinOps is to foster greater and value-driven relationships with teams, vendors, and all the above FinOps practitioners, for enlarged scope of sourcing and vendor management.

-Satyendra Pasalapudi

Under this quora of procurement, the personas include sourcing analysts, vendor management, or directors within procurement teams. The core work of procurement teams is to identify the sourcing and purchasing of products and services within the cloud platform vendor.

To ensure prices and terms are negotiated and the contract nature is fulfilled and streamlined, a win-win procedure for cloud contract is grounded without any complications. Meeting the objectives: vendor relationships, volume commitment or enterprise-grade cloud offers, and relationships with cloud platform providers are the primary focus areas for procurement.

Though procurement has a great level of commitment to their objectives, a lack of visibility on cloud cost data and centralized processes for cloud commitments challenges underlie. In this case, standalone FinOps helps to:

- Perform proper industry research to identify the suitable and best cloud costs available so that your enterprise can choose what aligns with your business objectives.

- Generate the billing data as per the utilized cloud resources.

- Enabling deeper visibility makes cloud costs based on the resources, technologies, licenses, and contracts, possible.

Core personas build and develop a world-class FinOps culture, as key decision-makers are responsible for driving the necessary and most crucial changes. All the core personas foster higher cloud resource or cloud cost visibility and optimization, with a focus on establishing discipline across diverse teams on an enterprise scale.

Allied personas

In our strategic ways of driving FinOps discipline within enterprises, we have seen those allied personas, who majorly intersect their nature of work with framework capabilities. This approach to involving associated teams enhances accountability within teams. These allied personas include IT service management, asset management, sustainability, security developers or managing individuals, and IT financial management.

Let us decode how these personas contribute for greater compelling benefit for enterprises:

- **ITSM/ITIL**: After achieving successes with many large-scale and mid-level enterprises, we found that nearly 50%-60% of enterprises still face challenges in standardizing their IT operations. Here, the role of **IT service management** (**ITSM**) collaborates closely with FinOps practitioners to not only set IT operations but also enhance service quality and reliability, ensuring that IT services meet agreed-upon service levels and performance goals by balancing against cloud cost management priorities. The responsibilities of ITSM/ITIL teams include:

  o   Service design.

  o   Service operations and optimizations.

  o   Service level monitoring.

  o   Change management.

  o   Cost analysis and optimization.

  o   Documentation and reporting.

  o   Collaboration with stakeholders.

- **ITAM**: The team takes care of assessing the impacts caused by cloud usage. The **IT asset management** (**ITAM**) collaborates with FinOps practitioners to exponentially increase efficiency, transparency, and value by embracing the expertise and data from both the disciplined professionals, ensuring that costs are optimized, compliance requirements are met, and strategic objectives are aligned against cloud cost management priorities. With FinOps, the ITAM focuses on meeting the following objectives:

  o   Asset discovery and inventory.

  o   Asset auditing and compliance.

  o   Managing license costs.

  o   Analyzing and optimizing costs.

  o   Documentation and reporting.

  o   Stakeholder collaboration.

- **Sustainability**: With increased cloud consumption, carbon emissions are substantial, and enterprises are regaining their focus on reducing carbon emissions by 30%-50%, which is the need of the hour. To our surprise and advantage, FinOps makes us achieve a better world. For stakeholders to achieve such sustainable goals, teams collaborate with FinOps practitioners who develop strategies and implement best practices to optimize cloud computing for environmental impact. This aligns broader sustainability goals with cloud cost utilization. The sustainable goals, when intersected with FinOps, include the following objectives:

  o Perform optimizations for sustainable initiatives.

  o Waste reduction.

  o Meeting policy and compliance requirements.

  o Efficiency and optimization analysis.

  o Documentation and reporting.

  o Collaboration with stakeholders.

- **Security**: Security-related cloud resources are underutilized in most enterprises. To optimize security cloud spending, improve IT security financial governance, and strengthen the security posture, the IT security teams intersect with FinOps to achieve the following objectives:

  o Monitoring and anomaly response.

  o Anomaly investigation and analysis.

  o Policy and compliance.

  o Identity and access management.

  o Documentation and reporting.

  o Stakeholder collaboration.

- **ITFM/TBM**: Aligned towards informed decision-making, allowing transparency into IT spending, and cloud and IT investments meet business objectives, the IT financial management is responsible for adding value to the organization. The primary responsibilities are as follows:

  o Budgeting.

  o Cost accounting and optimization.

  o Financial analysis.

  o Prioritizing the investments.

  o Financial reporting.

  o Continuous process improvements.

  o Documentation and reporting.

  o Stakeholder collaboration.

FinOps phases

Skipping analysis, ignoring preplanning and preparation for cloud costs, and unforeseen risks are the paranoid within any enterprise of any scale. That is why teams working in any business unit can be involved in any FinOps phase at any given time. Here, the primary job of FinOps practitioners is to find ways to improve cloud usage and create documentation to empower the teams and individuals to embrace the change and accelerate overall value.

The biggest impact is the analysis paralysis; quick actions on a regular cadence save everyone from losing track of everything. These quick actions reinforce a series of best practices, through small steps, later growing into the size and scope of the team's collaboration through a very thorough experience and momentum.

However, the final goal is to work relentlessly on strategies and reimagine workflows that encompass FinOps capabilities to measure results, make incremental improvements, and reinvent the cyclic process of these phases.

Inform, **optimize**, and **operate** are three FinOps phases that are aimed at improving cloud cost value and benefiting your business with higher ROI. Let us take you deeper into each one of these phases and how these phases can tune the maximum value ever:

- **Inform (Granular visibility, effective allocation)**: In the inform phase, FinOps activities involve identifying data sources for cloud cost, usage, and efficiency data. Using this data for allocation, analysis, and reporting empowers teams to develop capabilities in budgeting, forecasting trends, building KPIs for benchmarking, and developing metrics that will reveal the business value of an organization's cloud spend. Accurate allocation of cloud spends based on tags, accounts, or business rules enables accurate reporting. Business and financial teams must ensure they are driving ROI while staying within budget, accurately forecasting spend and carbon costs, and avoiding surprises. Benchmarking against others or between teams provides organizations with metrics to understand how effectively they are operating. By combining all of the cloud cost data with other data about sustainability, efficiency, utilization, and the performance benchmarks for the organization, teams should be able to see the key performance indicators and unit metrics related to the organization's cloud use. The on-demand and elastic nature of the cloud, coupled with complex pricing discounts, requires organizations to continuously revisit activities that inform their business objectives through data-driven decisions using accurate and timely visibility of their cloud usage.

- **Optimize (Relentless improvements for effective resource utilization)**: In the Optimize phase, FinOps activities involve identifying opportunities to enhance cloud efficiency by leveraging the data and capabilities developed in the Inform Phase. Cloud providers offer multiple options to optimize cloud resources. This involves building capabilities to right-size underutilized cloud resources, take advantage of modern architectures, manage workloads, and automate the elimination of waste from unused resources. Additionally, cloud providers offer options to optimize cloud rates. This involves visibility, analysis, and reporting capabilities to empower the purchase and management of commitment discount and committed use discount pricing models such as **Reserved Instances (RI)**, **Savings Plans (SP)**, and **committed use discounts (CUD)**. This phase is also about collaboration across teams to optimize visibility, reporting, and management processes for areas where unit metrics indicate cloud performance is not aligned with the organization's cloud value goals. Optimization options may result in competing paths. Still, the underlying goal is to develop a robust set of opportunities that will help the organization achieve greater value from its cloud investment.

- **Operate (Full stack implementation to evolve and transform)**: In the operate phase, FinOps activities involve implementing organizational changes to operationalize FinOps using the data and capabilities developed in the inform and optimize phase. This includes establishing cloud governance policies, monitoring compliance, and empowering individuals through the development of training programs, team guidelines, and automation policies that align with organizational objectives. FinOps success requires organizations to build a culture of accountability where engineering, finance, and business teams collaborate on continuous, incremental action based on the data generated in the Inform phase, selecting the best opportunities identified in the Optimize phase, and using a bias for action developed throughout the organization. Working through this phase, keep in mind the goal to iteratively develop strategies and refine workflows; this involves looping back to the inform and optimize phases to mature the activities adopted from the framework capabilities, evaluate introducing new capabilities and evolving FinOps operations for the organization.

FinOps domains

Without having an idea for a business, it is impossible to sustain it. As an enterprise, your focus should be whirling in the maximum of possible outcomes through the FinOps implementation. As part of this, identifying the domains and how you can utilize each one of them across the capabilities delivers significant outcomes.

The primary objective of FinOps domains is to define the fundamental business outcomes and, subsequently, quantify them through the establishment of FinOps. Practicing FinOps enables enterprises to drive each of the domains in a streamlined manner, accelerating overall operational efficiency while bolstering the business bottom line.

Understand cloud usage and cost

At the heart of FinOps lies the fundamental capability to understand cloud usage and cost. Think of it as the first step in a dance; without mastering it, the rest of the performance falters. This capability requires a meticulous approach to tracking and analyzing how cloud resources are utilized and how much they cost.

That is the reason why visibility in cloud usage is paramount. By leveraging detailed billing reports, resource tagging, and cost allocation methods, organizations can break down their cloud expenses with surgical precision. This is not just about knowing what was spent but understanding why it was paid. Are specific departments consuming more resources? Are there unexpected spikes in usage? By evaluating these questions, businesses can uncover insights that drive better decision-making.

Moreover, it is crucial to move beyond raw data and develop meaningful metrics that resonate with stakeholders. Clear, actionable reports, and dashboards should translate complex usage patterns into straightforward narratives. By doing so, organizations empower their teams to take proactive steps in managing and reducing cloud costs.

Domain capabilities include:

- Data ingestion

- Allocation

- Reporting and analytics

- Anomaly management

Each of these domain capabilities will help the enterprises to:

- Identify, define, and ingest all cloud cost and usage data.

- Normalize data as a necessity across sources, utilizing FOCUS datasets as priority.

- Develop an allocation strategy for aligning all costs to internal users.

- Redefine policies and techniques for allocating shared costs and resources.

- Create and define standard reporting tools, parameters, and methods.

- Allocate the relevant reporting data to personas based on their way of operations.

- Identify and document the needs of allied personas across the enterprise for understanding cloud costs and usage.

Quantify business value

Once cloud usage and costs are understood, the next leap is to quantify the business value derived from these expenditures. This capability bridges the gap between financial metrics and business outcomes, transforming cloud spending from a mere cost center to a strategic investment.

Quantifying business value involves evaluating the ROI for cloud initiatives. This means aligning cloud costs with business goals and outcomes, such as revenue growth, customer satisfaction, or operational efficiency. It is about asking the critical question: How does our cloud spend contribute to our business objectives?

A key aspect of this capability is stakeholder communication. Decision-makers need to see the tangible benefits of their cloud investments. By correlating cloud expenses with business metrics, organizations can demonstrate value in terms that resonate with executives and business units. This might involve showing how cloud-based innovations have accelerated time-to-market, improved customer experiences, or enabled cost savings in other areas.

When it comes to boosting value for enterprises, the following domain capabilities are aligned as part of FinOps culture:

- Planning and estimations

- Forecasting

- Budgeting

- Benchmarking

- Unit economics

These capabilities enable:

- Estimation of cloud needs and planning involved that gives an overview of cloud cost, impact, and usage data.

- Teams plan budgets consistently, reducing the likelihood of budget overruns.

- Benchmarks for the defined techniques and models that are linked to business value.

- Exceptional business value of cloud-based solutions, as objectively measured using relevant metrics.

Optimize cloud usage and cost

Optimization is the lifeblood of FinOps, ensuring that every dollar spent on cloud services is maximized. This capability revolves around continuous improvement; constantly seeking ways to enhance efficiency and reduce waste.

Optimization starts with rightsizing, which means adjusting cloud resources to match actual needs. This involves scaling down over-provisioned resources, eliminating unused instances, and selecting the most cost-effective service options. It is akin to tuning an engine for peak performance, ensuring that the organization gets the most bang for its buck.

Additionally, leveraging cost-saving strategies is essential. This includes utilizing Reserved Instances, Spot Instances, and other pricing models that cloud providers offer. Automation tools play a significant role here, enabling organizations to adjust resources based on real-time demand dynamically.

Optimization is not a one-off task but an ongoing process. Regular reviews and audits of cloud usage and costs help maintain efficiency. By fostering a culture of continuous improvement, organizations can ensure that their cloud investments consistently deliver high value.

For continuous optimization, the enterprises must focus on the following domain capabilities:

- Architecting for cloud
- Rate optimization
- Workload optimization
- Cloud sustainability
- Licensing and SaaS

At its core, the capabilities help enterprises in:

- Analyzing and managing the commitments on cloud and resources spend.
- Optimizing resource utilization and respective efficiency by creating manual and automated policies that help teams use cloud resources across the infrastructure.
- Maximizing business value and achieving performance, scalability, and operational objectives through cost-effective design solutions.
- Focusing on strategic metrics and criteria by incorporating sustainability goals into their FinOps capabilities.
- Understanding and optimizing the use of software licenses and SaaS investments.

Managing the FinOps practice

The final capability is managing the FinOps practice itself; building and nurturing a structured approach to cloud financial management. This involves establishing processes, roles, and governance frameworks that ensure the FinOps discipline thrives across the organization.

Central to managing FinOps is the creation of a cross-functional FinOps team. This team typically includes representatives from finance, engineering, and operations, working together to align financial and technical goals. Effective communication and collaboration among these stakeholders are vital, as they ensure that financial objectives are embedded into daily operational decisions.

Governance frameworks are also crucial. Setting clear policies and guidelines for cloud spending, implementing budget controls, and enforcing best practices create a disciplined environment. Regular training and awareness programs can help instill a cost-conscious culture within the organization.

Aligning with all the FinOps strategic imperatives, the FinOps practices are embedded as domain capabilities, including:

- FinOps practice operations
- Cloud policy and governance
- FinOps assessment
- FinOps tools and services
- FinOps education and enablement
- Invoicing and chargeback
- Onboarding workloads
- Intersecting disciplines

All these FinOps capabilities assist enterprises in the following ways:

- Run a highly skilled FinOps team leader who can be a driver of FinOps at its every phase.
- Create and manage an A-player FinOps team, who become cloud-mature at every FinOps phase.
- Define and implement processes and workflows so that core and allied personas can drive FinOps capabilities into their daily activities.
- Define criteria for FinOps capability assessment and set milestones for a matured FinOps practice.
- Develop education and training to embrace FinOps across the enterprise.
- Support cloud cost management initiatives on a high scale that align with organization's use case and maturity level.

By mastering these FinOps capabilities, organizations can transform their approach to cloud financial management, driving not only cost efficiency but also strategic value from their cloud investments.

FinOps maturity model

Adopting a FinOps maturity model guides organizations through different stages of capability development, from initial cost tracking to advanced optimization and strategic financial management. This structured approach helps organizations scale their FinOps practices as they grow, ensuring sustained financial health and strategic advantage in the cloud.

Start with simple steps, implement A/B testing for your environment, and consistently improve FinOps Capabilities as per your defined needs.

-Venkat Reddy

The FinOps principles majorly reflect that **business value should drive decision-making**. An enterprise that has anomaly detection in the Walk stage, can experience a few cost spikes that it may have encountered previously. The solution is to invest time in developing FinOps capabilities that land immediate benefits. The *Walk, Crawl, and Run* stages are recognized as the key stages of the FinOps maturity model, where organizations achieve the highest business value.

When implementing this model, the goal is to perform at your maturity level depending on the complexity of the environment, rather than rushing to Run and Go, losing huge through workforce management and crippled processes. Continually assess your existing environment and go with the flow. If the focus shifts to the Run phase without any initial establishment, it is beyond your current skill, leading to overconsumption of resources.

Every capability and functional activity need not be in sync; but they function at different levels of maturity as per the business needs and enterprise requirements. Let us see the maturity level characteristics and KPIs for each of these phases to get a basic understanding of this model.

Crawl

The maturity level characteristics are:

- Very low reporting and tools usage.
- Existing measurements in this phase give insight into the benefits of maturing the capability.
- The setting of basic KPIs is accomplished to measure the success.
- Ground-level processes and policies are defined around the capability.
- Everyone is aware of the capability, but is not followed by major teams within the enterprise.
- Planning is done to address the low hanging fruits.

The sample goals/KPIs are:

- Able to allocate a minimum of 50%.
- Resource-based commitments discount target coverage of ~60%.
- The accuracy variance between forecast spending and actual spend is 20%.

Walk

The maturity level characteristics are:

- Capability is clearly defined and implemented within the organization.
- Difficulties within the enterprise are identified and efforts to resolve are estimated but business decisions are not taken.

- Most of the processes are automated to meet the capability requirements.
- Medium to high goals/KPIs are set for the measurement of success.

The sample goals/KPIs are:

- At least 80% of resources must be allocated.
- Resource-based commitments discount target coverage is 70%.
- The variance of Forecast spend to actual spend accuracy is 15%.

Run

The maturity level characteristics are:

- Capability is followed by all the teams.
- Most of the difficult edge cases are being addressed.
- Very high goals/KPIs are set to measure success at scale.
- Close to 100% automation is achieved.

The sample goals/KPIs are:

- More than 90% of cloud spend can be allocated.
- Resource-based commitments discount target coverage is approximately 80%.
- Forecast spend to actual spend variance is 12%.

Transformation with FinOps maturity model

Transitioning from one stage of maturity to the other is required as business complexity increases. Here is our practice that we recommend for enterprises that help you progress from one stage to the other:

- **Crawl to Walk phase**:
  - o **Define policies**: Create and implement enterprise-wide policies for cloud cost management that include role definition, responsibilities, and processes, focused on optimizing costs.
  - o **Visibility and reporting**: Set up deeper visibility tactics into cloud costs with tracking and reporting. With the help of cost management and optimization tools, derive insights into usage patterns, cost trends, and forecasting.
  - o **Stakeholder engagement**: Engage stakeholders by stating why FinOps plays a crucial role in optimizing cloud costs.
  - o **Optimization methods**: Plan the cost overruns through optimization. Implement cost-saving methods to prevent yourself from overrunning cloud costs.

- o **Train**: Educate the teams on FinOps tasks and principles, such as alerting on cost overruns or tagging of resources.

- o **Automate**: Automate simple FinOps tasks to enhance resource efficiency and team productivity.

- **Walk to Run phase**:

  - o **Advanced automation**: Handle the most complicated FinOps processes through advanced automation, as rightsizing of resources or predictability can play a crucial role.

  - o **FinOps in business process**: Integrate the full stack of FinOps processes into your business.

  - o **Forecasting and budgeting**: A cling on the more sophisticated forecasting models can be the need of the hour for highly accurate future cloud spending. Align this predicted cloud spend with your budgets.

  - o **Continuous improvement**: Review the processes, tools, and policies regularly, and look for areas of improvement whenever the business or market demands.

  - o **Strategic business alignment**: FinOps practices must align with broader business objectives, facilitating business decisions for cost optimization and growth.

This is the how the FinOps maturity model turns the stone for you and spins the business with great momentum to save cloud costs, driven by greater flexibility and automation features. Now, let us look at the FinOps Capabilities that enhance and streamline entire FinOps culture.

FinOps capabilities

The FinOps capabilities are as follows:

- **Allocation**: **Define strategies to assign and share cloud costs**:

  - o Allocation is the bedrock of effective FinOps, ensuring that every dollar spent in the cloud is transparently assigned and tracked. Imagine trying to navigate a ship without a compass; without a clear allocation strategy, cloud costs can quickly spiral out of control, with no one accountable for the overspend. In FinOps, allocation is all about:

    - ▪ Defining strategies to assign and share cloud costs.

    - ▪ Going beyond just dividing costs; making sure these costs are accurately apportioned to those who won them.

    - ▪ Leveraging account structures, tags, labels, and derived metadata to categorize and assign costs effectively.

- Understanding the cost of cloud resources to make informed decisions that drive efficiency and cost savings.

- Resource-level naming conversions and tags or labels within the cloud environment.

- Leveraging other sources like the organization's **configuration management database (CMDB)**, observability, or utilization data can enhance the granularity and accuracy of shared cost allocation.

- **Anomaly management: Detect, identify, alert, and manage irregularities:**

  o In the world of cloud financial management, unexpected spikes or irregularities in usage and cost are like sudden storms at sea; they can disrupt even the best-laid plans if not managed swiftly. This is where anomaly management steps in, giving FinOps teams the tools and strategies to detect, identify, alert, and manage these unexpected events before they escalate. Anomaly management is crucial for:

    - Maintaining cost-effective cloud operations.

    - Identifying unexpected spending, ensuring that anomalies do not go unnoticed.

    - Distributing anomaly alerts to the relevant personnel who can investigate and resolve the issue.

    - Enabling FinOps teams to respond quickly to anomalies, thereby minimizing the financial impact on the business.

    - Reducing unnecessary costs on top of enhancing overall cloud governance and ensuring operations go smooth and predictable.

- **Architecting for cloud: Designing solutions with cost-awareness and efficiency:**

  o When it comes to building and modernizing solutions in the cloud, cost efficiency must be baked into the design from the start. Architecting for cloud is about making thoughtful decisions that maximize business value while meeting performance, scalability, and operational objectives. Think of it as constructing a building; you would not lay the foundation without first planning how the entire structure will stand. Similarly, cloud architecture must be designed with a clear vision of efficiency and cost-effectiveness. The goal of this capability is to:

    - Architect systems that not only meet the technical needs but also align with the financial goals of the organization.

    - Avoid building in technical debt that could prove costly to resolve later.

- Incorporation of cloud-native services and efficient design principles from the outset for cost efficiency.

- Necessity of continuous reassessment and architectural modernization for legacy systems or those migrating to the cloud.

- Analyzing the spending regularly, identifying inefficiencies, and modernizing architectures are critical tasks for any organization committed to optimizing its cloud estate.

- Maintaining a proactive approach to cloud architecture to ensure they are always in the best position to achieve their cost and performance goals.

- **Benchmarking: Evaluating cloud optimization and value:**

  o In FinOps, Benchmarking is like having a map that shows where you stand compared to others on the same journey. It provides the metrics and KPIs needed to evaluate cloud optimization and value, both internally within different parts of the organization and externally against industry peers. This capability is crucial for aligning FinOps practices with broader business objectives. Benchmarking indeed is classified as:

    - **Internal benchmarking**: Allows organizations to compare performance metrics between different teams or departments, fostering a competitive yet collaborative environment. By understanding how various segments utilize cloud resources, organizations can identify best practices, promote efficiency, and ensure that resources are used to their fullest potential.

    - **External benchmarking**: provides insights into how an organization compares to others in the industry. While care must be taken to protect sensitive pricing or usage information, external comparisons can provide valuable context and highlight areas for improvement.

  o Benchmarking also plays a critical role in decision-making. By providing a clear view of where optimization efforts are succeeding or falling short, it helps FinOps teams make informed decisions that align with the organization's financial and operational goals. Ultimately, effective benchmarking ensures that FinOps practices not only keep pace with but also exceed industry standards, driving continuous improvement and business value.

- **Budgeting:**

  o In the dynamic world of multi-cloud environments, budgeting is not just about setting limits but establishing a strategic framework that ensures cloud spending aligns with broader business objectives. Let us explore on a few variables of FinOps Budgeting:

- An ongoing process that is the financial backbone for cloud operations.

- Fund approvals to support planned cloud activities, tracking, and spending against these budgets, budget adjustments are the focus elements.

- Every enterprise must maintain a predictable flow of expenditure, allowing organizations to navigate the complexities of cloud spending with confidence.

- The budgeting cycle must be flexible, with built-in provisions for holdbacks and mid-cycle adjustments to accommodate unforeseen expenses and shifts in cloud usage.

- It is closely linked with forecasting, planning, and estimating.

- In dynamic environments, budgeting requires more frequent adjustments and potentially larger holdbacks to manage uncertainties.

- The budgeting processes must align with organizational growth and operational needs.

- Shortening the budgeting cycle or adjusting budget thresholds can help organizations stay agile in the face of change.

  o Over time, these practices become second nature, enabling organizations to handle even out-of-cycle changes with ease and ensuring that cloud budgeting supports, not hinders, their growth and innovation.

- **Cloud policy and governance:**

  o Cloud policy and governance are the guardrails that ensure cloud usage aligns with an organization's strategic goals while complying with regulatory requirements. These frameworks are crucial for maintaining control over cloud environments, preventing the chaos that can arise from unchecked cloud expansion. A cloud policy is a formal statement of intent, outlining how specific cloud-related activities should be carried out to enhance business value. Governance, on the other hand, encompasses the processes, tools, and controls that enforce these policies, ensuring that cloud resources are used efficiently and securely.

  o At the heart of cloud policy and governance is the alignment of cloud activities with organizational goals. This alignment ensures that cloud resources are deployed and utilized in a manner that maximizes ROI. By enforcing policies that promote best practices, organizations can ensure that cloud costs remain predictable and manageable.

  o Governance also plays a crucial role in safeguarding against known risks, providing a defense-in-depth strategy that enhances cloud security and compliance. By embedding these frameworks into their FinOps practices, organizations can optimize their cloud resources, drive efficiency, and achieve sustainable cloud success.

- **Cloud sustainability:**

  o As organizations increasingly rely on cloud services, the need for sustainable cloud practices becomes paramount. Cloud sustainability is about more than just reducing costs; it is about making environmentally responsible decisions that align with the organization's broader sustainability goals. This capability integrates sustainability criteria and metrics into cloud optimization, ensuring that financial value is balanced with environmental efficiency.

  o In a broader scope of FinOps, cloud sustainability optimizes cloud usage and cost domain. The cloud sustainability component helps enterprises in:

    ▪ Creating an impact through informed decisions that navigate the enterprises' financial and environmental objectives.

    ▪ Evaluating the total carbon emissions associated with the sourcing, production, and disposal of cloud infrastructure, as well as the operational efficiency of cloud workloads.

    ▪ Using the available data to make informed decisions that drive sustainable cloud practices. While data quality is important, the focus should be on using the data to make directionally correct recommendations, even if the data is imperfect.

    ▪ Positioning the enterprises as leaders in sustainable cloud practices.

- **Data ingestion:**

  o In the realm of FinOps, data is the lifeblood that drives informed decision-making. Data ingestion is the process of collecting, transferring, storing, and normalizing data from various sources to create a comprehensive, contextual dataset of cloud usage and cost information. This dataset is crucial for enabling analysis and supporting the activities of all FinOps Capabilities across the organization. As it is a continuous process, the data ingestion capability promotes:

    ▪ Overcoming challenges such as the ingestion of cloud cost and usage data from cloud service providers at scale.

    ▪ Providing a valuable, large, and granular dataset to the organization's current maturity level.

    ▪ Striking the right balance between data completeness and usability.

    ▪ Unlocking the full potential of cloud data through a robust data ingestion capability that drives effective FinOps practice and greater value from their cloud investments.

- **FinOps assessment:**

  o FinOps assessment is the cornerstone of a mature FinOps practice. It is a thoughtful, repeatable, and measurable process that allows an organization to take a step back and evaluate its FinOps capabilities within the broader context of the FinOps framework. This capability is more than just checking boxes; it is about gaining deep insights into the strengths and weaknesses of your FinOps activities, identifying gaps, and charting a course for continuous improvement. Conducting a FinOps assessment empowers to:

    - Measure its effectiveness, align its actions with organizational goals, and spotlight areas ripe for maturation.

    - Benchmark its current capabilities and prioritize efforts that will have the most significant impact on driving cloud value.

    - Bring diverse perspectives that may reveal the need to focus on different capabilities in various areas of the business.

    - Expand the scope so that FinOps remains robust and aligned with evolving business objectives.

    - Understand where you stand today, define where you want to be, and create a clear, actionable pathway.

    - Identify where current practices fall short and where additional focus is needed.

    - Foster a deeper understanding and cooperation across different teams and organizational levels, promoting a culture of cost awareness and continuous improvement.

- **FinOps education and enablement:**

  o The heart of a successful FinOps practice lies in education and enablement; training that builds a common language, shared understanding, and the practical skills needed to drive FinOps adoption across the organization. This capability is essential in creating a culture where every stakeholder, from engineers to finance to leadership, grasps the nuances of FinOps, understands their role within it, and feels empowered to contribute. The essentials of FinOps training are:

    - Embedding FinOps principles into the very fabric of your organization.

    - Ensuring everyone is involved in the cloud cost management process.

    - Fostering collaboration across disciplines and ensuring cloud-related decisions are made with broader business value.

    - Tailoring to the specific needs of different personas.

- ▪ Continuous reinforcement of all the modules for maintaining momentum and adapting to new challenges.

- ▪ Cultivating a sense of accountability for cloud costs throughout the organization.

- **FinOps practice operations:**

  o Running an effective FinOps practice is akin to orchestrating a complex, dynamic system where every component must function in harmony. FinOps practice operations is the capability that drives this system, ensuring that the FinOps team is not only operationally sound but also strategically aligned with the organization's goals.

  o This capability encompasses a wide range of activities, from the initial adoption of FinOps practices to the ongoing fine-tuning required as your FinOps maturity grows. FinOps practice operations involve establishing the frameworks, processes, and decision-making protocols that enable seamless collaboration among different teams and personas.

  o As part of this capability, organizations need to establish clear roles and responsibilities within the FinOps team and across the broader organization. This includes defining how decisions are made, how different teams interact, and how accountability is maintained. Continuous improvement is also a critical aspect, regularly revisiting and refining processes to adapt to new challenges and opportunities in the cloud landscape.

  o Ultimately, FinOps practice operations is about creating a resilient, scalable practice that not only meets the current needs of the organization but also evolves in tandem with the organization's growth and changing cloud strategies. By focusing on the operational aspects of FinOps, organizations can ensure that their cloud investments are managed effectively, delivering consistent value over time.

- **FinOps tools and services:**

  o The selection and integration of FinOps tools and services is a critical capability that can make or break your FinOps practice. This capability is all about developing a thoughtful strategy for adopting tools and services that align with the FinOps Framework and empower your team to manage cloud costs effectively.

  o Before diving into tool selection, it is crucial to have a clear understanding of your organization's cloud strategy, goals, and the policies that govern tool usage. This preemptive clarity helps avoid the common pitfalls of adopting tools that are misaligned with organizational needs or that duplicate existing solutions. The right tools and services should seamlessly integrate with your cloud environment, support your FinOps practices, and align with your overall business objectives.

o When selecting FinOps tools or services, it is essential to establish a set of requirements that clearly identifies where external help is needed. This might include capabilities such as automated cost tracking, real-time usage monitoring, anomaly detection, or reporting and analytics that are crucial for your specific cloud environment. The selected tools should enhance your team's ability to manage and optimize cloud spend, while also providing the flexibility to grow and adapt as your FinOps practice matures.

o In addition to tool selection, this capability also involves developing methodologies for effective tool integration. This includes ensuring that tools are configured correctly, that data flows seamlessly between systems, and that users are adequately trained to maximize the benefits of the tools. Regular reviews and updates to the toolset are also necessary to keep pace with technological advancements and changing business needs.

- **Forecasting**

    o Forecasting in the context of FinOps is about more than just predicting future cloud costs; it is about creating a detailed, data-driven model that anticipates the financial and operational impact of your cloud investments. This capability leverages statistical methods, historical spending patterns, planned changes, and various related metrics to provide a clear picture of what lies ahead.

    o At its core, forecasting serves as a foundational input to the budgeting capability, establishing the baseline for financial planning and allocation. However, its influence extends far beyond budgeting. Forecasting informs key decisions at every level of the organization, from IT capital planning to anomaly detection, enabling teams to make proactive adjustments before issues arise.

    o Forecast models are not static; they are living documents that must be updated regularly to reflect changes such as the integration of new features, shifts in usage patterns, or modernization of application architectures. The dynamic nature of forecasting requires close collaboration among engineering, product, finance, and leadership teams to ensure that forecast models remain aligned with business goals and that any variances are addressed promptly.

    o The tight integration between forecasting, estimating, and budgeting is essential for maintaining financial discipline and accountability. While these capabilities may appear to overlap, particularly in smaller organizations, they each play a distinct role in the broader FinOps practice. Forecasting sets the expectations, estimating defines the cost, and budgeting allocates the resources; together, they create a cohesive financial strategy that supports the organization's cloud journey.

- **Intersecting disciplines:**

    o FinOps does not operate in a vacuum. The intersecting disciplines capability recognizes the critical need to coordinate activities with other IT disciplines and frameworks that have responsibilities extending beyond cloud management. This capability focuses on fostering collaboration and integration between FinOps and other key personas, including **IT asset management (ITAM)**, **IT financial management (ITFM)**, sustainability, and security, among others.

o   As cloud usage becomes more pervasive, traditional IT disciplines face new challenges and opportunities. The goal of this capability is to ensure that these disciplines are not working in isolation but are instead aligned with the broader organizational cloud strategy. This alignment is essential for maximizing the value of cloud investments while also managing risks and ensuring compliance with regulatory requirements.

o   The interactions between FinOps and other disciplines often involve shared responsibilities and overlapping objectives. For example, ITFM and FinOps both focus on cost management, but from different perspectives. Similarly, ITAM and FinOps must work together to track and optimize cloud assets. By establishing clear lines of communication and collaboration, organizations can ensure that these disciplines work in harmony, supporting each other's efforts and contributing to the overall success of the cloud strategy.

o   This capability also involves establishing and maintaining standards and best practices that guide the interactions between FinOps and other IT disciplines. These standards should be flexible enough to accommodate the unique needs of each discipline while also ensuring consistency and alignment with the organization's cloud objectives.

- **Invoicing and chargeback:**

o   Invoicing and chargeback is a critical capability that bridges the gap between the FinOps practice and the organization's finance and accounting functions. This capability involves developing specific workflows, reporting mechanisms, and reconciliation processes to ensure that cloud costs are accurately allocated to the appropriate cost centers and that chargebacks are aligned with the organization's accounting requirements.

o   Managing cloud invoices is not just about processing payments; it is about ensuring that every dollar spent on cloud resources is accounted for, reported correctly, and charged back to the appropriate business units. This requires close collaboration between the FinOps team and finance personas, with input from product and engineering personas to ensure that cost data is aligned with budgets and financial reporting needs.

o   The goal of this capability is to support the finance team in accurately and transparently allocating costs, in the formats and at the intervals required by the organization. This includes not only managing invoices and creating chargeback reports, but also maintaining the data and reporting integrity necessary to support evolving cloud practices and changing accounting requirements.

Appendix C
References

1. https://www.nops.io/blog/top-finops-practices-to-effectively-manage-cloud-costs/

2. https://www.lucidity.cloud/blog/finops-best-practices

3. https://www.finops.org/framework/principles/

4. https://focus.finops.org/

5. https://www.finops.org/wg/finops-kpis/?prod_kpis%5BrefinementList%5D%5Bcapabilities.title%5D%5B0%5D=Allocation

6. https://docs.aws.amazon.com/whitepapers/latest/tagging-best-practices/building-a-cost-allocation-strategy.html)

7. https://www.finops.org/wg/cloud-cost-allocation/

8. https://www.finops.org/assets/use-cases/refunds-by-subaccount/

9. https://www.finops.org/assets/use-cases/allocate-application-multi-currency/

10. https://www.finops.org/wg/finops-tools-and-services/

11. https://docs.aws.amazon.com/wellarchitected/latest/management-and-governance-guide/cloudfinancialmanagement.html

12. https://spot.io/resources/cloud-cost/cloud-cost-optimization-15-ways-to-optimize-your-cloud/

13. https://www.oracle.com/in/cloud/cloud-cost-optimization/

14. https://www.lucidity.cloud/blog/multi-cloud-cost-optimization

15. https://medium.com/buildpiper/roadmap-to-cloud-cost-optimization-3fba51770072

16. https://www.europeclouds.com/blog/mastering-finops-multi-cloud-environments-best-practices-for-2024#:~:text=A%20key%20element%20for%20success,view%20of%20their%20cloud%20spending.

17. https://airwalkreply.com/finops-within-a-multi-cloud-environment

18. https://www.c-facts.com/blogs/measuring-cloud-computing-costs-8-best-practices/

19. https://cloud.google.com/architecture/framework/cost-optimization/monitor

20. https://docs.aws.amazon.com/whitepapers/latest/establishing-your-cloud-foundation-on-aws/cost-monitoring-and-reporting.html

21. https://www.imperva.com/learn/data-security/cloud-governance/

22. https://www.geeksforgeeks.org/cloud-governance-and-its-need/

23. https://www.redhat.com/en/topics/automation/what-is-cloud-governance

24. https://www.tatacommunications.com/knowledge-base/cloud-governance/

25. https://www.vmware.com/topics/cloud-cost-management.html

26. https://www.linkedin.com/pulse/cloud-finops-industry-overview-futuristic-trends-3mmof/

27. https://devops.com/what-the-future-holds-for-finops-and-devops/

28. https://medium.com/@bijit211987/top-trends-driving-multi-cloud-adoption-and-automation-eeadec5eeb17

29. https://www.finops.org/insights/the-evolution-of-finops-keynote-themes-from-finops-x-2024/

30. https://www2.deloitte.com/us/en/pages/consulting/articles/the-next-ten-years-for-cloud-big-things-are-on-the-horizon-Deloitte-on-cloud-podcast-cloud-computing-multi-cloud-supercloud-AI-cloud-value-observability-finops-governance.html

31. https://blog-idceurope.com/the-new-era-of-finops-and-greenops/

Index

www.ingramcontent.com/pod-product-compliance
Lightning Source LLC
Chambersburg PA
CBHW061808210326
41599CB00034B/6918